STUDIES IN THE HISTORY AND TRADITIONS OF SEPPHORIS

STUDIES IN JUDAISM IN LATE ANTIQUITY

EDITED BY

JACOB NEUSNER

VOLUME THIRTY-SEVEN

STUART S. MILLER

STUDIES IN THE HISTORY AND TRADITIONS OF SEPPHORIS

LEIDEN
E. J. BRILL
1984

STUDIES IN THE HISTORY AND TRADITIONS OF SEPPHORIS

BY

STUART S. MILLER
Assistant Professor of Hebrew and Judaic Studies
University of Connecticut (Storrs)

LEIDEN
E. J. BRILL
1984

ISBN 90 04 06926 7

PRINTED IN THE NETHERLANDS BY E. J. BRILL

For Laura

TABLE OF CONTENTS

PREFACE

This work represents a revised version of my doctoral dissertation which was originally completed under the direction of Professors F. E. Peters, B. A. Levine and L. H. Schiffman at New York University in October, 1980. I first conceived the idea of working on a Galilean city in Professor Peters' seminar on Greco-Roman cities of the Near East. I am grateful to Professor Peters for his continued interest in my research and, most of all, for introducing me to the history and cultures of the Greco-Roman Near East. Professor Levine, with whom I studied Bible and Aramaic, was an enthusiastic adviser throughout my undergraduate and graduate days at New York University. His interest in the cult of Ancient Israel played at least a subconscious role in my selection of "The Priests" as one of the studies which appear below. Professor Levine's enthusiasm for a subject obviously carried over to this student as it must to all others. Professor Schiffman directed each step of my doctoral research and offered many helpful suggestions towards the revision and preparation of this work for publication. It was in his Talmud seminars that I began to develop a systematic approach to rabbinic literature. Professor Schiffman's own scholarship and learning continue to be a constant source of inspiration.

I would like to thank Professor J. N. Neusner of Brown University for agreeing to publish this volume in his series *Studies in Judaism in Late Antiquity* and for his advice on the final editing of the manuscript.

Needless to say, whatever faults remain in this work are my responsibility.

The transliteration systems for Hebrew and Greek used throughout this volume are based on those suggested in the *Encyclopaedia Judaica* 1 (1971-2), pp. 90 and 92. Although an attempt has been made to be as consistent as possible, popular spellings have sometimes been preferred to the more scientific renderings. In many instances, these spellings correspond to those used in the entries of the *Encyclopaedia* (e.g., *amora, baraita*).

Unless otherwise indicated, the rabbinic and Greek texts presented herein have been translated by the author. Biblical verses have been rendered in accordance with the new translation series of the Jewish Publication Society. The older (1915) translation of the Society was resorted to for those books of the Bible which have not yet appeared in the new series.

Several institutions provided financial assistance in support of my research. These include the Memorial Foundation for Jewish Culture and the National Foundation for Jewish Culture. The Lane Cooper Fund should also be acknowledged for sponsoring my visit of relevant sites in Galilee and Golan during the Spring of 1979.

In connection with my research in Israel, I would like to thank Dr. Y. Meshorer, curator of archeology at the Israel Museum and Senior Lecturer in

Numismatics at Hebrew University for providing me with advance copies of his monographs on the coins of Sepphoris. I also gained much from my conversations with Dr. D. Urman of Ben-Gurion University of the Negev.

I am grateful to Natanel Tefillinsky, *zikhrono li-verakhah*, of Moshav Meron, who unfortunately did not live to see the fruition of my research. I gained much from Mr. Tefillinsky's knowledge of both Galilee and the Talmud and am thankful that I had the opportunity to meet him and benefit from his insight before his untimely passing.

I would like to acknowledge my in-laws, Mr. and Mrs. B. Nelson, and my parents, Mr. and Mrs. I. Miller for their assistance and support. My parents deserve special recognition for fostering my early academic interests.

Ms. S. Tiller of Rutgers University typed and helped edit the early versions of my manuscript.

Many of the ideas in the following pages were first shared with my wife, Laura, to whom this volume is dedicated in appreciation for her constant encouragement and support of my research. Indeed, this work is as much the product of her love as it is of my labor.

November 25, 1981 Stuart S. Miller
28 *Ḥeshvan*, 5742

ABBREVIATIONS

AJSr	Association for Jewish Studies Review.
ANET	J. Pritchard, ed., *Ancient Near Eastern Texts.*
Ant.	Josephus, Jewish *Antiquities.*
B.	Babylonian Talmud.
BASOR	*Bulletin of the American Schools of Oriental Research.*
BDB	F. Brown, S. R. Driver, C. A. Briggs, *Hebrew and English Lexicon of the Old Testament.*
BGU	*Ägyptische Urkunden aus den königlichen Museen zu Berlin. Griechische Urkunden.*
CRAIBL	*Comptes-rendus Académie des inscriptions et belles-lettres.*
HTR	*Harvard Theological Review.*
HUCA	*Hebrew Union College Annual.*
IEJ	*Israel Exploration Journal.*
JBL	*Journal of Biblical Literature.*
JPOS	*Journal of the Palestine Oriental Society.*
JPS	Jewish Publication Society.
JQR	*Jewish Quarterly Review.*
JRS	*Journal of Roman Studies.*
JTS	*Journal of Theological Studies.*
M.	Mishnah.
MGWJ	*Monatschrift für Geschichte und Wissenschaft des Judentums.*
MWJ	*Magazin für die Wissenschaft des Judentums.*
P.	Palestinian Talmud.
PAAJR	*Proceedings of the American Academy for Jewish Research.*
PJB	*Palästinajahrbuch.*
Rab.	(Midrash) *Rabbah.*
T.	Tosefta.
ZDMG	*Zeitschrift der Deutschen Morgenländischen Gesellschaft.*

INTRODUCTION

Any attempt to reconstruct the history of an ancient city is dependent upon the extant archeological and literary sources. The abundance and quality of these sources will, of course, have a direct bearing upon the emerging picture. Oftentimes, even a wealth of archeological or literary evidence will not yield a comprehensive account, and a more limited discussion of a city's history must be settled for. What follows is not urban history in the usual sense; the studies presented in this work are in no way intended to chronicle the day-to-day life of an ancient city within a given chronological framework. Instead, a more modest inquiry into some of the rabbinic traditions pertaining to Sepphoris, an important academic and administrative center in Greco-Roman Galilee, is attempted. The purpose is to illustrate how a critical examination of the relevant traditions, taking into consideration recent advances in talmudic studies, can provide some insight into selected aspects of the history of Sepphoris. A brief discussion of what is known about the city will precede a fuller consideration of the methodology employed and the reasons for its use.

Historical Data

The mound upon which the ancient city of Sepphoris once stood rises some 115 meters above the Bet Netofah valley in Lower Galilee.[1] The site, which is located approximately five kilometers (three miles) northwest of Nazareth, was known to the Arabs as *Saffuriye.*[2] The city is usually referred to as "*Ẓipporin*" in the Palestinian Talmud and as "*Ẓippori*" in other rabbinic sources.[3] Josephus

---

[1] L. Waterman *et al.*, *Preliminary Report of the University of Michigan Excavation at Sepphoris, Palestine, in* 1931 (1937), p. 1.

[2] Pronounced *Saffuri.* See W. F. Albright's review of the Waterman report (see n. 1) in *Classical Weekly* 21 (1938), 148. The village known by that name fell to the Israeli army in 1948. A *moshav* was established at the foot of the *tell* in 1949. See M. Avi-Yonah, "Sepphoris," *Encyclopaedia Judaica* 14 (1971), col. 1178. The location of the city is generally accepted. See S. Krauss, "Sepphoris," *The Jewish Encyclopedia* 11 (1905), 200.

[3] The name also appears sometimes as צפורים. See S. Klein, "*Ẓippori*" in his *Ma᾿amarim Shonim La-Ḥaqirat ᾿Ereẓ Yisrael* (1924), pp. 47f. Cf. Z. Frankel, *Mevo᾿ Ha-Yerushalmi* (1870), p. 3b and E. Y. Kutscher, *Studies in Galilean Aramaic* (1976), p. 36. According to Yeivin, the final ין or ים is a locative case ending. Yeivin maintains that the name צפורים or צפורין belonged to an earlier, pre-exilic settlement since the usual form in rabbinic sources is צפורי. See S. Yeivin, "Historical and Archaeological Notes," in Waterman, *Report*, pp. 17f. This explanation seems unlikely, however, since the forms צפורים and especially צפורין are well attested in the rabbinic sources.

The Babylonian Talmud (*Meg.* 6a) identifies Sepphoris with Qitron (Judges 1:30). This possibility is discussed below, pp. 25ff. The Talmud (*ad loc.*) also explains that the city is called *Ẓippori* because it sits on top of a mountain like a bird (Hebrew: *ẓippor*).

calls the city "Sepphoris" (Σέπφωρις), a name evidently derived from the Semitic designations.[4]

Most of what is known about Sepphoris comes from the writings of Josephus, the church fathers, and rabbinic literature. Sepphoris first enters history in the *Antiquities* of Josephus. The historian describes Ptolemy Lathyrus' unsuccessful attempt to capture the city when the Hasmonean Alexander Yannai became king (ca. 100 B.C.E.).[5] Josephus next mentions the city in connection with the events following the Roman conquest of Palestine. Gabinius, the proconsul of Syria (ca. 57-55 B.C.E.), dissolved the central government and divided the country into five districts, each having its own administrative council (*synedria*).[6] The fact that Sepphoris was chosen as the site of the Galilean council suggests that the city had already become the capital of Galilee.

Josephus also portrays Sepphoris as the foremost city of Galilee during the Herodian period. After the death of Herod (ca. 4 B.C.E.), the rebel Judas and his gang attacked the royal palace (τῷ Βασιλείῳ) at Sepphoris in order to obtain arms.[7] Herod had evidently considered the city important enough to be fortified. In any event, Varus, the legate of Syria, quelled the rebellion by destroying the city and selling its inhabitants into slavery. Sepphoris was soon rebuilt by Herod Antipas, who, according to Josephus, made the city "the ornament of all Galilee" and called it "Autokratoris."[8]

Sepphoris seems to have lost some of its prestige when Antipas later moved to Tiberias, but the city again became the capital of Galilee under the procurator Felix (52-60 C.E.).[9] During the First Revolt, the residents of Sepphoris appear to have wavered before taking a pro-Roman stand.[10] Josephus reports that he

---

[4] On the Greek and Latin forms of the name see E. Schürer, *Geschichte des jüdischen Volkes im Zeitalter Jesu Christi* (1901-9) II, 209f.

[5] *Ant.* XIII, 338.

[6] *Ant.* XIV, 91 and *War* I, 170.

[7] *Ant.* XVII, 271 and *War* II, 56.

[8] *Ant.* XVIII, 27. The rebuilding probably began shortly after the city's destruction by Varus and continued into the early years C.E. See Yeivin, "Notes," p. 19, n. 14. According to Schürer, the title "Autokratoris" indicates that the city was granted autonomy. See Schürer, *Geschichte* II, 211, n. 496 and cf. S. Freyne, *Galilee from Alexander the Great to Hadrian* 323 B.C.E. to 135 C.E.: *A Study of Second Temple Judaism* (1980), p. 148, n. 50. Hoehner suggests that αὐτοκράτωρ may mean "Imperator" and could have been intended in honor of Augustus. The title may also suggest that Sepphoris was a capital city. See H. W. Hoehner, *Herod Antipas* (1972), p. 86, n. 1.

[9] *Life* 38. The passage is discussed below, pp. 54f.

[10] In *War* II, 574 Josephus says that he permitted the residents of Sepphoris to erect walls around their city because they were affluent and "eager for war." In *War* III, 61, Josephus claims that he fortified the city before it had abandoned the Galilean effort. The city eventually asked the Romans for military support. See *Life* 373 and 394; *War* III, 30-34. According to Cohen, Sepphoris was pro-Roman as early as the time of Felix (ca. 52-60 C.E., see *Life* 38) and remained so during the First Revolt, as indicated by numismatic evidence (discussed below, n. 12). Cohen suggests that the Sepphoreans may have originally fortified their city but only to protect themselves from hostile Galileans living in the environs, not in preparation for war with the Romans. Josephus' claim that he was responsible for the fortification of Sepphoris, when at most he only *permitted* the erection of walls, may be the result of the historian's hyperbolic style. See S. J. D. Cohen, *Josephus in Galilee and Rome: His Vita and Development As a Historian* (1979), pp. 246ff.

himself led assaults against the city.[11] Independent testimony to the position of Sepphoris during the war comes from coins bearing the designation "City of Peace" (Eirenopolis), which were struck at Sepphoris in 67-68 C.E.[12]

Several of the church fathers refer to Sepphoris as Diocaesarea (Διοκαισάρεια), a title which the city seems to have received under Hadrian (ca. 130).[13] The church fathers, however, were interested in the later history of the city. Thus Epiphanius describes how an apostate from Judaism named Josephus received authorization from the Emperor Constantine (306-337 C.E.) to build a church in Sepphoris.[14] Jerome reports on the revolt under Gallus (ca. 351) which began

---

[11] In *Life* 82 Josephus claims to have captured Sepphoris twice. Cohen notes, however, that Josephus' own account does not seem to support this contention. In *Life* 373-380 Josephus' assault appears to have been terminated by a rumor of Roman intervention. Elsewhere, in *Life* 394-396 and in *War* III, 59-61, Josephus admits of other instances where he was forced to retreat. According to Cohen, Josephus attempts to show in his autobiography that he made every effort to prevent Sepphoris from remaining pro-Roman but, at the same time, did not deal with the city severely. See Cohen, *Josephus*, pp. 122, 151f. and 216.

[12] Y. Meshorer, following M. Narkis, understands Eirenopolis (εἰρηνόπολις) as a reference to the pro-Roman stance of Sepphoris. Meshorer notes that Josephus refers to the Sepphoreans who welcomed Vespasian at Ptolemais in 67 C.E. (*War* III, 30-31) as "people who think peace" (εἰρηνικὰ φρονοῦντες). See Y. Meshorer, "Sepphoris and Rome," *Greek Numismatics and Archaeology, Essays in Honor of Margaret Thompson* (1979), p. 160 and *idem*, "*Matbeᶜot Ẓippori Ke-Maqor Histori*," *Ẓion* 43 (1978), 186. Cf. M. Narkis, "*ʾAnshei Ẓippori Ve-ʾEspasianos*," *Yediᶜot Ha-Ḥevrah Ha-ᶜIvrit La-Ḥaqirat ʾEreẓ Yisrael Va-ᶜAtiqoteha* 17 (1953), 119. Cf. Cohen, *Josephus*, p. 246. Cohen claims that the coins under discussion, which also refer to Sepphoris as "Neronias," reflect pro-Roman sentiment which prevailed in the city even before 67-68 C.E. (see above, n. 10). H. Seyrig, who first established the readings Eirenopolis and Neronias, has suggested that Sepphoris received the surname Eirenopolis in connection with the closing of the temple of Janus in Rome, an act of *pax Romana* carried out under Nero in 64 C.E. See H. Seyrig, "Irenopolis-Neronias-Sepphoris," *Numismatic Chronicle* 10 (1950), 289. The fact that the coins mention Vespasian and were issued in 67-68 C.E. would seem to support the view that the name Eirenopolis was bestowed upon Sepphoris with the arrival of the military commander in Palestine. Various explanations have been proposed for the pro-Roman stance of Sepphoris. Yeivin suggests ("Notes," pp. 23f.) that the dependence of the city on external water sources made an anti-Roman posture impossible, as Sepphoris would never have been able to withstand a siege once its water supply had been cut off. This explanation has been questioned by Hoehner (*Herod Antipas*, p. 87). Cf. Cohen, *Josephus*, p. 244. Perhaps the havoc wrought by Varus upon Sepphoris in 4 B.C.E. was remembered resulting in a disinclination to challenge the Romans. See Yeivin, "Notes," p. 19 and Freyne, *Galilee*, p. 68. More likely, however, is the suggestion that Sepphoris realized that its status as capital of Galilee was dependent upon the good graces of the Romans. See Cohen, p. 244, n. 4 and Freyne, p. 128.

[13] Coins bearing the name first appear under Antoninus Pius, but a milestone from 130 C.E. indicates that the city was known as Diocaesarea already in the time of Hadrian. See B. Lifschitz, "*Sur la date du transfert de la legio VI Ferrata en Palestine*," *Latomus* 19 (1960), 110f. and M. Hecker, "*Kevish Romaʾi Legio-Ẓippori*," *Yediᶜot Ha-Ḥevrah La-Ḥaqirat ʾEreẓ Yisrael Va-ᶜAtiqoteha* 25 (1961), 183f. The new name would have been in honor of Hadrian who had adopted the title Zeus, Olympus (= Dio). See E. M. Smallwood, *The Jews Under Roman Rule* (1976), p. 432.

[14] The text from Epiphanius' *Panarion* (30) is reproduced in S. Klein, *Sefer Ha-Yishuv* I (1939), pp. 68ff. There is no way of determining the earliest date for the settlement of Christians at Sepphoris. In 1926, however, S. J. Case published an article entitled "Jesus and Sepphoris" (*JBL* 45 (1925), 14-22). In this study, Case argued that Jesus, who was from the nearby village of Nazareth, must have frequently visited Sepphoris where he was exposed to a more cosmopolitan environment. Case tries to show that events in the history of Sepphoris deeply affected Jesus. While Case's study is suggestive, it is not based upon any concrete evidence. Moreover, A. Alt has shown that the orientation

when the Jews killed some Roman soldiers during the night and stole their weapons. Gallus, relates Jerome, subdued the rebels and burned Diocaesarea (Sepphoris), Tiberias and Diospolis (Lydda).[15] Sozomenus, Socrates, and others single out Sepphoris as the center of the revolt and note that the city was destroyed by Gallus.[16] While the extent of the revolt and the resulting destruction has been questioned,[17] the participation of Sepphoris in the insurrection is certain. Still, Sepphoris seems to have recovered quickly as Theodoretus states that the city was completely Jewish in the time of Valens (364-378).[18] An inscription found at Sepphoris also suggests that the Christians had succeeded in establishing a community there sometime during the fifth century.[19]

The numerous references to Sepphoris (*Ẓippori*) in rabbinic literature provide much insight into periods and aspects of the city's history which would otherwise remain obscure. The general picture which emerges is that of an important tannaitic and amoraic center. The city had already become the home of leading scholars well before Rabbi Judah Ha-Nasi moved there ca. 200 C.E.[20] It continued to be an important academic center until the close of the Palestinian Talmud.[21] Rabbinic literature preserves many details concerning the social, economic and political life of Sepphoris. Since the rabbis were not interested in the city *per se*, this information is not presented within any kind of chronological or historical context. For this reason, the mere collating of the references to Sepphoris would only result in a general, rabbinic account of questionable historical reliability.[22] A more analytical approach to the material will be suggested below.

---

of Nazareth was southward rather than northward to Sepphoris from which it was separated by the contour of the land. See A. Alt, "*Die Stätten des Wirkens Jesu in Galiläa territorialgeschichtlich betrachtet*" in *idem, Kleine Schriften zur Geschichte des Volkes Israel* (1953-64), II, 441ff. Cf. F. W. Boelter, "Sepphoris—Seat of the Galilean Sanhedrin," *Explor* 3 (Winter, 1977), 41f.

[15] Jerome, *Chronicon, Olymp.* 282.

[16] Sozomenus, *Hist. eccl.* IV, 7; Socrates, *Hist. eccl.* II, 33. For others, see S. Lieberman, "Palestine in the Third and Fourth Centuries," reprinted in *idem, Texts and Studies* (1974), p. 121 and M. Avi-Yonah, *The Jews of Palestine* (1976), p. 184, n. 76.

[17] By Lieberman, in the article mentioned in the previous note.

[18] Theodoretus, *Hist. eccl.* IV, 22.

[19] The inscription is actually from the early sixth century, but it reports the renewal of an earlier church. See M. Avi-Yonah, "A Sixth Century Inscription from Sepphoris," *IEJ* 11 (1961), 184-187 and below, p. 6. The establishment of a Christian community at Sepphoris during the fifth century appears to have been more successful than the earlier attempts to do the same. Cf. M. Schwabe, "*Eine griechische Inschrift aus Sepphoris*," *JPOS* 15 (1935), 95ff.

[20] P. *Kilaʾyim* 9, 32b and P. *Ketubot* 12, 35a report that Judah lived in Sepphoris the last seventeen years of his life. See A. Guttmann, "The Patriarch Judah I—His Birth and His Death," reprinted in *idem, Studies in Rabbinic Judaism* (1976), pp. 239ff. On the scholars who lived in Sepphoris see Klein, "*Ẓippori*," pp. 57ff. During Judah's time, the Sanhedrin was probably located at Sepphoris. See B. *Rosh Ha-Shanah* 31a-b.

[21] The Palestinian Talmud is generally believed to have been edited in the early fifth century. Much of its material emanated from the discussions in the academy at Sepphoris. See H. L. Strack, *Introduction to the Talmud and Midrash* (1931), p. 65.

[22] Klein's article "*Ẓippori*" represents such a collation. It is discussed below, p. 7.

Archeological Findings

The *tell* upon which the ancient city of Sepphoris is located was partially excavated in 1931 by L. Waterman of the University of Michigan in collaboration with S. Yeivin, N. E. Manasseh and C. S. Fisher.[23] On the northwest slope, the excavators uncovered part of a Roman theater which, according to W. F. Albright, belongs to the late second or third century.[24] The theater had a seating capacity of between 4000 and 5000 persons.[25] Part of a 2.4 meters thick wall, perhaps from the Crusader period, was found over the ruins of the theater. This wall seems to have at one time encompassed the entire acropolis (Other traces can be seen on the eastern edge of the *tell*.), forming a citadel approximately 180 meters long and 90 meters wide.[26] Not far from the theater, but about twenty-four meters below it, an oil press was found.[27] On the northwest end of the summit the excavators discovered what they believed to be a Christian basilica, but M. Avi-Yonah has since contended that it was a Roman villa.[28] To the east, an extensive aqueduct was examined, but its relationship to the many cisterns on the *tell* could not be determined.[29]

A small fort standing on the summit of the *tell* was also inspected. Its construction testifies to several different periods of occupation at Sepphoris. While the walls of the upper story were built by Abdul Hamid (1876-1909),[30] the western corner and the lower courses belong to the period of the Crusades. Many of the cornerstones are really Roman sarcophagi adapted for building purposes. Traces of a building which may go back to the early centuries C.E. were found below the fort.[31]

Among the artifacts discovered were a Rhodian jar handle and fragments of Arretine ware.[32] Most of the potsherds belong to the Hellenistic through the Byzantine periods, but one jar rim has been dated to Early Iron II (1000-900

---

[23] The results of this excavation were published in the Waterman report referred to in n. 1. In the Spring of 1979, the present writer, under a grant from the Lane Cooper Fund, surveyed many of the ruins including the theater and the fort reported on here.

[24] Both Waterman and Yeivin had concluded that the theater was built by either Herod or Antipas. See Yeivin, "Notes," p. 29. Albright, however, contends in his review of the Waterman report (*Classical Weekly* 21 (1938), 148) that the masonry and ornamentation are Roman, not Herodian. He, therefore, prefers a late second or third century dating.

[25] See N. E. Manasseh, "Architecture and Topography," in Waterman, *Report*, p. 6.

[26] *Ibid.*, p. 2.

[27] *Ibid.*, p. 12.

[28] The view of the excavators is reported by Manasseh, *ibid.*, pp. 4ff. See, however, M. Avi-Yonah, "Sepphoris," *Encyclopedia of Archaeological Excavations in the Holy Land* 4 (1978), 1053f.

[29] Manasseh, "Architecture," p. 15. The aqueduct seems to have irrigated the local fields besides providing water for the city. See Z. Gorodazki, "*ᶜOreq Ha-Ḥayyim Shel-Ẓippori*," *Ha-Tevaᶜ Ve-Ha-ʾAreẓ* 19 (July-August, 1977), 226-229.

[30] He appears to have built upon earlier construction belonging to the period of Zahir al-ᶜAmr, the governor of Galilee in the beginning of the eighteenth century. See Manasseh, "Architecture," p. 3.

[31] *Ibid.*, pp. 3f.

[32] Yeivin, "Notes," pp. 26f. and Avi-Yonah, "Sepphoris," p. 1053.

B.C.E.).[33] Many coins were found in the theater. The earliest of these are four Seleucid issues and eight of Alexander Yannai. There are also coins of the Herodian dynasty, Bar Kokhba (one), several from the cities of Ashkelon, Tyre, Sidon and Dor, and other Roman, Byzantine and Arab issues.[34]

Several inscriptions have been found in the vicinity of the *tell.* In 1909 a mosaic believed to be part of a synagogue floor was accidentally uncovered. The mosaic contains the words: "Remembered be for good Rabbi Yudan, the son of Tanḥum, the son ... who gave...."[35] In 1930-31 E. L. Sukenik conducted excavations in behalf of the Hebrew University. Sukenik devoted his attention to the burial caves in the area, one of which also contained an inscription referring to a Rabbi Yudan.[36] Another grave, known locally as the Tomb of Jacob's Daughters, has been assigned to the second or third century C.E.[37] Some Greek inscriptions have also been found, including one which describes the refurbishing of a church by the bishop Marcellinus (ca. 518 C.E.).[38]

Sepphoris in Rabbinic Literature

The value of rabbinic literature as a source for the history of Sepphoris has long been acknowledged. In 1909, A. Büchler published *The Political and the Social Leaders of the Jewish Community of Sepphoris in the Second and Third Centuries.* Büchler posited the existence of a conflict between the rabbis and the official (Jewish) leaders of Sepphoris. The rabbis attacked the character of the leaders who often took advantage of the people, especially in matters of taxation. In return, the wealthy leaders spread malicious slander concerning the scholars and refused to support the rabbinical students.[39] Büchler assumed that statements attributed to rabbis who lived in Sepphoris could be used as evidence regardless of whether they specifically mention the city. Büchler argues that general statements regarding life in Galilee certainly apply to Sepphoris, the greatest city of that region.[40] While this assumption may at times be correct, in most cases there is no way of

---

[33] Yeivin, "Notes," p. 24.

[34] The coins have been catalogued by C. S. Bunnel in Waterman, *Report*, pp. 35ff. Cf. Avi-Yonah, "Sepphoris," pp. 1053f.

[35] Translation is that of Avi-Jonah, *ibid.*, p. 1055. On the mosaic and its inscription, see C. Clermont-Ganneau, "*Mosaique juive a inscription de Sepphoris*," *CRAIBL* (1909), pp. 677ff. and J. Naveh, *ʿAl Peseifas Ve-ʾEven* (1978), pp. 51f.

[36] See E. L. Sukenik, "*Mi-Seridei Ẓippori*," *Tarbiz*, 3 (1931), 107f.

[37] See N. Avigad, "*Qever Benot Yaʿaqov She-Le-Yad Ẓippori*," *ʾEreẓ Yisrael* 11 (1973), 41ff. Cf. Sukenik, "*Mi-Seridei Ẓippori*," pp. 108f. and Avi-Yonah, "Sepphoris," pp. 1154f.
Sukenik has also published two short inscriptions found on tombstones at Sepphoris. These refer to rabbis. See E. L. Sukenik, "*Shetei Maẓevot Yehudiyot Mi-Ẓippori*," *Yediʿot Ha-Ḥevrah Ha-ʿIvrit La-Ḥaqirat ʾEreẓ Yisrael Va-ʿAtiqoteha*, 12 (1945-6), 62ff.

[38] See Avi-Yonah, "Sixth Century Inscription," pp. 184-187.

[39] A more lengthy summary of Büchler's findings appears on pp. 77f. of his book. Some other evidence regarding the social conflict has been studied by M. Beer in "*ʿAl Manhigim Shel Yehudei Ẓippori Be-Meʾah Ha-Shelishit*," *Sinai* 74 (1974), 133-138.

[40] Büchler, *Political and Social Leaders*, p. 4.

knowing whether the statement of a Sepphorean rabbi refers to his hometown unless he explicitly says so. Generalities concerning Galilean life may apply to Sepphoris, but then again, they may not. Furthermore, many of the halakhic concerns and aggadic interpretations of the rabbis could very well have been of purely academic interest. In his "*Familienreinheit und Sittlichkeit in Sepphoris im zweiten Jahrhundert*" (1934),[41] Büchler examined the composition of the Jewish community of Sepphoris and relations among its social groupings. Here again undue consideration is given to statements which may not have referred to Sepphoris. Büchler wrote one other study of interest here, "*Über die Minim von Sepphoris und Tiberias im zweiten und dritten Jahrhundert*" (1912).[42] In this work he attempted to identify those *minim* who were reported to have conversed with Sepphorean (and Tiberian) rabbis. Unfortunately, Büchler assumed that these conversations took place in Sepphoris. His conclusion that most of the *minim* concerned were "Bible reading heathen" probably reveals more about the *minim* in general than about those living in Sepphoris. To be sure, Büchler's compilation of evidence in the three works mentioned is impressive, but it is difficult to discern how much of it is relevant.

Unlike Büchler, S. Klein concentrated on rabbinic traditions and reports which specifically refer to Sepphoris (*Ẓippori*). In his article, "*Ẓippori*" (1924),[43] Klein collated many of these references and attempted a topical study of their substance. Klein deals with such subjects as the structure of the city, its environs, history and social composition. His considerable knowledge of Galilee serves him well in his elucidation of topographical and geographical matters.

Both Büchler and Klein are to be credited with emphasizing the importance of rabbinic literature for any inquiry into the history of Sepphoris.[44] The question to be addressed here, however, is how the information provided in rabbinic literature is to be used for such an inquiry. We have already pointed out the difficulties with Büchler's approach. Klein's study provides much useful information, but the general reliability of the sources is taken for granted. The Tosefta, Mishnah, Talmudim and Midrashim do not pretend to offer a historical profile of Sepphoris or for that matter any other city in ancient Palestine.[45] The rabbis,

---

[41] *MGWJ* 78 (1934), 126-164.

[42] In *Festschrift zu Hermann Cohens Siebzigstem Geburtstage* (1912), pp. 271-295. The article reappeared in English as "The Minim of Sepphoris and Tiberias in the Second and Third Centuries," in A. Büchler, *Studies in Jewish History* (1956), pp. 245-274.

[43] Referred to above, n. 3. Klein also collected many of the rabbinic references to Sepphoris in his *Sefer Ha-Yishuv* I, pp. 130-141. Cf. the article on Sepphoris by I. Z. Horowitz in the encyclopedia *ʾOẓar Yisrael* 9 (1913), 51-54.

[44] For a recent attempt to collate the rabbinic material and integrate it with the archeological data, see K. Mukhtar, "*Ẓippori Bi-Yemei Bayit Sheni, Ha-Mishnah Ve-Ha-Talmud*" (M. A. Thesis, Tel Aviv University, 1974).

[45] In his *Caesarea Under Roman Rule* (1975), L. I. Levine has utilized rabbinic literature in addition to archeological, numismatic and classical sources to reconstruct the history of Caesarea. The variety of sources available to Levine enabled him to clarify many aspects of the city's history. The sources for the history of Sepphoris are more limited resulting in a greater dependence upon the rabbinic material.

after all, were not historians; their incidental references to Sepphoris are usually made in the context of other halakhic and aggadic concerns.[46] As such, the rabbinic evidence must be utilized with extreme caution.

Attempts to extrapolate historical information from rabbinic literature are made even more complicated by the nature of the sources. Seemingly relevant information can often be found in contexts which give no obvious indication of the time or place intended. Or else, the composite nature of the material may suggest several different possibilities. Even when the text or its contents can be reasonably assigned to a particular period or locale, it is by no means certain that the historical information it provides is original to it. Very often, parallels found in other collections lack the information, expand upon it, or contradict it altogether. As much of the material was redacted long after the time it reflects, it is difficult to discern what constitutes an editorial gloss and what is germane to the text. Finally, we are dependent upon those manuscripts and editions available to us.[47] Indeed the obstacles to fruitful historical inquiry seem formidable.

Several attempts, however, have been made to investigate historical topics using the rabbinic sources critically. S. Lieberman, in several works, has shown how philological considerations and knowledge of the Greco-Roman milieu can contribute immeasurably to our understanding of Palestinian life as portrayed in rabbinic literature.[48] He has especially noted the importance of papyri and inscriptions.[49] With regard to the usage of rabbinic sources, Lieberman has stated, "Every single passage of Talmudic literature must be investigated both in the light of the whole context and as a separate unit in regard to its correct reading, meaning, time and place."[50] According to Lieberman, much of the material appearing in the Palestinian Talmud and early Midrashim belongs to the third and

[46] In his "Preface to the Second Printing" of *There We Sat Down* (1978), p. xvii, J. Neusner states: "A study of rabbinic sources will not provide much, if any, evidence that we have eyewitness accounts of great events or stenographic records of what people actually said. On the contrary, it is anachronistic to suppose the Talmudic rabbis cared to supply such information to begin with." On the disinterest of the rabbis in history cf. Cohen, *Josephus*, pp. 253ff.

[47] For many a rabbinic work, a critical edition has yet to appear. A survey of some of the available editions and manuscripts appears in I. Meiseles, "Talmud, Recent Research," *Encyclopaedia Judaica Yearbook* 1974, pp. 266f. Also, B. M. Bokser, "An Annotated Bibliographical Guide to the Study of the Palestinian Talmud," *Aufstieg und Niedergang der römischen Welt* pt. 2, vol. 19.2 (1974), 139-256, and in the same volume, D. Goodblatt, "The Babylonian Talmud," pp. 265f. and 267f.

[48] Some of Lieberman's historical studies appear in his *Hellenism in Jewish Palestine* (1962); *Greek in Jewish Palestine* (1965) and *Texts and Studies* (1974). Also, see his "The Martyrs of Caesarea," *Annuaire de l'Institut de Philologie et d'Histoire Orientales et Slaves* 7 (1939-44), 395-445 and "*Redifat Dat Yisrael*," in the *Salo Baron Jubilee Volumes* (1975), III, 213-245.

[49] See Lieberman's *Greek in Jewish Palestine*, p. 5. By way of comparison see G. Allon, *Meḥqarim Be-Toledot Yisrael* I (1967) and II (1970). These volumes contain articles by Allon which originally appeared elsewhere. Allon fully understood the value of rabbinic literature for historical inquiries and, like Lieberman, was adept at using external sources.

[50] "Martyrs of Caesarea," p. 395.

fourth centuries and is, therefore, particularly valuable for the history of Palestine during that period.[51]

Also relevant to our discussion are the recent works of D. Sperber, *Roman Palestine* 200-400: *Money and Prices* (1974) and *Roman Palestine* 200-400: *The Land* (1978). In these studies, Sperber is cognizant of the difficulties involved in the use of rabbinic literature for historical inquiries. He pays particular attention to the variants found in parallel texts and recognizes the need to determine whether these were part of the original text. As Sperber explains, "...it is crucial to distinguish the original authentic form of a statement (as far as is possible) from its re-edited or reworded form. Likewise, it must be seen whether a term belongs historically to its own chronological stratum, or whether it is merely being used as a literary device, an archaism, etc."[52] In many cases, Sperber's reconstruction of the monetary system and agrarian life of Palestine in the Roman period is aided by his critical examination of the sources.[53]

Although primarily interested in Midrash, R. Bloch has formulated an approach to aggadic traditions which is helpful with regard to rabbinic material in general. In her "*Note Méthodologique pour l'étude de la littérature rabbinique*,"[54] Bloch suggests a two stage approach beginning with an "external" comparison of the traditions with others appearing in writings outside of Palestinian rabbinic Judaism. Since the dates of many of the external sources are known, they can help establish a *terminus ad quem* for rabbinic traditions. The second stage is an "internal" comparison which would trace a single tradition through the various documents in which it appears. According to Bloch, the purpose of this stage is "to distinguish the most primitive elements and the variants, the developments, the additions and the revisions; it takes account of the diversity of literary genres and historical situations."[55] Although Bloch fails to recognize the importance of the context from which the traditions are drawn,[56] her articulation of the problem and her suggested solution are instructive.

Perhaps the most ambitious attempt to formulate an epistemological framework for historical inquiries into rabbinic literature has been made by J. Neusner. In his *Development of a Legend: Studies on the Traditions Concerning Yohanan ben Zakkai* (1970), Neusner compares different versions of stories and shows that those appearing in later collections are in fact dependent upon those found in

---

[51] *Ibid.*

[52] *Money and Prices*, p. 21.

[53] Sperber, however, relegates much of his textual analysis to the notes. For a chapter in which he does not, see "Underselling and the Law of *ʾOnaʾah*," in *The Land*, pp. 136-159.

[54] *Researches de Science Religieuse*, 43 (1955), pp. 194-227. This article has recently been translated into English by W. S. Green and W. J. Sullivan in *Approaches to Ancient Judaism: Theory and Practice*, ed. W. S. Green (1978), pp. 51-76. The English translation will be referred to here.

[55] *Approaches*, p. 60.

[56] Cf. Green's remarks in his introduction to *Approaches*, p. 4. For some of the difficulties of Bloch's approach with regard to Midrash see E. P. Sanders, *Paul and Palestinian Judaism* (1977), pp. 26f.

earlier collections. They are, therefore, later in origin.[57] In *The Rabbinic Traditions about the Pharisees Before 70* (three volumes, 1971), Neusner proposes a method for dating traditions attributed to a given rabbi. Neusner considers a tradition to be verified if it is quoted or alluded to by a later authority. The period in which the later authority taught can be regarded as a firm *terminus ante quem* for the tradition. Before that time, the substance and form of the tradition must have been known.[58] In his *Eliezer Ben Hyrcanus: The Tradition and the Man* (two volumes, 1973), Neusner claims that those traditions attested to at Yavneh (70-120 C.E.) and Usha (140-165 C.E.) bring us closest to the Eliezer of history.[59] The later the tradition, the less likely it is to reflect the concerns of Eliezer. Those traditions which are first attested to in amoraic materials probably reflect the Eliezer of legend.[60]

Neusner refined his approach in *A History of the Mishnaic Law of Purities* III, *Kelim* (1974). In this work, he pays particular attention to laws attributed to named *tannaim* but unattested to by later authorities. Neusner found that, as a rule, these laws do not rely upon traditions attributed to later authorities. As such, they can be dated to the period of the scholar in whose name they appear. Anonymous traditions which are related to or contradict these dated laws can then be assigned to the same period. By investigating the relationship of anonymous traditions to those which have been dated, Neusner attempts to assign the former to either Yavneh or Usha.[61]

Other methods of verifying traditions can, of course, be suggested. As mentioned earlier, parallels found in sources external to rabbinic literature can be used to verify a particular tradition.[62] Unfortunately, this type of information is not always available. The date of compilation of a collection in which a tradition appears can also be used to establish a *terminus ante quem* for that tradition. This approach, however, does not always permit as precise a dating as possible. Thus Neusner's method provides a useful alternative.[63]

Neusner, of course, realized that rabbinic literature does not permit the writing of history in the ordinary sense. It is for this reason that he turned instead to the analysis of individual traditions. By studying the development and forms of these traditions, and applying his method of "attestations" to them,

---

[57] *Development*, p. 265.

[58] See Neusner's *Rabbinic Traditions* III, 180ff. Cf. his *From Politics to Piety* (1973), pp. 92ff.

[59] Eliezer himself lived during the Yavnean period, but a contemporary could also attest to his words.

It should be noted that Neusner originally used the terms "verify/verification" but later adopted "attest/attestation." They are, therefore, used interchangeably in the discussion here.

[60] *Eliezer* II, 92ff.

[61] See *Purities* III, 237-249.

[62] See p. 9.

[63] Neusner considers the other methods in *Rabbinic Traditions* III, 180ff. and *From Politics to Piety*, 92ff.

Neusner was better able to discern their historical reliability and implications.[64]

Any historical inquiry which utilizes rabbinic literature as its main source must consider the problems addressed by Lieberman, Bloch, Sperber and Neusner. The mere collating of data and harmonization of divergent sources can no longer be considered a valid approach to this type of inquiry. The studies presented below attempt to illustrate how philological, literary, textual and historical considerations can help elucidate some of the rabbinic traditions pertaining to Sepphoris.[65]

The point of departure is, of course, the text of each relevant tradition. Each passage has been translated taking into consideration significant variants found in the available manuscripts and editions. Parallels appearing in other collections are considered individually. Although traditions appearing in later collections are generally presumed to be late, the variants they contain must still be examined carefully. The *amoraim*, in particular, preserved earlier tannaitic material in the form of *baraitot*. It is not always clear when a variant belongs to the original text and when it has been interpolated into a *baraita*. Parallels also offer useful information as to when a tradition circulated and how it was understood by other rabbis or schools.[66] Since the context of a passage is likewise helpful in this regard, it too has been fully elucidated.

Traditional commentaries to rabbinic literature have been routinely consulted. The Geonim and *rishonim*[67] in particular often provide invaluable insight into a passage and its context. When the plain meaning is not apparent, these commentators often provide relevant information from other rabbinic sources. Sometimes a commentary will even preserve a reading not found in the extant manuscripts. Although the commentaries must be read critically to avoid interpretations which have been read into the text, they should not be overlooked.[68]

While philological, literary and textual considerations are invaluable for establishing the correctness and meaning of a tradition, they do not guarantee its veracity. After all, the best form of a tradition may only represent what a later editor wanted us to know.[69] Only after the best text is recovered, however, can

---

[64] For a more in-depth discussion of Neusner's methodology, see A. J. Saldarini, "'Form Criticism' of Rabbinic Literature," *JBL* 96 (1977), pp. 262ff.

[65] The intention here, of course, is not to subject each tradition or rabbinic passage to all of the considerations mentioned. Such an effort is beyond the limits of this study. Philological, literary, textual and historical considerations are taken into account only insofar as to determine the historical value of a passage.

[66] Or, in many cases, how it was understood by the editor(s) of the text, who is (are) often responsible for the way a parallel is used in a later context.

[67] The *rishonim* are commentators who lived between the end of the Geonic period (eleventh century) and the middle of the fifteenth century. See I. M. Ta-Shma, "*Rishonim*," *Encyclopaedia Judaica* 14 (1971), cols. 192f.

[68] On the importance of traditional commentaries, cf. L. H. Schiffman, *The Halakhah at Qumran* (1975), pp. 16f.

[69] Cf. Neusner, *There We Sat Down*, pp. xv-xvi.

the historicity of a tradition be discussed. Because of the difficulties with the usage of statements made by Sepphorean rabbis,[70] only traditions containing direct references to Sepphoris (*Ẓippori*) will be considered in the studies presented below. Most of the evidence will consist of incidental realia and data in need of interpretation vis-à-vis the known historical evidence (literary sources, archeology, etc.). Passages preserving events in the history of Sepphoris are considered, but usually because they contain other pertinent information. When the event itself is important, an attempt is made to verify it using external sources.[71] Even when the historicity of an event cannot be determined, the tradition is still elucidated since it may reveal the attitude or perspective of those who preserved it.

The primary purpose, of course, is to learn something about the Sepphoris with which the *tannaim* and *amoraim* were familiar. Two subjects will be investigated here. Part One focuses on an institution, the military encampment or *castra* which rabbinic sources report was located at Sepphoris. According to the Mishnah (*ʿArakhin* 9:6), the *castra* of Sepphoris was in existence since the days of Joshua bin Nun. This and other traditions concerning the *castra* will be elucidated in order to determine the nature and importance of this institution. An attempt is also made to ascertain the various periods in which the *castra* functioned and to relate its history to that of the city itself.

Part Two deals with a particular segment of Sepphorean society, the priests. It is commonly accepted that the priestly course of *Yedaʿyah* settled at Sepphoris. Indeed, priests are reported to have resided in Sepphoris as early as the Second Temple period. All those traditions which seem to be of importance for the history of priestly settlement at Sepphoris will be discussed below.

Although the subjects themselves suggest various lines of inquiry, in the end, each tradition is permitted to speak for itself. The intent is not to look for some predetermined information but to listen to whatever the sources have to say. Only then can their historical value be fully appreciated. Finally, it should be noted that the choice of subjects was necessarily selective; the application of the methodology adopted here to all of the rabbinic references to "*Ẓippori*" would have required several volumes.

---

[70] See above, pp. 6f.

[71] See the discussion of the Joseph ben Elim material below, pp. 74ff.

PART ONE

THE CASTRA

FOREWORD

Rabbinic sources mention the existence of a *castra* (קסטרא, קצטרה, קצרה, גסטרא, ''military encampment'')[1] at Sepphoris. Unfortunately, no other sources use this term in relationship to Sepphoris.[2] The rabbis, furthermore, only mention the *castra* in passing; they were not interested in the institution itself. The context of the references, therefore, assumes an importance of its own and must be carefully examined if anything is to be gleaned concerning the *castra*. The following study analyzes the passages in which the references occur in order to determine the meaning and historicity of the *castra shel-Ẓippori* (*castra* of Sepphoris).

---

[1] All of the Semitic forms have been understood as variants of Latin *castra*. S. Krauss, in his *Griechische und lateinische Lehnwörter im Talmud, Midrasch und Targum* (1898-9), I, 129, suggests that the emphatic sound of צ compensated for the elision of T in the form קצרה. Another example would be בוצרה for Bostra. For the interchange of ס for צ and ג for ק in both western and eastern Aramaic, see G. Dalman, *Grammatik des jüdisch-palästinischen Aramäisch und aramäische Dialektproben* (1960), pp. 99, 104 and J. N. Epstein, *Diqduq ʾAramit Bavlit* (1960), p. 19. G. Preisigke, in his *Wörterbuch der griechischen Papyrusurkunden* (1925-58), III, 205, has documented the form γαστρῆσις for Greek χαστρησιῶν which is the equivalent of Latin *castrensis*, a word derived from *castra* (see P. G. W. Glare, ed., *Oxford Latin Dictionary* (1968-), II, 283). Thus the same G for K phenomenon occurs in the Greek form χάστρα.

The word קצרה meaning *castra* should not be confused with a similarly spelled word denoting ''a fuller.'' For general definitions of the Semitic forms, see the appropriate entries in J. Fuerst, *Glossarium Graeco-Hebraeum* (1890); A. Kohut, *ʿArukh Ha-Shalem* (reprinted, 1970); Krauss, *Lehnwörter*, and J. Levy, *Wörterbuch über die Talmudim und Midraschim* (1883).

On *castra* as a ''military encampment'' see Glare, p. 282. Cf. E. A. Sophocles, *Greek Lexicon of the Roman and Byzantine Periods* (1914), p. 632.

For the sake of consistency, the Latin form, *castra*, is used throughout this chapter as the transliteration of the Semitic word.

[2] According to F. Lebrecht (*Bether, die fragliche Stadt im Hadrianisch-juedischen Kriege* (1877), p. 40), the *Sabure siue Veterocariare* mentioned in the *Notitia Dignitatum* (ed. O. Seeck (1876), p. 73) is equivalent to *Vetera* (''old'') *Castra-Saphurei*, i.e. the old *castra* of Sepphoris. Lebrecht also identifies the city of Bether with Vetera making Bether and Sepphoris one and the same! These views, although widely repeated (see, for example, Kohut, *ʿArukh Ha-Shalem* II, 89; 123 and S. Krauss, *Antoninus und Rabbi* (1910), pp. 118f.), cannot stand up to criticism. See S. Klein, ''*Ẓippori*,'' p. 53, n. 6. Cf. *idem.*, *Beiträge zur Geographie und Geschichte Galiläas* (1909), p. 34, n. 3.

CHAPTER ONE

THE "OLD" *CASTRA*

The Castra in Tannaitic Sources

Mishnah ʿ*Arakhin* 9:6 reads as follows:[3]

> עיר שגגותיה[4] חומתה ושאינה מוקפת חומה מימות יהושע בן נון אינה כבתי ערי חומה ואילו הן בתי ערי חומה שלש חצירות שלשני שני בתים מוקפות חומה מימות יהושע בן נון כגון קצרה הישנה שלציפרין[5] וחקרה של גש חלב ויותפת[6] הישנה וגמלה וגדור[7] וחדיד ואונו וירושלם וכן כיוצא בהן

> (Houses in)[8] a city whose roofs (*gagoteha*) form its wall, and/or that was not encompassed by a wall since the days of Joshua bin Nun are not considered "dwellings in walled cities" (*battei ʿarei ḥomah*).
>
> (Houses in any of) these are considered "dwellings in walled cities": (A city which has no less than) three courtyards, each having two houses, which have been encompassed by a wall since the days of Joshua bin Nun, such as (*kegon*): *castra ha-yeshanah* (the old encampment) of (*shel-*)[9] Sepphoris, the *ḥakra*[10] (citadel) of Gush Ḥalav (Gischala),[11] old (*yeshanah*) Jotapata,[12] Gamala,[13] Gedor,[14] Ḥadid,[15] Ono,[16] Jerusalem and others like them (*kayoẓe bahen*).

---

[3] The text presented here is that of Ms. Kaufmann.

[4] Ms. Cambridge has שגנותיה (*she-ganoteha* "whose gardens") instead of שגגותיה (*she-gagoteha*). The latter, however, appears in the better Mss. and makes better sense.

[5] Ms. Parma has שבציפורין. Codex Jerusalem and Ms. Cambridge have של צפורים which agrees with the printed editions.

[6] Most of the Mss. read יודפת but יותפת is closer to the Ἰωτάπατα of Josephus. For the location of this city see below, n. 12.

[7] The better Mss. have גדור. Codex Jerusalem and some of the printed editions of the Talmud read גדוד. Ms. Munich (95) of the Talmud has גרור, but the ensuing discussion of the *gemara* has . For the location of Gedor, see below, n. 14.

[8] This phrase and "houses in any of" further on in the text are understood from the context. Cf. M. ʿ*Arakhin* 9:3.

[9] Or, according to Ms. Parma (above, n. 5), "the *castra ha-yeshanah* which is in (Sepphoris)."

[10] This word also appears in rabbinic literature as אקרא. Krauss (*Lehnwörter* I, 61; II, 125; 252f.) identifies it with Greek ἄκρα = "Burg" or "Castell." H. G. Liddel and R. Scott in *A Greek-English Lexicon* (1976), p. 54 define ἄκρα as a "hilltop" or a "citadel" overhanging a town like an acropolis. The word appears often in Josephus and in the Books of Maccabees. See S. Klein's entry in the German *Encyclopaedia Judaica* (1928-34), I, cols. 38ff., for the references and a comprehensive discussion of the term. In order to remain as faithful as possible to the Greek form, the word חקרה will be transliterated as *ḥakra* (rather than *ḥaqrah*).

[11] This city in upper Galilee is known today as Al-Jish. See M. Avi-Yonah, *The Holy Land*[2] (1977), p. 133.

[12] Jotapata was identified by Schultz with Khirbet Jifat due north of Sepphoris. See E. G. Schultz, "*Mittheilungen über eine Reise durch Samarien und Galilaea*," *ZDMG* 3 (1848), 49ff. Cf. the "*Anmerkungen*" of H. Gross in the same volume, pp. 59ff. Also F. M. Abel, *Geographie de la Palestine* (1933) II, 366.

[13] For the location of Gamala, see note 41 below.

The Mishnah in which this passage appears elaborates upon the biblical laws pertaining to the redemption of houses in walled cities. According to Leviticus 25:29-30, a house within a walled city could be redeemed for one full year after it had been sold. If it was not redeemed during that time, it became the property of the purchaser (and his descendants) and was not "released" in the year of Jubilee.[17] The section in the Mishnah immediately preceding our passage discusses "a house built within a wall" (בית הבנוי בחומה).Two mid-second century *tannaim*, Judah ben Ilai and Simeon ben Yoḥai, disagree as to whether this type of structure constitutes a dwelling in a walled city.[18] Our passage is a further clarification of the matter: a city "whose roofs form its wall" is in effect a place where all the peripheral houses are built within the wall.[19] Thus it may be assumed that the text we have cited belongs to the same circle of second century *tannaim* whose opinions precede it.[20] Here, however, the stipulation that the wall must be in existence "since the days of Joshua" is introduced. A concise definition of *battei ʿarei ḥomah* is also provided (ואילו הן בתי ערי חומה): Only a dwelling in a city of "no less than three courtyards, each having two houses which have been

---

[14] Gedor is believed to be identical with Tell Gadur adjoining Es-Salt in Peraea (Transjordan). See Abel, *Geographie* II, 154, S. Klein, *ʾEreẓ Ha-Galil* (1967), p. 6, n. 24, and A. H. M. Jones, *The Cities of the Eastern Roman Provinces* (1971), p. 258. Cf. H. St. J. Thackeray's note to Josephus, *War* IV, 413 (*Loeb Classical Library*).

[15] Ḥadid is modern El Hadithe near Lod. See M. Avi-Yonah, *Map of Roman Palestine* (1940), p. 16 and S. Klein, *ʾEreẓ Yehudah* (1939), pp. 20 and 60.

[16] Ono, today known as Kefar ʿAna, is also in the vicinity of Lod. See Klein, *ibid.*, p. 20. Cf. Jones, *Cities*, p. 280.

[17] A house in an unwalled town could be redeemed at any time and did return to the original owner in the Jubilee year. See Leviticus 25:31. According to S. Baron, these laws took into consideration the "destitute peasants" who lived outside of the (walled) cities in rural areas. These people were constantly losing their property through expropriation. See S. Baron, *A Social and Religious History of the Jews* I[2] (1952), 85f. The reasoning behind the tannaitic laws will be explained later in this study.

[18] M. *ʿArakhin* 9:5. Cf. T. *ʿArakhin* 5:14. R. Judah says it does not qualify as a house in a walled city. R. Simeon maintains that the outer wall of the house can serve as the city wall. The *tannaim* may have understood Joshua 2:15 differently. See B. *ʿArakhin* 32a and *Tosefot Yom Tov* on the Mishnah.

[19] This is in accordance with the interpretation of R. Samuel Strashun. Rabbenu Gershom explains that "the entire wall was full of roofs" (איכא דאמרי שכל החומה סביב מלאה גגות), i.e. the roofs of the houses formed the top of the wall. Similarly, Israel Lipschutz, in his commentary, *Tiferet Yisrael*, explains that the wall of a "house built within a wall" formed part of the city wall and rose higher than the house itself. The wall of a house in a city "whose house-roofs form its walls," on the other hand, did not extend higher than the house but merged with the roof so as to give the impression that the roof and wall were one. Cf. the Talmud's (B. *ʿArakhin* 32a) explanation of a "vaulted roof" (שור איגר). Admittedly, there are many possible explanations (See *Encyclopedia Talmudit* (1947-), V, 18 for a summary.), but it is clear that this discussion is related to the one preceding it in the Mishnah. The same idea underlies both cases: Part of a house, either its wall or its roof, constitutes a section of the city wall.

[20] For the dating of anonymous traditions (in this case, the entire passage) based on their relationship to attributed sayings (the opinions of R. Judah and R. Simeon), see the discussion above, p. 10.

encompassed by a wall since the days of Joshua bin Nun" is included in this category. Examples of cities which fulfill these requirements are then presented.

This chapter of the Mishnah is based upon the relationship of the sale of property to the laws of Jubilee.[21] Since there are indications in rabbinic literature that these laws were not implemented during the Second Temple period,[22] it might be suggested that the *halakhot* pertaining to the redemption of dwellings in walled cities are merely theoretical. A. Gulak has convincingly argued otherwise.[23] This scholar admits that much of the Jubilee legislation could not have been observed during the Second Temple period because the "release" of lands depended upon the biblical order of tribal settlement. Once this arrangement was disturbed,[24] many laws could no longer be observed. The *halakhot* of our passage, however, did not become obsolete because they were not dependent upon the ancient tribal arrangement. Even during the biblical period, the settlers within walled cities were of a mixture of tribes.[25] The Bible, therefore, is not concerned with the return, during the Jubilee year, of the houses purchased by these settlers to any particular tribe. Houses which were not redeemed within a year after their sale were to "pass to the purchaser beyond reclaim throughout the ages."[26] This law remained in effect during the days of the Second Temple precisely because it was never contingent upon the tribal order of settlement.[27] Gulak further explains that cities which were walled after the time of Joshua were not considered "walled cities" (*ʿarei ḥomah*) because they were originally regarded as courtyards and fields to which the Jubilee law of release was applicable.[28] Regardless of whether Gulak is correct that the *halakhah* of *battei ʿarei ḥomah* was still in effect during the Second Temple period, his elucidation of the law explains the emphasis in the Mishnah on the antiquity of the walls. The use of the phrase "since the days of

---

[21] See Leviticus 25:8ff. For a discussion of the entire chapter of the Mishnah, see J. Neusner, *A History of the Mishnaic Law of Holy Things* IV (1979), 71-84.

[22] See, for example, B. *ʿArakhin* 32b where it is reported that the Jubilee was annulled when the tribes of Reuben and Gad and the half tribe of Menasseh were exiled. Also see the discussion and sources quoted by A. Gulak, *Le-Ḥeqer Toledot Ha-Mishpat Ha-ʿIvri Bi-Tequfat Ha-Talmud* (1929), p. 45, n. 2.

[23] Gulak, *ibid.*, pp. 36ff.

[24] The tribal confederacy began to be undermined by the transformation of Israel into a dynastic monarchy. Tribal independence was already disregarded by Solomon when he reorganized the land into administrative districts. See J. Bright, *A History of Israel*[3] (1974), pp. 218f. The notion of tribal distinctiveness persisted, however, as can be seen in Ezekiel 47:13-23 and 48.

[25] Gulak, *Ḥeqer*, p. 36. The tribal notion seems to have been the basis of many biblical laws. See Liver, "The Israelite Tribes," in *The World History of the Jewish People* III, *Judges* (1971), 191f. On the observance of the biblical Jubilee year, see Baron, *History* I, 332, n. 30.

[26] Leviticus 25:30. Houses in unwalled villages, however, returned to their original owners during the Jubilee year. See the following verse in Leviticus.

[27] Gulak (*Ḥeqer*, p. 36) contends that the tendency was to permit the final sale of property outside of the walled cities. Despite the fact that the surrounding areas lost their tribal distinctiveness, the redemption law of walled cities was not expanded to the countryside. Only in cities walled "since the days of Joshua" could homes be redeemed during the year following the sale.

[28] Cf. the Sifra version of the law presented below, p. 19.

Joshua bin Nun" by the *tannaim* indicates that they assumed that the tribal arrangement during the biblical conquest of Palestine was the reason for the *halakhah* of *battei ʿarei ḥomah.*[29]

The words, "since the days of Joshua bin Nun" are, therefore, to be understood literally. The antiquity of the walls was taken seriously and the cities cited in the Mishnah were believed to have been ancient, going back to the biblical conquest. It is interesting, however, that only one of the cities, Jerusalem, is mentioned in the biblical lists of fortified cities.[30] The mishnaic list is obviously a reflection of a later time, but the inclusion of Jerusalem suggests a date earlier than the destruction of that city in 70 C.E.[31] It will be shown below that several other cities mentioned in the list flourished in the pre-70 period.

The same list of cities is also presented in a parallel to the Mishnaic passage found in the Sifra:[32]

---

[29] Perhaps, for this reason, the *halakhah* was not expanded to areas which later lost their tribal identity. See n. 27.

It should be noted that according to B. *ʿArakhin* 29a, the *halakhot* of *battei ʿarei ḥomah* were observed only when the Jubilee laws were still in effect. Gulak believes, however, that this *baraita* was taught following the destruction of most of the cities mentioned in the Mishnah during the First Revolt. He points to M. *ʿArakhin* 9:4 as proof that the *halakhot* were still observed during the Second Temple period. That passage indicates that Hillel implemented a *taqqanah* which enabled the redeemer to deposit his money in a Temple chamber should the buyer hide himself on the last day of the year in order to prevent the transaction from taking place. (On the Hillel tradition, see J. Neusner, *Rabbinic Traditions* I, 215f.) Gulak contends that the other laws which according to the *baraita* of B. *ʿArakhin* 29a were not observed once the Jubilee had been suspended, also remained in effect for a time during the Second Temple period. See Gulak, *Ḥeqer*, p. 38 and especially note 1. All this, however, has no bearing on the point made here, i.e. the *tannaim* understood the relationship of the redemption laws to the biblical notions of settlement.

[30] Fortified cities are referred to as *ʿarei mivẓar* in the Bible. (The root b/ẓ/r means "to enclose," see *BDB*, p. 130). See, for example, Num. 32:36, Joshua 10:20 and II Kings 18:13. A list is presented in Joshua 19:35-38. The walls of Jerusalem are mentioned in many places, for example, I Kings 3:1, 9:15. The city is characterized as *beẓurah* (fortified) in Ez. 21:25. On the meaning of *ʿarei mivẓar*, cf. F. S. Frick, *The City in Ancient Israel* (1977), p. 31.

[31] According to Klein (*ʾEreẓ Ha-Galil*, p. 7), the list had to have been composed before 70 since Jerusalem was no longer a Jewish city after that date. It could, however, be argued that Jerusalem was selected as an example merely because it was a well known walled city whose biblical tradition was well established. Still, the other cities in the list were not as well known and, as will be shown, were places whose importance was in the pre-70 era.

A tradition preserved in a *baraita* (*B. Babaʾ Qammaʾ* 82b and *ʾAvot de-Rabbi Natan*, chap. 25) states that the sale of houses could never become final in Jerusalem. If this were true, the *halakhah* of *battei ʿarei ḥomah* would never apply to Jerusalem. Thus one *amora* postulated the existence of two Jerusalems! See B. *ʿArakhin* 32b and the discussion below, pp. 21f. Guttmann has suggested that the *baraita* reflects a "theoretical *halakhah*" created to emphasize the eternal superiority of Jerusalem. *Halakhot* of this nature were, in the final analysis, disregarded by the redactors of the Mishnah. See A. Guttmann, "Jerusalem in Tannaitic Law," reprinted in his *Studies in Rabbinic Judaism* (1976), pp. 236-260. According to Sperber, the *halakhah* of *battei ʿarei ḥomah* originally applied to Jerusalem but was later rescinded with respect to that city. See D. Sperber, "Social Legislation in Jerusalem during the Latter Part of the Second Temple Period," *Journal for the Study of Judaism in the Persian, Hellenistic and Roman Periods* 6 (1975), 91ff.

[32] *Be-Har, parashah* 4:1, here quoted from the 1545 ed. Venice (Jerusalem, 1971). Cf. the parallel of the *Yalqut* 665.

ואיש כי ימכור בית מושב עיר חומה יכול אפילו הקיפוה חומ׳ מיכן ולהבא ת״ל בית מושב עיר חומה המוקפת חומה מימות יהושע בן נון ולא שהקיפוה מיכאן ולהבא ואילו הן בתי ערי חומה שלש חצירות של שני[33] בתים המוקפות חומה מימות יהושע בן נון כנון קצרה הישנה של ציפורים וחקרה של גוש חלב ויודפת הישנה וגמלה הרי בגליל ונדור הרי בעבר הירדן וחדיד ואונו וירושלם הרי ביהודה[34] אמר רבי ישמעאל ב״ר יוסי לא מנו אילו אלא שקידשום כשעלו בני[35] הגולה אבל הראשונות בטלו כיון שבטלה הארץ

"(And) if a man sells a dwelling house (*bet moshav*) in a walled city" (Leviticus 25:29): It could even be that they (the people living there) encompassed it later on (after the days of Joshua)! Thus the text states: "a dwelling house *in* a walled city," i.e. one which is encompassed by a wall since the days of Joshua bin Nun and not which they encompassed later on. (Houses in any of) these are considered dwellings in a walled city: (A city which has no less than) three courtyards, each having two houses, which have been encompassed by a wall since the days of Joshua bin Nun, such as (*kegon*): *castra ha-yeshanah* (the old encampment) of Sepphoris, the *ḥakra* (citadel) of Gush Ḥalav, old (*yeshanah*) Jotapata and Gamala, (which are) in Galilee (*harei be-galil*); Gedor, (which is) in Transjordan (*harei be-ʿever ha-yarden*) and Ḥadid, Ono and Jerusalem, (which are) in Judah (Judea; *harei bi-yehudah*). Rabbi Ishmael ben Yose said, "They (the *tannaim*) only specify those (cities) which the exiles (to Babylonia) sanctified upon their return. The (sanctity of the) original (cities of the conquest period) was suspended when (that of) the entire land was suspended."

Here the *halakhah* is expounded as an exegesis of Leviticus 25:29 with the emphasis again upon the antiquity of the walls. The biblical verse reads "a dwelling house *in* a walled city" indicating that the city had to have been walled at the time of its settlement.[36] The Sifra text is similar to that of the Mishnah except for the addition of the parenthetical phrases, *harei be-galil, harei be-ʿever ha-yarden*, and *harei bi-yehudah*, which will be shown to be interpolations. The view of Ishmael ben Yose (late second century) which also appears elsewhere,[37] seems inappropriate here. There is no need to explain that the *tannaim* "only" specify (לא מנו אילו אלא) cities which were sanctified by the returnees from Babylonia. The text explicitly states that the cities mentioned are examples (*kegon*, such as). Ishmael's excuse for the selectivity of the list is unnecessary. His opinion appears to have been appended to the original exegesis and list of cities.

---

[33] The word *shenei* (שני) is repeated in the Codex Vatican 31 as well as in all of the Mss. of M. *ʿArakhin* which parallel this section. See p. 15.

[34] Codex Vatican 31 reads הרי היא ביהודה implying that the explanation was only intended to clarify the location of Jerusalem. Perhaps the editor of this Ms. knew of the view that there were two Jerusalems (See n. 31)!

[35] Codex Vatican 31 has *min* (מן) instead of בני. Cf. the Tosefta parallel (below, pp. 22f.) and B. *ʿArakhin* 32b.

[36] Elijah b. Solomon Zalman (the *Gaon* of Vilna) explains that the cities which the Jews came upon when entering the land were already walled by the non-Jews living there. The *halakhah* was applied to these cities and not to those later walled by the Jews. See the *Gaon*'s commentary on this text.

[37] T. *ʿArakhin* 5:16 and B. *ʿArakhin* 32b. See below, pp. 22f.

A *baraita* found in the Babylonian *gemara* to Mishnah *ʿArakhin* 9:5 may help to clarify the Sifra text:[38]

תנא גמלא בגליל וגדוד[39] בעבר הירדן וחדיד ואונה[40] וירושלים ביהודה

It was taught (*tenaʾ*): Gamala in Galilee[41] (*be-galil*), Gedor in Transjordan (*be-ʿever ha-yarden*) and Ḥadid, Ono and Jerusalem in Judah (Judea, *bi-yehudah*).

---

[38] B. *ʿArakhin* 32a, ed. Vilna. It should be noted that there is no extant Palestinian *gemara* to *ʿArakhin*.

[39] Ms. Munich (95) appears to have נדור. It is difficult to discern whether the last letter is a ר or a ד.

[40] A corruption of אונו.

[41] This *baraita*, like the Sifra text, considers Gamala as a city in Galilee. Josephus, however, places the city in lower Gaulanitis (Golan). See *War* IV, 2. The Gamala known to Josephus seems to have been a well known fortress. The historian reports that Gamala's southern hill formed a natural citadel (ἄκρα) because of its height. *War* IV, 8 reads: ὁ νότιος δ' αὐτῆς ὄχθος εἰς ἄπειρον ὕψος ἀνατείνων ἄκρα τῆς πόλεως ἦν. Josephus further states that he fortified the city with walls despite its impregnable nature (*War* IV, 9. Cf. II, 574). Of course, there could have been another well known city by the name of Gamala which the *tannaim* preferred for their list. There are, in fact, two sites known as Hirbet "Jumeiliya." (See *Reshumot Yalqut Ha-Pirsumim*, *Reshumot* 1091 (1964), pp. 1356 and 1364 where the coordinates for both are provided.) Neither of these places, however, is known to have been a Jewish stronghold.

Still, S. Klein appears to have had one of these sites in mind when he suggested a place in upper Galilee known as "Dschebl Dshamle" for the Gamala referred to by the *tannaim*. (See Klein's "*Zur Geographie Palästinas in der Zeit Mischna*," *MGWJ* 61 (1917), pp. 139ff.) Klein refers to T. *Makkot* 3:5 as evidence for a Galilean Gamala:

שלש ערים הפריש יהושע בארץ כנען והיו מכוונות כנגד שלש שבעבר הירדן...אע"פ שהפרישו קדש בגליל לא היתה קולטת הפרישו גמלה תחתיה עד שכיבשו את קדש

Joshua set aside three cities in the Land of Canaan (as cities of refuge) and they corresponded to the three in Transjordan.... Even though they (Israel) set aside Qedesh in Galilee, it did not offer asylum; they set aside Gamala instead (of it) until they conquered Qedesh.

The text explicitly states that the three cities of refuge in Transjordan had their counterparts in Canaan proper. Thus Klein believed that just as Qedesh was in Upper Galilee, its temporary replacement, Gamala, had to be located there as well. The problem with this hypothesis is that the area to which Klein assigns Gamala (See his map in *ʾEreẓ Ha-Galil* at the end of the illustration pages) was certainly not conquered before Qedesh. (If in fact it was conquered at all. The Bible (Judges 1:31-33) reports that both Asher and Naphtali failed to complete the conquest of their assigned areas (in upper Galilee) after the death of Joshua. Qedesh, however, was conquered earlier, during Joshua's lifetime. See Joshua 12:22.) If, however, it is assumed that part of the Golan was sometimes referred to as "Galilee" the problem of the location of the city can be solved. Josephus refers to the rebel Judas both as "the Galilean" (*War* II, 118 and 433; *Ant.* XVIII, 23; XX, 102. Cf. Acts 5:37) and as a "Gaulanite from a city called Gamala" (*Ant.* XVIII, 4). The historian certainly knew the location of the city but used the popular designation of the area when he referred to "Judas, the Galilean." Josephus also reports that his command as general included the two Galilees (upper and lower) along with Gamala, the strongest city of the region (*War* II, 568. Cf. D. M. Rhoads, *Israel in Revolution* 6-74 C.E. (1976), p. 48). There can be no doubt that the eastern shores of the "Sea of Galilee" (as the Kinneret is called in the New Testament, for example, Matt. 4:18) were sometimes considered part of Galilee. Gamala has recently been identified by archeologists as a site not far from the north-eastern limit of the sea. For a report on the initial excavations, see S. Guttman, *Gamala* (1977). Also see D. Urman, "The Golan during the Roman and Byzantine Periods: Topography, Settlements, Economy" (Ph.D. dissertation, New York University, 1979), pp. 227-231. For a discussion of a "greater" Galilee, see E. Meyers, "Galilean Regionalism as a Factor in Historical Reconstruction," *BASOR* 221 (1976), 93-101, and cf. G. Stemberger, "Galilee—Land

This concise reformulation of the list of the Mishnah serves as an introduction to the amoraic discussion of the cities. The passage actually omits three items included in the Mishnah and the Sifra: the old *castra* of Sepphoris, the *ḥakra* of Gush Ḥalav and old Jotapata. It also does not suggest that the locations mentioned are merely examples as the other accounts do.[42] The list is otherwise similar to that of the Sifra in that it states the areas in which the cities are located (*be-galil* etc.). Here, however, these parenthetical remarks are an integral part of the *baraita* whose purpose seems to be to identify the regions in which the cities are located.[43] Thus the *baraita* is followed by the question, "what does this mean?" (*ma'i ka'amar* מאי קאמר), i.e. What is the purpose of these designations? Are there not other cities in these regions to which the *halakhah* can be applied?[44] The ensuing amoraic discussion is confined to interpretations of this particular *baraita* with its abbreviated list of cities.[45] In the Sifra version, the parenthetical phrases are superfluous and were probably interpolated by someone familiar with this *baraita*. Similarly, the statement of Rabbi Ishmael seems to be addressed to the same problems which the *amoraim* are concerned with and fits in better in the *gemara*, where it is in fact reproduced.[46] What is original in the Sifra is the exegesis concerning the antiquity of the walls. The editors combined this exegesis with the list of the Misnah and the parenthetical elements of the *baraita*.[47]

The *amoraim* were puzzled by both the selectivity and the identification of the cities mentioned in the *baraita*. According to Abaye (278-338 C.E.), Leviticus 25:29-30 applied to all the walled cities in existence since the days of Joshua bin Nun "up to" (*ʿad*) Gamala in Galilee and "up to" Gedor in Transjordan, as well as to Ḥadid, Ono and Jerusalem in Judea.[48] Thus Abaye regards Gamala and Gedor as mere geographical limitations of the areas in Galilee and Transjor-

---

of Salvation" in W. D. Davies, *The Gospel and the Land: Early Christianity and Jewish Territorial Doctrine* (1974), pp. 409ff.

The identification of the Gamala of the Mishnah (and *baraita*) with the city known to Josephus in Gaulanitis is important for our discussion of the origins of the list of walled cities. See below, pp. 24f.

[42] The Mishnah and Sifra have *kegon*, "such as," before the list. The Mishnah also has *kayoẓe bahen* ("others like them") at the conclusion of the list. Cf. the remarks of *Tosafot* on the *baraita* in B. *ʿArakhin* 32a.

[43] *Baraitot* introduced by *tena'* often complete or explain the Mishnah. Thus they are usually later in origin than the *mishnah* they complement. See H. Albeck, *Mavo' La-Talmudim* (1969), pp. 46ff. and cf. J. N. Epstein, *Mavo' Le-Nusaḥ Ha-Mishnah*² (1964), I, 137ff.

[44] See the commentary of Rashi on the words *ma'i ka'amar*.

[45] B. *ʿArakhin* 32b.

[46] *Ibid.* Cf. the Tosefta version presented below, pp. 22f.

[47] It is unlikely that the Talmud borrowed from the *Sifra* as the former does not seem to be familiar with the midrashic work. See Albeck, *Mavo' La-Talmudim*, pp. 113ff. According to Neusner, the Sifra actually represents a protest against the Mishnah's use of logic to decide *halakhah*. The purpose of the Sifra is to demonstrate that the only reliable basis for *halakhah* is exegesis of biblical verses. Thus the exegetical interpolations of the Sifra are actually dependent upon the legal traditions found in the Mishnah (and Tosefta). See J. Neusner, *Purities* VII, *Negaim* (1975), 1-12 and 211-230.

[48] אמר אביי הכי קאמר עד גמלא בגליל עד גדוד בעבר הירדן וחדיד ואונו וירושלים ביהודה

dan in which there were walled cities of the appropriate size dating to the period of the conquest.[49] Rava (d. 352 C.E.) suggests that the phrases *be-galil* ("in Galilee"), *be-ʿever ha-yarden* (in Transjordan) and *bi-yehudah* ("in Judah") were necessary in order to exclude cities having the same names in other areas of the country.[50] This view is supported by Rav Ashi (ca. 335-427/8 C.E.) who suggests that there were in fact two Jerusalems![51]

Thus by the fourth century (the time of Rav Ashi), little unanimity existed in the interpretation of the list of walled cities presented in the *baraita*. The terseness of the *baraita* perplexed the *amoraim* who did not want it to be misconstrued as a definitive list of *all* the walled cities to which the *halakhah* applied. The Mishnah, on the other hand, clearly stated that its list only contained examples of such cities. The *baraita* would not have been problematic for the *amoraim* had they assumed that its purpose was merely to note that the list of the Mishnah contained examples from each region of the country.[52] The division of *Ereẓ Yisrael* into the regions of Judea, Transjordan, and Galilee is often referred to in the Mishnah.[53] The cities mentioned in the mishnaic list were evidently selected with this tripartite division in mind. The parenthetical phrases, *be-galil, be-ʿever ha-yarden* and *bi-yehudah*, found in both the Sifra and *baraita* versions would seem to substantiate this. As for the list itself, the remarks attributed to Ishmael ben Yose clearly suggest that many other cities could have been included:[54]

א״ר ישמעאל ברבי יוסי וכי אין לנו מוקפות חומה אלא אלו בלבד הרי הוא אומר ששים עיר כל חבל ארגוב וגו׳ כל אלה ערים בצורות חומה גבוהה וגו׳ אלא כיון שגלו ישראל לבבל בטלה מהן מצות ערי חומה וכשעלו מן הגולה מצאו אלו שמוקפות חומה

---

[49] Klein explains that the *baraita* itself suggested this interpretation to Abbaye since three cities in Judah were mentioned but only one in each, Galilee and Transjordan. See S. Klein, "ʿ*Arim Muqafot Ḥomah Mi-Yemot Yehoshuʿa bin Nun*" in ʿ*Azkarah Li-Khevod Ha-Rav Kook* (1937), pt. 5, p. 76.

[50] רבא אמר גמלא בגליל לאפוקי גמלא דשאר ארצות גדוד בעבר הירדן לאפוקי גדוד דשאר ארצות אינך דלא איכא דכותייהו לא איצטריך

According to Rabbenu Gershom and Rashi, the *castra ha-yeshanah shel-Ẓippori, ḥakra shel-Gush Ḥalav* and *Yodfat* (Jotapata) *ha-yeshanah* were omitted from the *baraita* because no other cities could be confused with them. See their comments on the passage.

[51] רב אשי אמר לאו אמר רב יוסף תרי קדש הוו ה״נ תרי ירושלים הוו

Actually, Rav Ashi's statement was an attempt to answer the objection that the sale of houses was never final in Jerusalem (above, n. 31). Accordingly, the Mishnah meant a different Jerusalem. Klein ("ʿ*Arim*," p. 77) suggests that the "other" Jerusalem was outside the walls of the original city, but there is no support for his claim.

[52] See note 42. It is at least possible that the *baraita* represents the original list of cities of the Mishnah. In this case the references to the old *castra* of Sepphoris, the *ḥakra* of Gush Ḥalav and old Jotapata would have been interpolated into the Mishnah, perhaps by *amoraim* who found the brevity of the list problematic. The fact, however, that the *amoraim* paraphrase the *baraita* with its parenthetical elements (see nn. 48, 50) indicates that only the list of the *baraita*—not that of the Mishnah—was found to be difficult. To the *amoraim*, who knew the locations of the cities, the designations *be-galil, be-ʿever ha-yarden* and *bi-yehudah* were superfluous and warranted elucidation.

[53] See M. *Baba*ʾ *Batra*ʾ 3:2, M. *Sheviʿit* 9:2 and M. *Ketubot* 13:10. Cf. B. *Sanhedrin* 11b and P. *Sanhedrin* 1, 18d. Also see M. Guttmann, ʾ*Ereẓ Yisrael Be-Midrash Ve-Talmud* (1927), pp. 14f.

[54] Tosefta ʿ*Arakhin* 5:16, as it appears in ed. Vilna of the Babylonian Talmud (1973 reprint).

מימות יהושע בן נון וקדשום ולא אלו כלבד אלא כל שתבא לך במסורת שמוקפות חומה מימות יהושע בן נון כל המצוה הזאת נוהגת בה ושקדשום מכאן ואילך כל המצוה הזאת נוהגת בה

> Rabbi Ishmael ben Rabbi Yose said, "Are there not other (cities) besides these which were encompassed by a wall? Behold, it (Deut. 3:4-5) states: '...sixty towns, the whole district of Argob, etc. ... All these towns were fortified with high walls....' But when Israel was exiled to Babylonia the commandment concerning walled cities was suspended. And when they ascended out of exile they found these (the listed cities) which were encompassed by a wall since the days of Joshua bin Nun and they sanctified them. And this entire commandment does not apply to these (cities) alone, but to any concerning which a tradition is brought to you that it was encompassed by a wall since the days of Joshua bin Nun. (And) once they sanctified them, from then on this entire commandment applies to them."

That the rabbis knew of other walled cities to which the *halakhah* of *battei ʿarei ḥomah* was applicable cannot be doubted. The question which concerns us, however, is why were these particular cities selected as examples?

Rabbi Ishmael's remarks indicate that the oldest traditions were associated with cities known to have been in existence during the return from Babylonia (after 538 B.C.E.). During the talmudic period, the returnees were credited with the reestablishment of the ancient territorial boundaries within which the *halakhah* was applicable. The area "possessed by those who ascended from the Babylonian Exile" (שהחזיקו עולי בבל) was regarded as the true *Ereẓ Yisrael.*[55] The *tannaim* probably reckoned that cities which, according to their traditions, were sanctified by the returnees had to have been in existence when the boundaries were first established in the time of the biblical conquest. That the cities went back to the days of Joshua bin Nun was probably only an assumption.

Nevertheless, several of the locations are known to have existed even earlier than the conquest of Palestine under Joshua (ca. 1250-1200 B.C.E.). Jerusalem is mentioned in the Egyptian Execration Texts of the Middle Kingdom (21st to 18th centuries).[56] Ḥadid and Ono are included in the rolls of cities of returnees in the books of Ezra and Nehemiah.[57] Ono, however, also appears among the lists of cities conquered by the Egyptian Thutmose III (ca. 1490-1436).[58] Pottery fragments from Gush Ḥalav indicate that that location was inhabited in the early

---

[55] See M. *Sheviʿit* 6:1, T. *Sheviʿit* 4:11, P. *Sheviʿit* 6, 36c and *Sifre Deut.* 51. Cf. M. Avi-Yonah, "Historical Geography," *The Jewish People in the First Century* I, eds. S. Safrai *et al.* (1974), 104 and Guttmann, *ʾEreẓ Yisrael*, pp. 12f.

[56] *ANET*, p. 329.

[57] Ḥadid and Ono are mentioned together with Lod in Ezra 2:33 and 7:37. Neh. 11:35 does not include Ḥadid. Rashi believes that Lod should be included in the list of the Mishnah. See his comments on B. *Megillah* 4a and cf. Klein's discussion in "*ʿArim*," p. 71.

The fact that these cities occur in the lists of returnees could have suggested to R. Ishmael ben Yosi that the cities in M. *ʿArakhin* were sanctified upon the return from Babylonia.

[58] *ANET*, p. 243.

Israelite period.[59] Finally, an Iron I (1200-1000 B.C.E.) potsherd has been found at Jotapata, which appears as *Ia-at-bite* in the register of cities captured by Tiglath-pileser III in 732 B.C.E.[60] Thus the sites of at least five of the eight cities under discussion were occupied rather early.[61]

It could, therefore, be maintained that the *tannaim* actually knew of the antiquity of these cities. The fact, however, that not one of the cities, with the exception of Jerusalem, is mentioned in Jewish sources earlier than Ezra and Nehemiah indicates that the selection of the cities was based on other considerations. Furthermore, while some of the cities may have been traditionally connected with the return from Babylonia, the terms *castra* and *ḥakra* (ἄκρα) indicate that the list was compiled considerably later. As mentioned earlier, the inclusion of Jerusalem suggests a *terminus ad quem* of 70 C.E. for the period reflected by the list.[62] The places mentioned in the Mishnah must have been cities with Jewish populations or else the *halakhah* of *battei ʿarei ḥomah* could not have applied to them.[63] The *castra ha-yeshanah* of Sepphoris and the *ḥakra* of Gush Ḥalav formed cities in which Jews resided.[64] Since it is unlikely that Jews could have maintained military strongholds after 70, the use of these terms confirms that date as a *terminus ad quem*.[65]

Josephus claims that he was responsible for the fortification of nineteen sites, four of which were Sepphoris, Jotapata, Gamala, and Gischala (Gush Ḥalav).[66]

---

[59] See E. Meyers *et al.*, "Preliminary Report on the 1977 and 1978 Seasons at Gush Ḥalav (el-Jish)," *BASOR* 233 (1979), 35ff. Also *idem*, "The Meiron Excavation Project: Archeological Survey in Galilee and Golan, 1976," *BASOR* 230 (1978), 1.

[60] See Meyers *et al.*, "Meiron," p. 6. Cf. A. Saarisalo, "Topographical Researches in Galilee," *JPOS* 9 (1929), 39. For *Ia-at-bite*, see E. Fohrer, *Die Provinzeinteilung des assyrischen Reiches* (1920), p. 61, H. Tadmor, "*Kibbush Ha-Galil Bi-Yedei Tiglat Pileser Ha-Shelishi Melekh ʾAsshur,*" *Kol ʾEreẓ Naftali*, ed. H. Z. Hirschberg (1968), p. 64 and Klein, "*ʿArim*," p. 70, where *Sa-at-bite* appears to be a printing error.

[61] The single, Early Iron II potsherd found at Sepphoris (above, p. 5) cannot be regarded as conclusive evidence of an early settlement on the site. The literary evidence for a pre-exilic settlement at Sepphoris will, however, be examined below. See pp. 25ff.

[62] This does not mean that the list was composed by that time but rather that it was created intentionally with pre-70 C.E. sites in mind.

[63] The cities likely to have been selected as examples would have had to fit all criteria for walled cities. The *tannaim* did not choose these particular cities merely because they had ancient walls. See next note.

[64] It is assumed here that the *tannaim* did not select gentile cities in which Jews resided as examples of walled cities. It seems more likely that they would have selected Jewish cities to illustrate places to which the *halakhah* of *battei ʿarei ḥomah* applied. That several of the cities were in fact Jewish is evident from their history during the Maccabean and First Revolt periods. See the ensuing discussion in the text.

[65] 70 C.E. has been selected as a general date. The *castra* may have come to an end earlier in the First Revolt. See below, p. 57.

[66] *War* II, 573-574; *Life* 187-188. Josephus uses either τειχίζω or οἰκοδομέω τείχη both meaning to fortify with walls. Walls have been uncovered at Gamala (Guttman, *Gamala*, p. 16) and at Jotapata. See A. C. Sandberg Jr., "Josephus' Galilee Revisited," *Explor* 3 (Winter, 1977), 44ff. It should be noted that Josephus claims in *War* II, 574 that the inhabitants of Sepphoris erected their own walls because they were affluent and "eager for war." In *War* III, 61, however, he says he was responsible

Ḥadid, which Josephus informs us was a garrisoned camp of Vespasian, had been fortified earlier by Simon the Maccabee (ca. 140 B.C.E.).[67] Gamala, Sepphoris, Ḥadid and perhaps Gedor also appear to have been strongholds in the days of Alexander Yannai (103-76 B.C.E.).[68] These cities and of course Jerusalem would have been obvious choices as illustrations of walled cities. S. Klein, furthermore, has noted that cities which were in existence in the Hellenistic period[69] and which played a role in Maccabean history must have had their origins in the earlier, post-exilic, Persian period.[70] Thus while a date in the Maccabean period is likely as a *terminus post quem* for the period reflected by the list, Ishmael ben Yose's claim that these cities were specifically sanctified by those returning from Babylonia is not so farfetched.[71]

Sepphoris and Qitron

The possibility of a pre-exilic settlement at Sepphoris must now be considered. In B. *Megillah* 6a, the third century *amora*, Rabbi Zeira,[72] identifies Sepphoris with Qitron, a city which appears only once in the Bible (Judges 1:30) and about which little is known.[73] The passage reads as follows:[74]

אמר זעירא קטרון זו ציפורי ולמה נקרא שמה ציפורי שיושבת בראש ההר כצפור[75]
וקטרון ציפורי היא והא קטרון בחלקו של זבולון הואי דכתיב זבולון לא הוריש את

---

for fortifying the city. See above, p. 2, n. 10. Cohen claims that Josephus exaggerated his role in the fortification of Galilean cities. Cohen only questions Josephus' involvement; he admits that several of the cities appear to have been fortified in the latter part of the first century. See Cohen, *Josephus*, pp. 205, n. 45 and 243.

The rabbis, of course, did not believe that the first century walls were from the days of Joshua. Fortifications which existed in their own days on sites which were believed to have been occupied at a much earlier date were the most likely choices for examples of walled cities. The original walls did not have to remain according to the *halakhah*. See the statement of R. Eliezer ben Yose in B. *ʿArakhin* 32a.

[67] I Maccabees, 12:38 where Αδιδα is Ḥadid. Cf. The Αδδίδα of Josephus: *Ant.* XIII, 203 and *War* IV, 48.

[68] For Gamala, see *Ant.* XIII, 394; Sepphoris, *Ant.* XIII, 338; Ḥadid, *Ant.* XIII, 393 and Gedor, *Ant.* XIII, 356. On Gedor, cf. Thackeray's note to *War* IV, 413 (Loeb Classical Library) and E. M. Smallwood, *The Jews Under Roman Rule*, p. 15, n. 38. What appear to be fragments of a first century wall have been discovered at Sepphoris. See Yeivin, "Notes," p. 27.

[69] There have been Hellenistic pottery finds at Sepphoris and Gamala. See Meyers *et al.*, "Meiron," p. 7.

[70] Klein, "*ʿArim*," p. 74.

[71] The lack of substantial archeological evidence, however, seems to indicate that Galilee was not greatly populated between the sixth and third centuries. See E. Meyers and J. F. Strange, "Survey in Galilee, 1976," *Explor* 3 (Winter, 1977), 12 and Meyers *et al.*, "Meiron," p. 8.

[72] Zeira was a Babylonian who later emigrated to *Ereẓ Yisrael*. He seems to have flourished towards the end of the third century. See Albeck, *Mavoʾ La-Talmudim*, pp. 233ff.

[73] W. F. Albright and A. Alt have identified Qitron with locations in the Acco valley. Both of their suggestions have been rejected by Mazar. See B. Mazar, *ʿArim U-Gelilot Be-ʾEreẓ Yisrael* (1975), pp. 121, n. 3 and p. 165. The place remains unidentified.

[74] In ed. Vilna.

[75] Ms. Munich has א"ר פפא שיושבת בראש ההר כצפור.

יושבי קטרון ואת יושבי נהלול[76] וזבולון מתרעם על מדותיו הוה[77] שנאמר זבולון עם חרף נפשו למות[78] מה טעם משום[79] דנפתלי על מרומי שדה אמר זבולון לפני הקב"ה רבונו של עולם לאחיי נתת להם שדות וכרמים ולי נתת הרים וגבעות....

ואי סלקא דעתך קטרון זו ציפורי אמאי מתרעם על מדותיו והא הויא ציפורי מילתא[80] דעדיפא טובא וכי תימא דלית בה זבת חלב ודבש והאמר ריש לקיש לדידי חזי לי זבת חלב ודבש דציפורי והויא ששה עשר מיל על ששה עשר מיל....

אפ"ה שדות וכרמים עדיפא ליה[81]

> Zeira said, "Qitron is Sepphoris, and why is it called Sepphoris (*Zippori*)? Because it sits on the top of a mountain like a bird (*Zippor*)." But is Qitron Sepphoris? Surely Qitron is in the territory of Zevulun. For it is written: "Zevulun did not dispossess the inhabitants of Qitron or the inhabitants of Nahalol" (Judges 1:30). But Zevulun was discontented with its portion (of land) as it is said: "Zevulun is a people that mocked at death" (Judges 5:18). For what reason? Because Naphtali was "on the open heights" (Judges 5:18). Zevulun (himself) said before The Holy One Praised be He, "Master of the world, to my brothers you gave fields and vineyards, but to me you gave mountains and hills...."
>
> Now if you maintain that Qitron is Sepphoris why was (the tribe of) Zevulun discontented with its portion? Surely, Sepphoris was very desirable! And if you say that it does not flow with milk and honey did Resh Lakish not say, "I myself have seen the flowing milk and honey of Sepphoris and it (covers an area of) sixteen miles by sixteen miles?..."
>
> Even so, fields and vineyards are (more) desirable to it (the tribe of Zevulun).

The view of Zeira that Sepphoris is Qitron is found to be difficult. Qitron was located within the territory of Zevulun, a tribe which was dissatisfied with the lands apportioned to it. Zevulun himself is said to have complained that he received mountains and hills rather than fields and vineyards.[82] It is pointed out, however, that the area of Sepphoris was particularly desirable because of its milk and honey.[83] Obviously, Qitron and Sepphoris could not have been identical otherwise Zevulun would have been perfectly content with the productivity of the lands he acquired. The *gemara* concludes, however, that Qitron and Sepphoris were indeed identical; the tribe of Zevulun merely preferred fields and vineyards to the milk and honey of the mountainous country it received.

---

[76] Ms. Munich omits ואת יושבי נהלול.

[77] הוה is omitted in Ms. Munich.

[78] Ms. Munich completes the verse: ונפתלי על מרומי שדה.

[79] Ms. Munich has מ"ט זבולון עם חרף נפשו למות משום

[80] Ms. Munich omits מילתא and reads והא הוה ליה צפורי.

[81] Ms. Munich has שדות וכרמים הוו עדיפי ליה.

[82] Zevulun had other complaints but these have been omitted because they are irrelevant to the point made here.

[83] That the entire area surrounding Sepphoris, i.e. the territory of Zevulun, flowed with milk and honey is obvious from the statement of Resh Lakish. The fact that Sepphoris (Qitron) itself had milk and honey would have been irrelevant since Zevulun was said to have been unable to dispossess Qitron.

Earlier in the *gemara*,[84] the *amoraim* considered whether the city of Tiberias had been encompassed by a wall in the days of Joshua bin Nun. Some doubt was expressed because the *amora* Ḥezekiah was said to have read the *Megillah* (Book of Esther) in Tiberias on both the fourteenth and the fifteenth of *Adar*. According to the Mishnah (*Megillah* 1:1), the *Megillah* was to be read on the fourteenth in unwalled settlements and on the fifteenth in cities walled "since the days of Joshua bin Nun." Ḥezekiah read it on both days because he was unsure as to whether the city had actually been walled in the time of Joshua. The *amoraim* discussed the identity of Tiberias during the biblical period and decided that it was identical with the fortified city of Raqqat (Joshua 19:35). In the process of arriving at this conclusion, it was suggested that Raqqat was Sepphoris. Having rejected this possibility, the *gemara* introduced Zeira's remark concerning the identity of Sepphoris. Evidently, the *amoraim* were hard pressed to identify Sepphoris with a biblical city because of the tannaitic tradition connecting it with those cities encompassed by a wall since the days of Joshua.[85] As we have seen, even Zeira's identification was questioned. It is obvious from the discussions concerning both Tiberias and Sepphoris that the *amoraim* did not preserve indisputable traditions concerning these cities.

Besides the talmudic report, the only evidence for a pre-exilic settlement at Sepphoris is a single, Early Iron II potsherd found in a cistern on the *tell* during the 1931 excavation.[86] A more recent survey of the *tell* failed to turn up any sherds from periods earlier than the Hellenistic.[87] It was shown earlier that the list of walled cities presented in the Mishnah was composed with sites settled during the Hellenistic and Roman (pre-70) periods in mind.[88] These facts fail to lend any credence to Zeira's contested report. Thus the identification of Sepphoris with Qitron or any other biblical city must remain in doubt until more reliable archeological evidence can be found.[89] In any case, the "*castra*" of Sepphoris certainly belonged to a much later period.

---

[84] B. *Megillah* 5b-6a.

[85] Or as Yeivin puts it: "It is quite obvious that the later scholars merely sought to justify the early tradition, which assigned the 'old citadel of Sippori' to the days of the conquest and looked for a plausible settlement mentioned in the Bible with which they could associate it." See Yeivin, "Notes," p. 26. More recently, Levine has suggested that the talmudic discussion concerning the identity of Sepphoris (B. *Megillah* 6a) reflects resentment felt by fourth century Sepphoreans towards the city of Tiberias. See L. Levine, "R. Simeon b. Yoḥai and the Purification of Tiberias: History and Tradition," *HUCA* 49 (1978), p. 177.

[86] See above, pp. 5f.

[87] See Meyers *et al.*, "Meiron," p. 7. Yeivin claims that the cistern in which the Early Iron II potsherd (a jar rim) was found was originally a rock cut tomb belonging to the same period. Yeivin, however, uses the potsherd to date the supposed tomb. See his discussion in "Notes," pp. 22, 24f.

[88] Above, pp. 23ff.

[89] Klein has noted that a *tanna* by the name of Simeon of Qitron (*shimᶜon ʾish qitron*) appears in the *Mekhiltaʾ* to Exodus 14:15. Klein concludes from this that Sepphoris and Qitron could not be one and the same since the former was certainly known as *Ẓippori* in the time of Simeon. Klein suggests instead that Qitron was a village near Sepphoris. Curiously, a variant reading, *shemaᶜyah ʾish kefar qitron* (Shemayah of the village of Qitron), does appear. See H. S. Horovitz, I. A. Rabin, *Mechilta*

The Castra and the City

As previously mentioned, the earliest historical reference to Sepphoris occurs in the *Antiquities* of Josephus. The Jewish historian reports that Ptolemy Lathyrus made an unsuccessful attempt to capture Sepphoris during his campaign against Alexander Yannai.[90] Sepphoris must have been an important military encampment as early as the Maccabean period for it to have successfully repulsed the large forces led by Ptolemy. Both Sepphoris and Gush Ḥalav were fortified during the first century when they acquired reputations as strongholds.[91] The *tannaim* of the mid-second century were familiar with the military nature of these cities and, consequently, used the designations *castra* and *ḥakra* in referring to them. Since the Mishnah is concerned with walled *cities*, it is probable that the rabbis believed that the *castra* and *ḥakra* themselves constituted such places.

The term חקרא (*ḥakra*) is used in the *targumim* to refer to the entire city of Jerusalem and to fortified cities in general.[92] *Castra* is similarly employed in several classical sources.[93] Sepphoris, to be sure, must have maintained a particular section of the city for its citadel or encampment. When Josephus and his men marched against the city after it had requested a garrison from Cestius Gallus, the alarmed residents fled to the acropolis (εἰς τὴν ἀκρόπολιν συνέφυγον) for safety.[94] Josephus himself, however, states that Vespasian considered the entire city a fortress whose allegiance was imperative if Rome was to secure Galilee:[95]

> Καὶ γὰρ οὐ μικρὸν ἐδόκει τὸ κινδύνευμα πρὸς τὸν μέλλοντα πόλεμον ἀφαιρεθῆναι τὴν Σέπφωριν μεγίστην μὲν οὖσαν τῆς Γαλιλαίας πόλιν ἐρυμνοτάτῳ δ' ἐπιτετειχισμένην χωρίῳ καὶ φρουρὰν ὅλου τοῦ ἔθνους ἐσομένην

D'Rabbi Ismael (1970), p. 99. Klein also discusses the mistaken identification, found in a medieval source, of Sepphoris with biblical Tirẓah (Tell al-Farᶜa, about eleven km. north of Shekhem). See Klein, "*Ẓippori*," p. 47.

[90] *Ant.* XIII, 338. Cf. above, p. 2.

[91] For Sepphoris' capabilities as a stronghold, see *War* III, 34 (quoted below, pp. 28f.). Gischala (Gush Ḥalav), while not an impregnable fortress (see *War* IV, 96), was the scene of a confrontation between John, the son of Levi, and Titus. It was also the last city taken by the Romans. See *War* IV, 92-120.

[92] For example, II Sam. 5:7: ואחד דוד ית חקרא דציון היא קרתא דדוד.
Cf. II Sam. 23:14, I Chr. 11:5,7. *Targum Yerushalmi* to Num. 32:17 (ed. M. Ginsburger) has קרוי חקרא for ערי מבצר again implying entire, fortified cities. Cf. *Targum Yerushalmi* to Deut. 3:5.

[93] See the entry κάστρον τό in G. W. H. Lampe, *A Patristic Greek Lexicon* (1961) for examples of *castra* (in Greek form) applied to a city and a monastery. Pompeius Trogus refers to the valley of Jericho as encircled with hills and in the form of a *castra*. See M. Stern, *Greek and Latin Authors on Jews and Judaism* I (1976), 336. According to Polybius (Bk. VI, 31, 10), the arrangement of a camp gave it the appearance of a town.

[94] *Life* 376.

[95] *War* III, 34. The translation presented here is that of H. St. J. Thackeray in the Loeb Classical Library.

> Indeed it appeared to him (Vespasian) that the loss of Sepphoris would be a hazard gravely affecting the impending campaign as it was the largest city of Galilee, a fortress in an exceptionally strong position in the enemy's territory, and adapted to keep guard over the entire province.

The summit of the hill upon which Sepphoris was located was well suited for an acropolis and was the logical site for any *castra* or encampment intended to guard the city.[96] As the acropolis was often the oldest part of a city, the *tannaim* assumed that it constituted the original settlement.[97] The city probably extended beyond the original fortification during the second century when the rabbis referred to the earlier, walled city as the "old" *castra* (*castra ha-yeshanah*).[98]

Curiously, the expression *Shushan Ha-Birah* ("Susa, the fortress") is similarly used in Nehemiah (1:1), Daniel (8:2) and Esther (*passim*) to refer to the entire city of Susa.[99] Apparently, cities known for their stronghold capabilities were commonly referred to as fortresses.[100] This usage seems to have persisted into the tannaitic period when the terms *castra* and *ḥakra* were used to refer to fortifications which were considered cities in and of themselves. Indeed, this explanation may help to elucidate a difficult *halakhah.* Mishnah *Megillah* 1:1, it will be recalled, states that cities[101] encompassed by a wall "since the days of Joshua bin Nun" are to read the *Megillah* (Book of Esther) on the fifteenth of *Adar.* Villages and large towns, i.e. unwalled settlements, were to read the *Megillah* on the fourteenth. This *halakhah* is derived from Esther 9:16-19. Since the festival of Purim was celebrated on the fifteenth in Shushan, Jews in all other walled cities were to commemorate their salvation on the fifteenth. The rabbis, however, were

---

[96] See above, p. 5, where the dimensions of the acropolis during the Crusader period are presented. R. de Vaux notes (*Ancient Israel* (1965), I, 234f.) that the acropolis of fortified capitals such as Samaria, Jerusalem, and Rabbah was usually surrounded by a wall forming an enclosed citadel (*migdal*) within the city. Such may have been true of Sepphoris, a city which served periodically as the capital of Galilee and, at least in the days of Herod and Herod Antipas, as a royal residence. During the first century, however, the entire city formed a fortress. See B. Bar-Kochva, "Notes on the Fortresses of Josephus in Galilee," *IEJ* 24 (1974), p. 115.

[97] Wycherley refers to the acropolis as the "historical nucleus" of a city and notes, "At an early stage there might be no distinction in meaning between 'polis' and 'acropolis.' " See R. E. Wycherley, *How the Greeks Built Cities*[2] (1962), p. 5.

[98] As in Jerusalem and Tiberias, there appear to have been both an upper and a lower market at Sepphoris. See B. *ʿEruvin* 54b and B. *Yomaʾ* 11a. The need for two markets may reflect an expanding population. On the markets see Klein, *ʾEreẓ Ha-Galil*, p. 86 and "*Ẓippori*," p. 49.

[99] The term *birah* is probably a loan word from Akkadian *birtu* meaning "fortress." It appears in Aramaic as *birtaʾ*. In addition to Susa, the cities of Ecbatane (Ezra 6:2) and Yeb (Elephantine papyri) appear to have been referred to by this term. See de Vaux, *Ancient Israel* I, 235 and Frick, *The City in Ancient Israel*, pp. 48 and 70, n. 147.

[100] See previous note. The definition given in BDB (p. 108) for *Shushan Ha-Birah* misses the point. Cf. the note on Esther 1:2 in H. L. Ginsberg, ed., *The Five Megilloth and Jonah* (1969), p. 89.

[101] The word used for cities in this Mishnah is כרכין. Schürer, *Geschichte* II, 227, suggests that the difference between a *kerakh* and an *ʿir* was merely that of size, the former being the larger. Other differences, however, may have been implied by these designations. See the sources referred to by S. Baron, *The Jewish Community* (1942), III, p. 8, n. 6, especially P. Romanoff, "Onomasticon of Palestine," *PAAJR* 7 (1936), 154ff.

perplexed by the stipulation "since the days of Joshua bin Nun," failing to comprehend its relevance to the reading of the *Megillah*. Thus the mid-second century *tanna* Joshua ben Korḥa suggests that the cities need only have been walled since the time of Ahasuerus.[102] However, the Palestinian *amora* Simeon ben Pazzi (late third century) claims in the name of Joshua ben Levi that the stipulation "since the days of Joshua bin Nun" was intended to honor (*la-ḥaloq kavod*) the cities of *Ereẓ Yisrael* which were desolate in the days of Ahasuerus.[103] The source of this confusion may very well have been the *halakhah* of *battei ʿarei ḥomah*. The *tanna* (or *tannaim*) responsible for Mishnah *Megillah* 1:1 could have assumed that the expression "since the days of Joshua bin Nun" applied to all *halakhot* pertaining to walled cities.[104] *Shushan Ha-Birah* could have easily been likened to the fortified cities in Mishnah *ʿArakhin*, in particular, the *castra* of Sepphoris and the *ḥakra* of Gush Ḥalav. This would have been even more likely had the terms *castra* and *ḥakra*, like *ha-birah*, been understood to refer to fortifications which constituted cities.

Summary

The mid-second century authorities who were responsible for Mishnah *ʿArakhin* 9:6 took for granted that the biblical order of settlement was the reason for the differentiation between walled and unwalled cities in Leviticus 25. For this reason, they maintained that the cities to which the *halakhot* of *battei ʿarei ḥomah* applied must have been walled "since the days of Joshua bin Nun." Although the walled cities with which the rabbis were familiar were firmly rooted in the last two centuries of the Second Temple period, traditions existed linking these cities (or their sites) with the return from Babylonia. As the *tannaim* could not have known the true age of these cities, the traditions were projected further back to the days of Joshua when the Israelites were known to have conquered other walled cities. This seems to have especially been the case with Sepphoris which, at least according to one *amora* (Zeira), was identical to the biblical city of Qitron. This tradition, however, lacks evidence to support it.

The *castra ha-yeshanah shel-Ẓippori* consisted of at least three courtyards each having two houses and was *believed* to have been in existence since the time of Joshua bin Nun. In actuality, the term *castra* referred to the oldest known settlement at Sepphoris which probably consisted of a fortified acropolis under Jewish control since the Maccabean era. This designation was used loosely during the second century to refer to the entire, walled city of Sepphoris.

---

[102] See B. *Megillah* 2b, P. *Megillah* 1, 70a and T. *Megillah* 1:1.

[103] P. *Megillah* 1, 70a. Cf. S. Lieberman, *Toseftaʾ Ki-Feshutah* (1955-73), V, 1122f.

[104] It should be noted that the expression "since the days of Joshua bin Nun" has also been applied, by many commentators, to M. *Kelim* 1:7 which states that lepers were to be sent out of walled cities. The antiquity of the walls, however, is not mentioned in the Mishnah itself. The commentators evidently likened these walled cities to those of *battei ʿarei ḥomah*. See the comments of R. Samson ben Abraham on the Mishnah. Cf. the discussion in Gulak, *Ḥeqer*, pp. 37f., n. 1.

CHAPTER TWO

THE NON-JEWISH *CASTRA*

The *castra* of Sepphoris is also mentioned in other rabbinic sources where it no longer appears as a Jewish institution but rather as an encampment for gentile soldiers. Tosefta *Shabbat* 13:9 reports:[105]

> נכרי שבא לכבות אין אומ׳ לו כבה ואל תכבה מעשה שנפלה דליקה בחצרו של יוסף בן סימאי משיחין[106] ובאו אנשי קצטרה[107] של צפורי[108] לכבותה ולא הניחן ירד ענן וכיבה[109] אמרו חכמים לא היה צריך אע״פ כן למוצאי שבת שלח להם סלע לכל אחד ואחד ולהפרכום[110] שבהן[111] שלח[112] חמשים דינרין

> (If) a gentile comes to extinguish (a fire on the Sabbath) they should not say to him, "Extinguish" or "Do not extinguish." It happened that (*maᶜaseh*) a fire broke out in the courtyard of Joseph ben Simai of Shiḥin[113] and the men of the *castra* of Sepphoris came to extinguish it. But he did not permit them. A cloud descended and extinguished (the fire). But the sages (*ḥakhamim*) said, "He did not have to (prevent them from extinguishing)." Nevertheless, on the night following the Sabbath (*moẓaʾei shabbat*) he (Joseph) sent to each of them (the men of the *castra*) a *selaᶜ* and to their prefect (he sent) fifty *dinarin*.

This passage is found among several *halakhot* concerning items which a Jew may or may not salvage from a conflagration on the Sabbath. The episode ac-

---

[105] This is the text of Ms. Vienna (ed. Lieberman).

[106] The *editio princeps* has *be-shiḥin* (in Shiḥin), but Ms. London also has *mi-shiḥin* (from Shiḥin). The passage implies, however, that the courtyard of Joseph ben Simai was in Shiḥin. Furthermore, the prepositions מ and ב are known to have been interchangeable in biblical Hebrew. A similar phenomenon has been suggested for the post-biblical language. See Schiffman, *The Halakhah at Qumran*, pp. 27f., n. 44.

[107] Mss. Erfurt and London have קצטרא.

[108] Ms. Erfurt has שבציפורי. Similarly, Ms. London has שבצפורי. Both could mean that the *castra* was part of the city and was not located outside of it.

[109] Ms. Erfurt reads וירד ענן מן השמים.

[110] The *editio princeps* has ולאפרכום. Mr. Erfurt reads ולהיפרכום. Cf. the Genizah fragment: להופורכום (S. Lieberman, *Toseftaʾ Moᶜed* (1962), p. 60). This word is discussed below, pp. 40ff.

[111] Ms. Erfurt has שלהן.

[112] Ms. Erfurt has שיגר instead of שלח. Cf. the parallel of the Babylonian Talmud below, p. 36.

[113] Shiḥin appears as "Asochis" in the works of Josephus. The historian notes that Sepphoris was not far from that city. See *Ant.* XIII, 338. Shiḥin was located in the western part of the Bet Netofah valley and has been identified by Saarisalo with Hirbet El-Lon. See Saarisalo, "Topographical Researches," pp. 34f. Other sites in the neighborhood of Hirbet El-Lon have also been suggested. See M. Avi-Yonah, "Shiḥin," *Encyclopaedia Judaica* 14 (1971) col. 1398. According to Avi-Yonah, the city is identical with Tell al-Badawiyya. Cf. Klein, *ʾEreẓ Ha-Galil*, p. 16 and *idem, Beiträge*, pp. 63-70.

tually changes the subject by introducing the role of the gentile. The introductory *halakhah*, which states that a person should not interfere with a gentile who attempts to extinguish a fire on his property on the Sabbath, also appears in the identical form in Mishnah *Shabbat* 16:6. There it is explained that a Jew is not responsible for the observance of the Sabbath by a gentile.[114] In contrast, a Jew is answerable for a Jewish minor's observance of the Sabbath and, consequently, must not permit him to put out the flames.[115] The Tosefta account produces the incident (*maʿaseh*) which precipitated this *halakhic* ruling. The law is predicated upon the reaction of the *ḥakhamim* to Joseph ben Simai's behavior.[116]

Joseph ben Simai believed that a gentile was not to be permitted to perform a service for a Jew on the Sabbath under any condition. The ruling of the *ḥakhamim* indicates that, in the case of a fire, Joseph's interpretation of the *halakhah* was unnecessarily strict. The Tosefta goes on to explain other cases in which a Jew is *not* permitted to *actively* seek the services of a gentile on the Sabbath.[117] Here, however, the "men of the *castra* of Sepphoris" came on their own volition. Joseph may have feared that someone would suspect that he himself had put out the fire on the Sabbath.[118] Whatever the case, his extreme piety is ap-

---

[114] Actually this *halakhah* would appear to be premised upon the rabbinic notion of *shevut*, which prohibited acts which were inconsistent with the proper observance of the Sabbath. Accordingly, the concept would have been extended to include the *ordering* of a gentile to do something for a Jew (in this case, to extinguish the fire). The *Mekhiltaʾ*, however, found a biblical precedent (Ex. 12:16) for not allowing a gentile to perform one's work on the Sabbath. See *Mekhiltaʾ De-Rabbi Yishmael, Pisḥaʾ* 9. Cf. the discussion of B. Cohen, *Law and Tradition in Judaism* (1959), p. 148. A law similar to that of the Mishnah was taught at Qumran. See L. H. Schiffman, *The Halakhah at Qumran*, pp. 104ff.

[115] It is explained in the *gemara* (B. *Shabbat* 121a) that the minor is aware that his act will be of benefit to the adult. Consequently, it is as though the adult himself extinguished the flames. The gentile, however, does not have to be prohibited because he is motivated by the reward. Cf. Rashi on the *gemara* and *Tosefot Yom Tov* on the Mishnah.

[116] Albeck contends that a *maʿaseh* which is presented after a halakhic ruling actually preceded the latter and was the basis of the teaching. Cf. the words of M. Elon: "... even when the selfstanding halakhic ruling is stated in the Mishnah before the *maʿaseh*, it does not exclude the possibility that chronologically speaking the *maʿaseh* preceded such a ruling and that the former is the source of the latter—except that the compiler of the Mishnah saw fit to state first the ruling and then the *maʿaseh*." The same can be assumed to apply to a *maʿaseh* found in the Tosefta. See Elon's discussion in the *Encyclopaedia Judaica* 11 (1971), cols. 641ff. and Albeck, *Mavoʾ La-Mishnah* (1967), pp. 92f. Also cf. M. Elon, *Ha-Mishpat Ha-ʿIvri*: *Toledotav Meqorotav, ʿEqronotav* (1978) I, 780; A. Kaminka, "*Ha-Maʿaseh Be-Tor Meqor Ha-Halakhah*," in *idem.*, *Meḥqarim Ba-Miqraʾ U-Va-Talmud U-Ve-Sifrut Ha-Rabanit* II (1951), 6ff. and E. Z. Melamed, "*Ha-ʿMaʿaseh' Ba-Mishnah Ke-Maqor La-Halakhah,*" *Sinai* 46 (1959-60), 156ff. According to Epstein, an incident entitled *maʿaseh* often suggests a different or stricter understanding of the *halakhah*. See the examples provided by Epstein, *Nusaḥ* I, 605f. In our case, the stricter practice of Joseph ben Simai is rejected by the *ḥakhamim*. For other instances where the *halakhah* is derived from the decision of the *ḥakhamim* (or individual sage) in a particular *maʿaseh*, see H. Albeck, *Shishah Sidrei Mishnah, Seder Moʿed*, p. 425 and Elon, *Ha-Mishpat Ha-ʿIvri* I, 772ff.

[117] The discussion presented here accepts the order of Ms. Vienna of the Tosefta. It should be noted, however, that several Mss. place the laws concerning services provided by a gentile later in the text. See Lieberman, *Toseftaʾ Moʿed*, p. 61.

[118] See the *Ḥiddushei Ha-ʾAggadah* of R. Samuel Edels on B. *Shabbat* 121a.

parent from the tone of the passage and the reaction of the *ḥakhamim*. A late midrashic parallel also emphasizes Joseph's righteousness.[119]

> מהו.... ובכל מאדך בכל ממונך מעשה ביוסי בן סימאי דמן שיחין שנפלה דליקה בחצרו בשבת ויצא ויורד קסדור של צפורין לכבותה ולא הניח להם אמ׳ היאך אני מקיים בכל ממונך

> What is meant by "with all your might (*meʾod*)?" (Deut. 6:5: "You shall love the Lord your God with all your heart and with all your soul and with all your might.") With all your money (is meant).[120] It happened to Yose[121] ben Simai from Shiḥin that a fire broke out in his courtyard on the Sabbath. And the *quaestor*[122] of Sepphoris (went out and) descended (to Shiḥin) to extinguish it and he did not permit them (to extinguish it). He (Yose) said, "How will I fulfill 'with all your money'?"

Apparently, the *ḥakhamim* of the Tosefta account interpreted the divine intervention ("A cloud descended...") as an indication of Joseph's extreme piety. His behavior was the result of an overzealous understanding of the law. The *ḥakhamim* therefore ruled that a Jew could not be responsible for the voluntary actions of a gentile on the Sabbath even if they were in his behalf.

Precise dating of this story is difficult especially since Joseph ben Simai is a relatively unknown figure in rabbinic history.[123] Certain aspects of the ben Simai passage, however, suggest a late, first century date. As mentioned above, the term *maʿaseh* indicates that the incident antedates the formulation of the halakhic decision: If a gentile comes to extinguish they should not say to him, "Extinguish" or "Do not extinguish." This anonymous ruling is found in the Mishnah following statements by Rabbi Simeon ben Nannus and Rabbi Yose

---

[119] *Deuteronomy Rab.*, Ms. Oxford (ed. Lieberman), p. 70.

[120] For a similar usage of *meʾod* for "money," see S. Schechter, *Documents of Jewish Sectaries*[2] (1970), p. 82, n. 17 and B. *Sanhedrin* 74a.

[121] Joseph ben Simai is frequently referred to as Yose ben Simai, especially in the parallels of the Palestinian Talmud. For the sake of consistency, only the name Joseph will be used in our discussion.

[122] Hebrew *qasdor* (קסדור) seems to have been confused with קצרה. That soldiers (plural) of the קצרה were intended, is indicated by the plural form *la-hem*, which would make no sense if it referred to a *quaestor*.

[123] Hyman, however, has proposed that the Abba Yose ben Simai who is mentioned in a *maʿaseh* in the Babylonian Talmud (*Yevamot* 115a) is identical with the person involved in the present context. See A. Hyman, *Toledot Tannaʾim Ve-ʾAmoraʾim* (1964), II, 752f. An argument can be made in favor of this identification. Both names appear without the title "rabbi" suggesting that the person (or persons) intended was (were) not ordained. The title, "*abba*" (father) which is often used as a token of respect may emphasize the fact that Abba Yose was not known as "rabbi." Only one Ms. (Munich) refers to Joseph ben Simai as a rabbi. See below, p. 36 and n. 139. On the title "*abba*" see R. Margaliot, *Le-Ḥeqer Shemot Ve-Kinnuyim Ba-Talmud* (1944), pp. 51f. Since it was not an official title, Joseph (or Yose) need not have been referred to as "*abba*" all the time. Abba Yose appears to have been a contemporary of R. Judah ha-Nasi (late second, early third century) in the passage of the Babylonian Talmud referred to above. If Abba Yose and Joseph ben Simai are one and the same, that person would have lived during the last half of the second century. Unfortunately, in a parallel to the text in which Abba Yose appears he is referred to as Abba Simai (P. *Yevamot* 16, 15d). Thus there is no way to be certain that these variants refer to Joseph ben Simai.

ben Ḥalafta concerning the extinguishing of fires on the Sabbath. Both of these *tannaim* lived during the first half of the second century. In the Tosefta, the halakhic principle also follows the statement of Rabbi Simeon ben Nannus. (The view of Rabbi Yose is omitted.) Nevertheless, it would have been possible for second century rabbis to report an event which happened considerably earlier. Thus the Tosefta narrative, which includes the ben Simai incident, is followed by a discussion of the sending of letters by means of a gentile on the Sabbath.[124] This discussion directly parallels the ben Simai story. Whereas the anonymous *halakhah* in this case states that it is not permissible to send a letter by means of a gentile on the Sabbath eve, the practice of a particular sage, Joseph Ha-Kohen (the priest), is produced as evidence for a stricter understanding of the *halakhah.* Joseph was reputed never to have sent a letter via a gentile carrier.[125] The similarity of the construction of this narrative with that of the ben Simai incident (*halakhah* followed by a stricter *maᶜaseh* or practice) is striking. Both narratives were, evidently, produced by the same second century circle of *tannaim* who drew upon events or practices familiar to them to illustrate the stricter *halakhah.* Joseph Ha-Kohen and Joseph ben Simai would have had to have lived in roughly the same period for their practices to be remembered and reported by a particular circle. Since Joseph Ha-Kohen lived during the first century and may have even been the *tanna* by that name who is reported to have been in Jerusalem while the Temple still stood,[126] it could be maintained that Joseph ben Simai also lived during that period.[127] It has been shown, however, that the *castra* of the Mishnah was a place where Jews resided before 70 C.E.[128] The fire incident could not have occurred while the acropolis of Sepphoris was still in Jewish hands. The "men of the *castra*" who came to rescue Joseph's property were gentiles com-

---

[124] In Ms. Vienna (see note 117). On the structure of this section of the Tosefta, see B. Cohen, *Mishnah and Tosefta: A Comparative Study*, Part I—Shabbat (1935), 120ff.

[125] T. *Shabbat* 13:11 (Ms. Vienna, ed. Lieberman) reads:

אין משלחין איגרות ביד גוי בערב שבת וברביעי ובחמשי מותר אמרו עליו על יוסף הכהן שלא נמצא כתב ידו ביד גוי מעולם

Letters should not be sent by means of a gentile on the eve of the Sabbath. But it is permissible on Wednesday and Thursday. It was said of Joseph Ha-Kohen that his correspondence was never found in the hand of a gentile.

[126] See, for example, M. *Ḥallah* 4:11. According to Hyman, however, the Joseph Ha-Kohen of this *mishnah* is not to be identified with the R. Yose (or Joseph) Ha-Kohen who never sent a letter via a gentile carrier. The latter did not officiate in Jerusalem but rather was a student of Yoḥanan ben Zakkai somewhat later in the first century. See Hyman, *Toledot* II, 740f. and 754f. Cf. W. Bacher, *Die Agada Der Tannaiten* (1884-90) I, 72ff.

[127] Another incident (*maᶜaseh*) reported in both the Mishnah and Tosefta involves Rabban Gamaliel II who succeeded Yoḥanan ben Zakkai as *Nasi* at Yavneh ca. 80. The *maᶜaseh* also is an illustration of a *halakhah* regarding services performed by a gentile for a Jew on the Sabbath. The fact that Rabban Gamaliel flourished at the end of the first and the beginning of the second centuries also points to a date during that period for the Joseph ben Simai account. See M. *Shabbat* 16:8, T. *Shabbat* 13:14 and cf. M. *ᶜEruvin* 4:2.

[128] See above p. 24.

manded by a non-Jewish prefect. This force could not have been identical with any of the quasi-Jewish forces which were likely to have served under the Herods, as there would be no question of the correct *halakhah* in that case.[129] Some scholars have suggested that the ben Simai incident occurred in the days of Agrippa II, but this view, while possible, will be shown below to have been arrived at through a misunderstanding of the sources. All that can be determined at present is that the episode took place sometime between the First Revolt and the mid-second century when it was preserved by the *tannaim* of the Mishnah and Tosefta. As we shall see, the real significance of the passage is not in the event itself but in the fact that the *castra* of Sepphoris was familiar to rabbis of the second century.

The passage has also been preserved in both the Palestinian and Babylonian *gemarot* to Mishnah *Shabbat* 16:6. The Palestinian version reads as follows:[130]

> מעשה שנפלה דליקה בחצר יוסי בן סימאי בשיחין וירדו בני קיצרה[131] שלציפורין לכבות ולא הניח להן אמ׳ להן הניחו לגבאי שיגבה חובו מיד קשר עליו הענן וכיבהו במוצאי שבת שלח לכל חד מהם סלע ולאיפרכום[132] שלהן חמשים דינר אמרו חכמ׳[133] לא היה צריך לעשות כן

> It happened that a fire broke out in the courtyard of Yose ben Simai in Shiḥin and the men of the *castra* of Sepphoris went down to extinguish (it). But he did not permit them. He said to them, "Let the (Divine) Treasurer[134] collect His debt." Immediately a cloud thickened above it[135] (the fire) and extinguished it. On the night following the Sabbath he (Yose) sent to each of them (the men) a *selaʿ* and to their prefect fifty *dinar*. The sages said, "He did not have to do this."

---

[129] See G. Allon, *Toledot Ha-Yehudim Be-ʾEreẓ Yisrael Bi-Tequfat Ha-Mishnah Ve-Ha-Talmud* (1935-56) I, 91. Since the Herods were Jewish kings, the order to extinguish the fire might also have ultimately been perceived as coming from a Jew. On the composition of the army of Herod the Great see A. Momigliano, "Herod of Judaea," *The Cambridge Ancient History* 10 (1976), p. 327 and M. Stern, "The Reign of Herod" in *The World History of the Jewish People* VII, *The Herodian Period* (1975), 96.

[130] This is the Ms. Leiden version of P. *Shabbat* 16, 15d. The passage also appears in P. *Nedarim*, 4, 38d and P. *Yomaʾ* 8, 45b. In *Nedarim* almost the entire *sugya* (discussion) is reproduced with only minor changes. In *Yomaʾ* only the material beginning with our passage appears. Although the passage remains unchanged, it is used to indicate that one need not have a gentile or a minor act for him in a life threatening situation on the Sabbath. The passage seems most appropriate in reference to M. *Shabbat* 16:6,and for this reason the version of P. *Shabbat* is produced here. Cf. the Babylonian version produced below, p. 36. On the problem of parallel *sugyot* in the Palestinian Talmud, see the sources referred to by Bokser in "Bibliographical Guide," pp. 179f.

[131] Ms. Leiden has קצרה in both of the parallels mentioned in n. 130.

[132] The Ms. Leiden version of P. *Yomaʾ* 8, 45b has ולאפרכום.

[133] P. *Nedarim* 4, 38d has אמר רבי חנינא but this appears to be a mistake. See B. Ratner, *ʾAhavat Ẓiyyon Vi-Yerushalayim* (reprinted, 1967), *Yomaʾ*, p. 97.

[134] For this usage of the term *gabbaʾi* see Kohut, *ʿArukh Ha-Shalem* II, 220 and M. Jastrow, *Sefer Millim*, p. 206. The entire phrase, "Let the (Divine) Treasurer collect his debt," appears in *Lamentations Rab.* 1:16 (ed. Buber) where it is clearly a reference to divine agency.

[135] For this rendering, cf. B. *Taʿanit* 20a (נתקשרו שמים בעבות) and Jastrow, *Sefer Millim*, p. 1432.

This version is included among several other incidents used in the *gemara* to illustrate the *halakhah* of the Mishnah. Each episode begins with the words "a fire broke out" (נפלה דליקה) and involves the reaction of a particular sage to a fire which broke out on the Sabbath. The introductory discussion revolves around one such response of Rabbi Ammi who headed the *yeshivah* at Tiberias at the end of the third century.[136]

Besides the context, there are other indications that this is a later version of the account found in the Tosefta. Unlike the latter, this account has Joseph cry out to the "men of the *castra*": "Let the Divine Treasurer collect His debt." This utterance suggests that Joseph believed that the resulting loss from the fire was divinely sanctioned. (After all, the conflagration occurred on, of all days, the Sabbath when he thought it was prohibited to accept gentile aid in extinguishing it.) Thus it merely serves as a legendary embellishment intended to emphasize Joseph's piety. Another indication that this is a later, less reliable account is the inclusion of the view of the sages at the end of the story rather than earlier in the text.[137] The intention of the words attributed to the sages is ambiguous since they might mean that Joseph did not have to reward the "men of the *castra*." Only the context of the *gemara* makes it clear that the words refer to Joseph's prevention of the attempt of the soldiers to extinguish the fire. One would not know this from the passage itself.

The account in the Babylonian Talmud reads:[138]

> ת״ר מעשה ונפלה דליקה בחצירו של יוסף[139] בן סימאי בשיחין ובאו אנשי גיסטרא[140] של ציפורי לכבות[141] מפני שאפטרופום של מלך היה ולא הניחן מפני כבוד השבת ונעשה לו נס וירדו גשמים וכיבו לערב שיגר לכל אחד מהן שתי סלעין ולאפרכום שבהן חמשים[142] וכששמעו חכמים בדבר אמרו לא היה צריך לכך שהרי שנינו נכרי שבא לכבות אין אומרים לו כבה ואל תכבה

> The rabbis taught (*teno rabbanan*): It happened that a fire broke out in the courtyard of Joseph ben Simai in Shiḥin and the men of the *castra* of Sepphoris came to extinguish it since he (Joseph) was a steward of the king (*ʾepitropos*[143] *shel-melekh hayah*). But he

---

[136] See A. Hyman, *Toledot*, I, 221f.

[137] Cf. the Tosefta version, p. 31.

[138] B. *Shabbat* 121a, ed. Vilna.

[139] Ms. Munich has ר׳ יוסי but it is unlikely that Joseph was a rabbi. See Lieberman, *Toseftaʾ Ki-Feshutah* III, 212f.

[140] A variant of קסטרה, see n. 1. Cf. R. N. Rabbinovicz, *Sefer Diqduqei Soferim* (reprinted, 1976) on this passage.

[141] A Ms. of the code of R. Isaac ben Jacob Alfasi (Rif) has ובאו אנשי טבריא ושל צפורי לכבותה but "Tiberias" (טבריא) is evidently a mistake. See Rabbinovicz, *ibid.* and Lieberman, *Toseftaʾ Ki-Feshutah* III, 213.

[142] The implication here is that the prefect received fifty *selaʿim* and not *dinarin* as in the Tosefta and Palestinian Talmud. Ms. Munich reads: ולאפרכום שלהן חמשים סלעים
Cf., however, the text of R. Isaac ben Jacob Alfasi (Rif) which has דינרין.

[143] Krauss, *Lehnwörter* II, 104 identifies אפטרופום (*ʾepitropos*) with Greek ἐπίτροπος. Liddel and Scott (*Lexicon*, p. 669) translate: "one to whom the charge of anything is entrusted, steward, trustee, administrator." The term is also equivalent to Latin, *procurator*, but the sense of "governor" is not intended here. See below, p. 39 and n. 159.

did not permit them out of respect for the Sabbath (*kevod ha-shabbat*). A miracle occurred in his behalf and rain fell and extinguished (it). In the evening, he sent two *selaᶜ* to each of them and fifty to the prefect. But when the sages heard (about) the matter, they said, "He (Joseph) did not have to (do) this since we taught that (if) a gentile comes to extinguish, they do not say to him, 'Extinguish' or 'Do not extinguish'."

As in the Palestinian Talmud, the *gemara* begins with a discussion of the view of Rabbi Ammi.[144] The incident involving Joseph ben Simai is then presented as a *baraita* with the usual introductory phrase: *teno rabbanan*, "the rabbis taught." The words "since he was a steward (*ʾepitropos*) of the king" have been inserted to emphasize the importance of Joseph ben Simai, thereby providing the reason the "men of the *castra*" came to his aid. A justification is also offered for Joseph's behavior; he is concerned about "respect for the Sabbath" (*kevod ha-shabbat*). The vague reference of the Tosefta and Palestinian Talmud to the formation of a cloud has been omitted, perhaps because the metaphor was not in vogue in Babylonia. Instead it is stated more precisely that a miracle occurred which resulted in rain and the extinguishing of the fire. The amount awarded to the men has been changed to two *selaᶜ* apiece and the prefect receives *selaᶜim* instead of *dinarim,* perhaps a reflection of Babylonian monetary values.[145] As in the Palestinian parallels, the view of the *ḥakhamim* has been inappropriately placed following the report of the reward. The inclusion of the terse halakhic ruling: If a gentile comes to extinguish they do not say to him "Extinguish" or "Do not extinguish" at the conclusion has been appended to clarify the intention of the *ḥakhamim*. This text is even more sophisticated than the reworking found in the Palestinian Talmud. The Tosefta account has undergone the least revision. Consequently, it must be considered the earliest and most reliable version of the ben Simai narrative.

Joseph ben Simai: The ʾEpitropos of Agrippa II?

Several scholars have proposed that the following passage of the Babylonian Talmud (*Sukkah* 27a) suggests a late, first century date for the Joseph ben Simai incident:[146]

שאל אפוטרופוס של אגריפס המלך את רבי אליעזר כגון אני שאיני רגיל לאכול אלא סעודה אחת ביום מהו שאוכל סעודה אחת ואפטר אמר לו בכל יום ויום אתה ממשיך

---

144 Here, however, an incident involving R. Ammi is not presented.

145 According to the Babylonian account, each of the men received twice as many *selaᶜim* while the prefect's reward was quadrupled (1 *selaᶜ* = 4 *dinarin*). These values may reflect temporal as well as geographic differences. The Babylonian *amoraim* could have adjusted the amounts of the rewards of the original *baraita* to correspond with the monetary scale of their own day. The adjustment emphasizes the redacted nature of this version. On the differing economic conditions of Palestine and Babylonia and their relationship to prices, see D. Sperber, *Money and Prices*, pp. 18f. To be sure, the Babylonian version may just as well have been in error. Even so, the different monetary sums may have been unconsciously introduced into the text by a scribe familiar with Babylonian economic life.

146 Ed. Vilna is presented here.

כמה פרפאות לכבוד עצמך ועכשיו אי אתה ממשיך פרפרת אחת לכבוד קונך ועוד שאלו כנון אני שיש לי שתי נשים אחת בטבריא ואחת בציפורי ויש לי שתי סוכות אחת בטבריא ואחת בציפורי מהו שאצא מסוכה לסוכה ואפטר אמר לו לא שאני אומר כל היוצא מסוכה לסוכה בטל מצותה של ראשונה

The steward of Agrippa the king (*ʾepitropos shel-ʾagrippas ha-melekh*) asked Rabbi Eliezer, "In my own case, I am used to eating only one meal during the day; if I were to eat one meal (in the *sukkah*) would I be released (from my obligation)?" He answered, "Every day you add several desserts out of respect for yourself; would you not add one dessert in honor of your creator?" He (the steward) asked him again, "In my own case, I have two wives, one in Tiberias and one in Sepphoris, and I have two *sukkot*, one in Tiberias and one in Sepphoris. If I were to go from one *sukkah* to the other, would I be released (from my obligation)?" He said to him, "No, for I maintain that whoever goes from one *sukkah* to another nullifies the commandment (Lev. 23:42) of the first."

This narrative is found in a passage which discusses the views of Rabbi Eliezer ben Hyrcanus pertaining to the commandment to observe the festival of *Sukkot* (Tabernacles). In the Mishnah (*Sukkah* 2:6), Eliezer's view that a person is obligated to eat fourteen meals in a *sukkah*, one each day and night of the seven day holiday, is presented. The *gemara* relates questions of *halakhah* put to Eliezer by the "steward (*ʾepitropos*) of Agrippa." First, the latter asks the rabbi whether he would fulfill his obligation by eating only one meal a day in the *sukkah* since that is his usual daily quota. Eliezer, who earlier in the *gemara* explains that the second meal need only consist of dessert-type foods, of course takes exception to this practice. Next the steward asks the rabbi whether it is permissible to eat the fourteen meals in two separate *sukkot* since he possesses one in each of his (two) residences. To this the rabbi also objects.

Since Eliezer ben Hyrcanus lived at the end of the first century, the Agrippa mentioned here must be Agrippa II.[147] Büchler and Graetz concluded from the fact that the steward of Agrippa had a *sukkah* in both Tiberias and in Sepphoris that the jurisdiction of the Jewish king must have extended over both of these cities.[148] That the territory of Agrippa did include Tiberias is known from the reports of Josephus[149] and is generally accepted.[150] The evidence for Sepphoris, however, is less convincing. Büchler and Graetz maintain that this passage confirms the report related by Photius (ca. 820-891 C.E.) in the name of Justus of

[147] On the date of Agrippa II's death and his career in general, see E. Schürer, *The History of the Jewish People in the Age of Jesus Christ* (175 B.C.-A.D. 135) I, eds. G. Vermes and F. Millar (1973), 471ff.

[148] See A. Büchler, "*Die Schauplätze des Bar-Kochbakrieges und die auf diesen bezogenen jüdischen Nachrichten*," *JQR* 16 (1904), p. 161 and H. Graetz, "*Agrippa* II *und der Zustand Judäa's nach dem Untergang Jerusalems, MGWJ* 30 (1881), 483f.

[149] *Ant.* XX, 159; *War* II, 252 and *Life* 9.

[150] See Schürer, *History* I (ed. Vermes-Millar), p. 473.

Tiberias that Vespasian enlarged the territory of Agrippa.[151] Thus Sepphoris was included in this expanded area of Agrippa.

There are several difficulties with this interpretation. First of all, neither Photius nor the passage under discussion explicitly states that Sepphoris was included in Vespasian's enlargement of Agrippa's territory. Photius only casually remarks that the emperor increased the realm (*arche*) of the Jewish king:[152]

> ...'Αγρίππα τοῦ ἑβδόμου μὲν τῶν ἀπὸ τῆς οἰκίας Ἡρῴδου ὑστάτου δὲ ἐν τοῖς 'Ιουδαίων βασιλεῦσιν ὃς παρέλαβε μὲν τὴν ἀρχὴν ἐπὶ Κλαυδίοι ηὐξήθη δὲ ἐπὶ Νέρωνος καὶ ἔπι μᾶλλον ὑπὸ Οὐεσπασιανοῦ...
>
> ...Agrippa, the seventh (sovereign) of the House of Herod and the last of the Jewish kings, who received the realm (*parelabe men ten archen*)[153] under Claudius had it increased under Nero and still more by Vespasian...

Actually, Photius claims that both Nero and Vespasian were responsible for the enlargement of Agrippa's realm. No specific cities or territories are mentioned. Furthermore, the term used by Photius for "realm," *arche* (ἀρχή), can also be understood as "power" or "authority."[154] In fact, the phrase *paralambano ten archen* (παραλαμβάνω τὴν ἀρχήν) is a technical expression used for a person who receives or succeeds to an office.[155] An increase in the administrative functions of the Jewish king may have been all that was intended.[156] Still, some expansion of Agrippa's territory is likely in view of his support of the Romans during the First Revolt.[157] Photius' passage, however, does not mention any specific territorial changes and cannot be accepted as conclusive evidence that any took place.

Thus Photius' vague paraphrase of the words of Justus of Tiberius can hardly be used to confirm information which is inferential to begin with. As G. Allon has noted, the fact that the ᵓ*epitropos* of Agrippa had a *sukkah* in Sepphoris is no indication that he served in an official capacity in that city.[158] In fact, the word ᵓ*epitropos* in this case may very well refer to a steward or guardian of the king's possessions and not to an administrator or official in charge of the area.[159] Agrip-

---

[151] *Bibliotheca* cod. 33. Photius summarizes a chronicle attributed to Justus of Tiberias concerning the "Jewish kings." A discussion of the passage and its sources appears in Cohen, *Josephus*, pp. 142f. Cf. Büchler, "*Schauplätze*," pp. 161f. and Graetz, "*Agrippa* II," p. 483.

[152] *Bibliotheca,* cod. 33 (ed. R. Henry). Translation is the writer's.

[153] See the ensuing discussion for an alternative rendering of *arche*.

[154] Liddel and Scott, *Lexicon*, p. 252. Cf. the translation of R. Henry (1959) who understands ἀρχή as "le pouvoir."

[155] See Liddel and Scott, *Lexicon*, p. 1315.

[156] H. Mason compares the non-territorial usage of *arche* to that of Latin *provincia* and *magistratus*. For examples see his *Greek Terms for Roman Institutions: A Lexicon and Analysis* (1974), p. 110.

[157] See Schürer, *History* I (ed. Vermes-Millar), p. 476f.

[158] Allon, *Toledot* I, p. 91.

[159] Ptolemy, the *epitropos* of Agrippa II mentioned by Josephus, appears to have been in charge of the king's valuables. (See *Life* 126 and *War* II, 595 where the large amount of gold and the cavalry escort would seem to indicate that the entourage was transporting valuables belonging to the king.) Similarly, Joseph, who according to Genesis 39:5 was in charge of Potiphar's household and "all that he owned," is described in the Talmud as the ᵓ*epitropos* of that official (B. *Berakhot* 63a). The

pa's *ʾepitropos* may have had a residence in Sepphoris merely because he had a wife there. Allon, furthermore, points out that Agrippa's sister Berenice had landed estates in the area of *Bet Sheʿarim* although the area was not part of the kingdom of Agrippa. Thus the *ʾepitropos* could also have possessed land or a *sukkah* outside of the king's area.[160]

The passage in the Babylonian Talmud in which Joseph ben Simai is described as the "*ʾepitropos* of the king" has been understood to refer to the same "*ʾepitropos* of Agrippa" mentioned here. Joseph ben Simai, however, lived in Shiḥin, as the fire-incident indicates.[161] Furthermore, those scholars who identify Joseph ben Simai as the *ʾepitropos* of Agrippa do so on the basis of similar rabbinic phrases: *ʾepitropos shel-melekh hayah* and *ʾepitropos shel-ʾagrippas ha-melekh* (אפטרופוס של מלך היה; אפוטרופוס של אגריפס המלך).[162] As mentioned earlier, the words *ʾepitropos shel-melekh hayah* only appear in the account of Joseph ben Simai in the Babylonian Talmud and not in the more reliable passages of the Tosefta or the Palestinian *gemara.*[163] Thus the supposed relationship between the passage in B. *Sukkah* and the Joseph ben Simai narrative is based upon a faulty premise.[164]

The Prefect and the Castra

The term הפרכוס (or אפרכוס),[165] a Greek loan word, occurs often in talmudic and midrashic sources and can be generally defined as a "prefect" (Latin,

ʾepitropos could, of course, have been in charge of royal lands, but there is no reason to assume that such was the case in the present context. On the *ʾepitropos* as the administrator of the emperor's domains, see Sperber, *The Land*, pp. 136f., n. 1.

[160] Allon, *Toledot* I, 91. Safrai has suggested that the *ʾepitropos* managed estates "which Agrippa, like his sister Berenice, owned in that district." Allon's argument, however, seems more tenable, especially in view of the fact that the *ʾepitropos* need not have been in charge of Agrippa's domains. (See the previous note.) For Safrai's view, see his "The Relations between the Roman Army and the Jews of *ʾEreẓ Yisrael* after the Destruction of the Second Temple," *Roman Frontier Studies* 1967, eds. M. Gichon and S. Applebaum (1971), pp. 226f. On the estates of Berenice, see *Life* 118f.

[161] Cf. Allon, *Toledot* I, 91. Klein, *ʾEreẓ Ha-Galil*, p. 55, contends that all three, Tiberias, Sepphoris and Shiḥin, belonged to Agrippa II! Graetz suggests that Joseph had residences in both Tiberias and Sepphoris and also maintained a "type of villa" in Shiḥin. See Graetz, "*Agrippa* II," p. 485.

[162] Klein, *ʾEreẓ Ha-Galil*, p. 53 and Büchler, "*Schauplätze*," p. 162.

[163] Above, p. 37.

[164] A late first century date for the ben-Simai incident is still tenable but cannot be proved from B. *Sukkah* 27a. If, for argument's sake, we accept that Joseph ben Simai was the *ʾepitropos* of Agrippa II, then the suggestion that Sepphoris was part of Agrippa's domain is even more faulty. As Allon notes (*Toledot* I, 91), the "men of the *castra* of Sepphoris" who came to extinguish the fire on the property of Joseph ben Simai were gentiles who, in all probability, were not in the service of a Jewish king. (Büchler, "*Schauplätze*," p. 162 n. 1, recognizes this fact but contends that they were "hired troops!")

[165] The Mss. of the Tosefta contain variants of הפרכום. Ms. Leiden of the Palestinian Talmud has forms of אפרכום for all of the ben Simai parallels. The Ms. Oxford of the Babylonian Talmud has ולהפרכום but Munich reads ולאפרכום. The terms are constantly confused in Aramaic. See *Corpus Inscriptionum Semiticarum* II, 1, # 207. Jones suggests that the term as it is used in the Nabatean inscriptions refers to some form of local official. See Jones, *Cities*, p. 291. The orthographic differences (א or ה) may denote a distinction in meaning. See next note.

praefectus) who had both civil and military functions and who was responsible to the king or emperor.[166] The prefect mentioned in our passages, however, appears strictly as a military official in charge of the forces which were garrisoned in the *castra* of Sepphoris. As the commander of "the men of the *castra*" the prefect receives the largest reward from Joseph ben Simai who believed him to be responsible for issuing orders to extinguish the fire.

The use of the Greek equivalent of "prefect" and the term *castra* together in the ben Simai account is particularly interesting because it brings to mind the Roman *praefectus castrorum*. This official, who served as quartermaster of the Roman camp and occasionally assumed authority when either the *legatus* or senior tribune were absent, is usually associated with a legionary fortification.[167] According to Josephus, Sepphoris had already declared its allegiance to the Romans before the arrival of Vespasian at Ptolemais in 67.[168] The garrison which was thereupon stationed at Sepphoris under the command of Cestius Gallus appears to have been nothing more than a token force to assure the people of Sepphoris of protection.[169] On the other hand, that Sepphoris was able to admit the six thousand infantry which were sent later by Vespasian, indicates that the city could (and perhaps did) provide for a legionary size force.[170] While this would seem to justify the usage of the term *castra* to describe the encampment at Sepphoris, there is no literary or epigraphic evidence indicating that Sepphoris was a base for a full-scale legion. Furthermore, some of the troops sent by Vespasian were probably removed after the war when a legionary size force would not have been necessary. To be sure, the strategic importance of Sepphoris, a city located in the heart of lower Galilee, could hardly have been overlooked by the Romans. This was especially true during the Hadrianic period (ca. 130) when a contingent would have been necessary to police the roads which led to Tiberias and to the legionary camp at Kefar ʿOtnay (Legio), but a unit or subunit of *auxilia* would have been adequate for this purpose.[171] The stationing, moreover, of

---

[166] Krauss, *Lehnwörter* II, p. 115, identifies the אפרכום with Greek ἔπαρχος and defines the word simply as "prefect." He equates the form הפרכום with ὕπαρχος or "Statthalter" (governor). The precise meaning of the word, however, depends on the particular passage under discussion. For an analysis of the word as it appears in midrashic passages, see I. Ziegler, *Die Königsgleichnisse der Midrasch beleuchtet durch die römische Kaiserzeit* (1903). For examples of the different usages of *praefectus*/ἔπαρχος see Mason, *Greek Terms*, pp. 138ff.

[167] On the *praefectus castrorum* see H. M. D. Parker, *The Roman Legions* (1928), pp. 197ff. and G. Webster, *The Roman Imperial Army* (1969), p. 117.

[168] *War* III, 31.

[169] The original force is described as a "garrison" (δύναμις or φρουρά). See *Life* 347 and 394. Cf. *War* III, 31-32 where Caesennius Gallus and not Cestius Gallus assures Sepphoris of military aid.

[170] *War* III, 59f. Cf. *War* III, 33 and *Life* 411 where the size of the force is not indicated. A legion ordinarily consisted of approximately five-thousand infantry and one hundred and twenty horsemen. (See Webster, *Imperial Army*, pp. 114ff.) Even if we allow for some exaggeration on the part of Josephus, his choice of numbers is significant as he was fully aware of Sepphoris' capabilities as a stronghold.

[171] And perhaps better suited. Under Hadrian the non-Roman *auxilia* were stationed along the frontiers specifically to police the borders. See G. L. Cheesman, *The Auxilia of the Roman Army* (1914),

the legion VI Ferrata at Kefar ʿOtnay ca. 130[172] renders Sepphoris, which was only some sixteen miles to the north (via the road connecting the two locations), an improbable site for a similar force.[173]

The prefect, of course, could have commanded a unit smaller than a legion. *Eparchoi* (ἔπαρχοι) frequently appear as prefects in charge of *auxilia* or even smaller units.[174] Such divisions are known to have been positioned in *castra.* Thus an Egyptian papyrus refers to "the prefect of the cavalry (εἴλης) of soldiers of the *castra* of Dionysias" (ἔπαρχος εἴλης στρατιωτικῶν κάστρων Διονυσίαδος).[175] This same *praefectus alae* is elsewhere referred to as a *praefectus castrorum.*[176] According to F. G. Kenyon, when a *castra* had only a single *ala* of auxiliary troops, the prefect who commanded that unit was also referred to locally as the *praefectus castrorum.*[177] Such may very well have been the case at Sepphoris. The *eparchos* could have been known as the *praefectus castrorum* even though in reality he was an official in charge of a unit considerably smaller.

Unfortunately, the ben Simai passage does not inform us of the type of unit stationed in the *castra* of Sepphoris. Perhaps the rabbinic sources provide a clue. The "men of the *castra* of Sepphoris," presumably travelled several miles from their station to the premises of Joseph ben Simai.[178] The distance must have been covered by horseback otherwise they would not have arrived on time to put out the fire. Thus the contingent at Sepphoris could very well have been an auxiliary unit, perhaps an *ala* (cavalry) or, more likely, a *cohortes equitatae* (mounted infantry). (The latter would have required less space since only a proportion of

---

p. 107. A military diploma from 139 C.E. mentions fifteen auxiliary and twelve infantry units in Palestine. See Smallwood, *The Jews under Roman Rule*, p. 458.

The road from Kefar ʿOtnay to Sepphoris was already in existence in 130 C.E. See B. Lifschitz, "*la date du transfert,*" p. 110 and Hecker, "*Kevish Romaʾi,*" p. 183. The road leading from Ptolemais to Sepphoris and terminating at Tiberias was probably built after the revolt (ca. 135 C.E.) as a security measure. See M. Avi Yonah, *The Holy Land from the Persian to the Arab Conquest* (536 B.C.-A.D. 640): *A Historical Geography*² (1977), p. 186 and Smallwood, pp. 458f.

[172] Lifschitz, "*la date du transfert,*" pp. 109ff., claims that the existence of a road from Kefar ʿOtnay to Sepphoris in 130 C.E. proves that VI Ferrata was already stationed in the former city prior to the outbreak of the revolt. Cf. *idem.*, "*Ligyonot Romiyim Be-ʾEreẓ Yisrael,*" *Yediʿot Ha-Ḥevrah La-Ḥaqirat ʾEreẓ Yisrael Va-ʿAtiqoteha* 23 (1959), 58; Hecker, "*Kevish Romaʾi,*" p. 184 and Smallwood, *The Jews Under Roman Rule*, p. 436f.

[173] At least until the end of the second century since VI Ferrata remained in Palestine until that time and was only completely removed in the middle of the third century. See Smallwood, *ibid.*, pp. 498f.

[174] See G. Preisigke, *Wörterbuch*, s.v. ἔπαρχος.

[175] F. G. Kenyon, *Greek Papyri in the British Museum* (1893-) II, 271ff.

[176] Actually, the Greek reads: πραιπόσιτος (*praepositus*) χαστρῶν but that position was equivalent to a *praefectus castrorum*. See Kenyon, *ibid.*, p. 269.

[177] *Ibid.*

[178] Assuming that the identification of Shiḥin with Hirbet El-Lon is correct (note 113 above), Joseph ben Simai's courtyard was some five miles from Sepphoris. It could, of course, be maintained that the men happened to be in the neighborhood. However, the rabbinic sources seem to suggest that they came directly from the *castra* as a result of the fire.

its men were mounted.)[179] Still, a comparatively late Talmudic source reports that a *numerus* was once stationed in Sepphoris:[180]

ביומוי דר׳ מנה הוות נימורה[181] בציפורין והוון בניהון[182] מישכונין גבין מדאתאי[183]
מיזל לון אפיק ר׳ מנא כדון[184] כהיא דר׳ אימי[185] אמר לא דאנא סבר כדעתיה[186]
אלא בגין ציפרייא[187] דלא יחלטון בניהון

> In the days of Rabbi Mana, there was a *numerus*[188] in Sepphoris and their (the Sepphoreans') sons were seized[189] by them (the troops of the *numerus*). When it was time for them to leave,[190] Rabbi Mana declared the law[191] in accordance with Rabbi Immi. He (Rabbi Mana) said, "I am not in agreement with him but (have ruled thus) for the sake of the Sepphoreans whose sons will not be forfeited."[192]

Earlier in the *gemara*, Rabbi Immi (or Ammi, late third century) is said to have permitted an owner who is in dire economic straits[193] to sell his house regardless of the fact that it had been rented to someone else. Lieberman has plausibly suggested that the sons of the Sepphoreans were levied by the *numerus* in lieu of the *aurum tironicum.*[194] Although he disagreed with Immi's ruling, Rabbi Mana declared that under these unusual circumstances, the Sepphoreans could sell their houses, even though they were occupied by tenants, in order to pay the *aurum tironicum.*

---

179 An *ala* had approximately five hundred men and was subdivided into smaller units (*turmae*) of some thirty men. The *cohortes equitatae* of an auxiliary infantry of five hundred men amounted to one hundred and twenty soldiers. These figures varied, however. See Webster, *Imperial Army*, pp. 146, 149; cf. Cheesman, *Auxilia*, pp. 26ff. The acropolis of Sepphoris could certainly have supported these.

180 P. *Pesaḥim* 4, 31b, Ms. Leiden.

181 A fragment from the *Genizah* (hereafter "Genizah") reads נומירה. See L. Ginzberg, *Ginzei Schechter* (1928-9) I, p. 443.

182 Genizah: בניהון דציפוריי

183 Genizah: מאתי

184 Genizah: כרוז ("announcement").

185 Genizah: אמי His name appears variously as Immi or Ammi.

186 Genizah: דכוותה

187 Genizah: ציפוריי

188 Some commentators take this word to be טמירא meaning "secrecy" and read into the passage a persecution from which the Sepphoreans were hiding. See, for instance, Z. W. Rabinovitz, *Shaʿarei Torat ʾEreẓ Yisrael* (1940), p. 222 and the sources referred to by S. Lieberman in his *Ha-Yerushalmi Ki-Feshuto* I (1934), p. 444. On the incorrectness of the rendering טמירא see Ginzberg, *Ginzei Schechter* I, 431. Lieberman argues against any reference in this passage to persecutions of the Jews in his "Palestine in the Third and Fourth Centuries," reprinted in *idem, Texts and Studies*, p. 136.

189 The word מישכונין can also mean pledged. See Lieberman, "Palestine," p. 135, nn. 178, 179.

190 The word לון is taken as a *dativus commodi* here. See Dalman, *Grammatik*, p. 226.

191 Or, according to the Genizah version (above, n. 184), "Rabbi Manna made an announcement." For the interpretation provided here see *Penei Moshe* on the passage.

192 On this rendering of יחלטון see Lieberman, "*Palestine*," p. 135, n. 179.

193 Actually, the text states that he was in danger of dying of starvation.

194 Lieberman, "*Palestine*," p. 136. On the *aurum tironicum*, see M. Rostovtzeff, *The Social and Economic History of the Roman Empire* (1957) I, pp. 467, 511.

This passage would seem to be important for our discussion because it actually names the type of unit located at Sepphoris during the time of Mana (fourth century).[195] It is commonly believed that *numeri* were ethnic units of a few hundred men which were stationed wherever relatively small forces were needed.[196] Sepphoris could probably have easily accommodated a *numerus* if such had been the case. Unfortunately, the meaning of the term *numerus* has recently been called into question. M. P. Speidel has shown that the word is a non-technical term meaning "unit." It could be applied to any size or type of regiment.[197] Thus the passage reveals nothing concerning the nature of the "unit" which was in Sepphoris in the fourth century. Moreover, the account suggests that the *numerus* had come to Sepphoris specifically to levy troops or collect the *aurum tironicum.* The unit could have been in Sepphoris for only a short while and may not have been stationed in the city.

Although the type of unit stationed in the *castra* of Sepphoris cannot be determined, it seems likely that, at least during quiet times, a small force would have been sufficient to patrol the countryside and maintain order.[198] Lieberman has suggested that the הפרכום (or אפרכום) in the ben Simai account was actually a *hipparchos* (ἵππαρχος).[199] This official, who had a force of mounted constables (διωγμῖται) at his command, served as a kind of "chief of police."[200] A small

---

[195] Actually, there were two Palestinian *amoraim* named Mana. The earlier of the two lived in the second and third quarters of the third century. He could not have disputed Immi's view since the latter flourished at the end of the century. See Sperber, *The Land*, p. 180.

[196] See Cheesman, *Auxilia*, pp. 85f. and Webster, *Imperial Army*, pp. 149f. Cf. E. N. Luttwak, *The Grand Strategy of the Roman Empire* (1976), pp. 122f.

[197] M. P. Speidel, "The Rise of Ethnic Units in the Roman Imperial Army," *Aufstieg und Niedergang der römischen Welt*, pt. 2, vol. 3 (1974), 202-208.

[198] Two other sources have been used to illustrate the occupation of Sepphoris and its neighborhood by Roman regiments. B. *Shabbat* 145b has a report in the name of Rabbi Isaac that there was no festival upon which a *boleshet* (בולשת) did not enter Sepphoris. This term may only refer to individuals on patrol rather than a troop. Cf. the statement in the name of Rabbi Ḥanina which follows Isaac's. Ḥanina clearly refers to different types of officers who came to Tiberias on the festivals. Cf. Klein's discussion in "*Ẓippori*," p. 53 and especially n. 3. Klein suggests that the statements of the two rabbis should be interchanged because Ḥanina was from Sepphoris and Isaac from Tiberias. However, there is no Mss. support for this emendation.

The second source, P. *ʿEruvin* 5, 22b, refers to the *burgi* (בורגנין.). R. Simeon ben Yoḥai (early second century) claims that he could stay in these *burgi* on his travels between Sepphoris and Tiberias. While the term *burgus* usually refers to a small road fort (see Luttwak, *Strategy*, p. 160), in rabbinic literature the term also means caravanserai. In addition, it often seems to have been connected with villiages and farms. See Safrai "Relations," pp. 227f. and especially 229f. Also, D. Sperber, "On the πύργος as a Farm Building," *AJSr* 1 (1976), 359-361 and *idem, The Land*, p. 53, n. 19. According to Krauss, the *burgus* and the *castra* in rabbinic literature refer to a φρούριον or φρουρά ("garrison"). See S. Krauss, "*Die römischen Besatzungen in Palästina*," *MWJ* 19 (1892), pp. 235ff. and the continuation of this article in *MWJ* 20 (1893), 124. Also, *idem*, "*Ha-Kerakh, Ha-ʿIr, Ve-Ha-Kefar Ba-Talmud*," *He-ʿAtid* 3 (1922), 20f. Cf. Romanoff, "Onomasticon," p. 155, n. 1 and Sperber, "On the πύργος as a Farm Building," p. 360.

[199] Lieberman, *Toseftaʾ Ki-Feshutah* III, 213. The Tosefta Mss. all have הפרכום (with a ה, see n. 165) so that Lieberman's suggestion is quite reasonable.

[200] See A. H. M. Jones, *The Greek City from Alexander to Justinian* (1940), pp. 212f.

detachment would have been all that was needed to extinguish the blaze on Joseph ben Simai's property, and this kind of service would have been provided by a local police force. But the use of the word *castra* and the strategic importance of Sepphoris suggests that, if not in the days of Joseph ben Simai, at least at other times during the history of the city a more sophisticated military unit was stationed there.

Summary: Castra Shel-Ẓippori in the Joseph ben Simai Narratives

The second century rabbis who preserved the Joseph ben Simai account incidentally revealed that they were aware of the existence of a gentile *castra* at Sepphoris. The rabbis who refer to a *castra ha-yeshanah* in Mishnah *ʿArakhin* have also been shown to have lived in the second century, but they seem to have had an older, Jewish institution in mind.[201] Regardless of when the ben Simai incident occurred, the *castra* must have been in existence well into the second century. At that time a unit of gentile cavalry under the command of a prefect or *hipparchos* was stationed at Sepphoris.

There is no evidence that Joseph ben Simai was the *ʾepitropos* of Agrippa II. For that matter, he may never have served as an *ʾepitropos* to any king; the text which describes him as such is an embellished version of earlier material. Nor is there any proof that Vespasian entrusted Agrippa II with jurisdiction over Sepphoris. Indeed, Josephus contrasts Tiberias, which had been given to Agrippa II by Nero, with Sepphoris which concomitantly became the administrative capital of Galilee.[202] There is no reason to believe that this situation changed under Vespasian.

---

201 Above, p. 24.

202 See the text quoted below, p. 54.

CHAPTER THREE

THE "OLD" ᶜ*ARCHEI*

In Mishnah *Qiddushin* 4:5, Rabbi Yose ben Ḥalafta, a resident of Sepphoris in the mid-second century,[203] mentions the "old ᶜ*archei* (archives, ארכי, ערכי) of Sepphoris."[204] This institution is curiously reminiscent of the "old *castra* of Sepphoris." Further elucidation of the passage in which Rabbi Yose's reference occurs will help to determine the relationship (if any) between the ᶜ*archei* and the *castra*. The Mishnah reads:[205]

ואין בודקין לא מן המזבח ולמעלה[206] ולא מן הדוכן ולמעלה ולא מן סנהדרין ולמעלה וכל שהוחזקו אבותיו[207] משוטרי הרבים וגבאי צדקה משיאין לכהונה ואין[208] צריך לבדוק אחריהן ר' יוסי אומר אף מי שהיה חתום עד[209] בערכי[210] הישנה של צפורי[211] רבי חנינה[212] בן אנטיגנוס אומר אף מי שהיה מוכתב באסטרטיא[213] של מלך

They do not examine descent (of a woman) beyond the Altar[214] or beyond the Platform (*dukhan*)[215] or beyond the Sanhedrin. And all whose fathers are known to have been public clerks (*shoterim*)[216] or managers of charity[217] may (also) marry into the

---

[203] On R. Yose ben Ḥalafta, see W. Bacher, *Tannaiten* II, 150ff.

[204] For ᶜ*archei* meaning archive(s), see Krauss, *Lehnwörter* II, 130 and 418f. Apparently, the word is a shortened form of Greek ἀρχεῖον (archive). The word ἄρχη is found in many papyri with the sense of "notary's office." See, Preisigke, *Wörterbuch*, s.v. ἄρχη.

[205] The text is that of ed. Vilna. Cf. the parallel version in *Numbers Rab.* 9:7.

[206] The *editio princeps* (Naples, 1492) and Ms. Kaufmann have *u-le-ma*ᶜ*alan* (ולמעלן) throughout. Ms. Parma has ולמעלה.

[207] Ms. Parma has להיות ("to be") after אבותיו with no מ on שוטרי

[208] The *editio princeps*, Ms. Parma and Ms. Kaufmann have ואינו.

[209] The word עד (witness) is included in the *editio princeps* and Ms. Kaufmann. In the confused text of Ms. Parma, the phrase (עד) אף מי שהיה חתום is first attributed to R. Yose and then to R. Ḥaninah. In the former attribution, the term עד is included, in the latter it is not. The passage then closes with R. Ḥaninah stating: אף מי שהיה מוכתב באיסטרטיא של מלך. Although Ms. Munich to B. *Qiddushin* 76a and Ms. Leiden to P. *Qiddushin* 4, 65a do not have עד it would seem that the reading was favored in the Ms. tradition of the Mishnah.

[210] The *editio princeps* and Ms. Kaufmann have בארכי.

[211] Mss. Parma and Kaufmann read: שלציפורין.

[212] The *editio princeps* and Ms. Kaufmann have חנניא.

[213] This word appears as באסרטיא in the *editio princeps* and as באסרטייא in Ms. Kaufmann. See Krauss, *Lehnwörter* II, p. 83, where he equates it with Greek στρατία (army). Cf. A. Kohut, ᶜ*Arukh Ha-Shalem* I, 175 and B. *Qiddushin* 76b. The personal guard of the king's court seems to be intended here. See the discussion below, n. 244 and cf. Jastrow, *Sefer Millim*, p. 91f.

[214] i.e. beyond an ancestor who served at the Altar, a priest.

[215] Upon which the Levites sang and the priests recited the Priestly Blessing. The reference here is probably to the Levites as opposed to the priests who served at the Altar. For the Levites and the *dukhan* (platform) see M. ᶜ*Arakhin* 2:6.

[216] R. de Vaux notes (*Ancient Israel* I, 155) that II Chron. 19:11 speaks of Levites serving as *shoterim* on the tribunals of Jerusalem. The root š/t/r/ in Akkadian means "to write," but, as de Vaux astutely observes, the *shoterim* are differentiated from the scribes in II Chron. 34:13. They

priesthood, and there is no need to examine (their descent) any further. Rabbi Yose says, "Also whoever was signed as a witness (*ḥatum ᶜed*) in the old archives of Sepphoris (*ᶜarchei ha-yeshanah shel-Ẓippori*)."[218] Rabbi Ḥaninah ben Antigonus says, "Also whoever was registered in the army of the king."

According to the Mishnah,[219] ten family stocks returned to *Ereẓ Yisrael* from the Babylonian Exile. Of these there were several impure or doubtful stocks which were not permitted to intermarry with the others. Thus the rabbis prescribed that a man[220] who wished to marry a woman of priestly descent had to examine her lineage through four maternal generations on both her mother's and father's sides. A man who wished to marry a woman of Levitical or Israelite descent had to trace her lineage even further.[221] Our passage specifies that this examination could be dismissed with, once it is determined that the woman's lineage includes either a Temple or public official.[222] The statements of Rabbi Yose and Rabbi Ḥaninah expand the list of persons whose stock is beyond reproach.

Interpreters of this *mishnah* have understood the words attributed to Rabbi Yose in various ways. Some medieval commentators explain *ᶜarchei* as a court which preserved records of one's lineage and determined who was fit to serve as a witness or judge.[223] However, the words *ḥatum ᶜed* (signed as a *witness*) seem to

---

seem to have been associated with the judges (for example, Deut. 16:18). De Vaux suggests "clerks" as a translation. The commentators consider *shoterei ha-rabbim* to be judges who handled cases which did not require a court of twenty three. See, for instance, Rashi on B. *Qiddushin* 76b. Halivni discounts their role as judges, suggesting instead that they were responsible for procedural order. See D. Halivni, *Meqorot U-Mesorot, Nashim* (1968), p. 440.

217 Adopting the translation of Jastrow, *Sefer Millim*, p. 206.

218 Rashi understood *ha-yeshanah* to be the name of a city near Sepphoris. Rashi took his clue from the city Ḥadashah (חדשה = new) which is mentioned in M. *ᶜEruvin* 5:6. There was also a biblical town called *Yeshanah* (II Chron. 13:19 and elsewhere), but Rashi may not have had this place in mind. See the comments of R. Samuel Straschun on B. *Qiddushin*, 76a. Straschun suggests that the word *yeshanah* was not understood as an adjective because it did not agree with the plural form, *ᶜarchei*. Cf. Rashi's comments on *castra ha-yeshanah shel-Ẓippori* in B. *ᶜArakhin* 32a.

219 M. *Qiddushin* 4:1.

220 The text seems to refer to any man who wished to marry a woman of priestly descent, but many of the commentators confine the *halakhah* to a priest. See the comments of H. Albeck in his ed. of the Mishnah, *Seder Nashim*, pp. 414f.

221 See M. *Qiddushin* 4:4 and cf. T. *Qiddushin* 5:4 and the comments of Lieberman, *Toseftaʾ Ki-Feshutah* VIII, 974f.

222 The commentators assume that it is still necessary to trace the lineage until such an official is found. See, for example, the remarks of R. Obadiah Bertinoro on this passage. On the appointment of officials of indisputable lineage, see S. Safrai, "*Ha-ᶜIr Ha-Yehudit Be-ʾEreẓ Yisrael Bi-Tequfat Ha-Mishnah Ve-Ha-Talmud," in Milḥemet Qodesh U-Martirologyah Be-Toledot Yisrael U-Ve-Toledot Ha-ᶜAmim, Ha-ᶜIr Ve-Ha-Qehillah* (1967), p. 229.

223 Cf. Rashi on B. *Qiddushin* 76a and the commentary of R. Obadiah Bertinoro on the Mishnah. These commentators apparently overlooked the word *ᶜed* (witness) or did not have it in the texts before them. They merely regard a person who is "signed" (*ḥatum*) or registered in the records of the court as being of worthy ancestry. Schürer, who incorrectly claims that the best Mss. do not include the word "*ᶜed*" (cf. n. 209 above), defines *ᶜarchei* as Greek ἄρχη. This word can refer to "power" or "authority," as mentioned earlier (p. 39), but it also has the extended meaning of "magistracy" or "office" (Liddel and Scott, *Lexicon*, s.v.). Schürer understands it to mean

imply something other than registration in the genealogical records of a court.[224] Indeed, Gulak has demonstrated that *ḥatum ʿed* is more readily understood once it is accepted that *ʿarchei* refers to an archive.[225] Gulak notes a tradition preserved in the name of Simeon ben Gamaliel II (first half of the second century C.E.) which states that only priests and Levites or Israelites (laymen) who may give their daughters in marriage into the priestly stock[226] could sign (*ḥotemin* from the same root as *ḥatum*) the *ketubah* (marriage document) of a woman as witness to the purity of her lineage.[227] The *ketubah* was placed in an archive both because of the monetary obligation stipulated therein[228] and in order to record the relationship. One who was *ḥatum ʿed* was a person whose name was recorded on a marriage document in an archive and whose stock was, therefore, unquestionable. According to Rabbi Yose, once a woman's lineage has been traced to such a person, her descent requires no further examination.[229]

There are several indications that the Jews possessed their own archives in the post-biblical period. A papyrus from Alexandria contrasts the *archeion* (ἀρχεῖον) of the Jews with the *politikon archeion* (πολιτικὸν ἀρχεῖον), or municipal archive, of

---

"government." He suggests that (1) the members of the old government were Israelites of pure descent, or (2) all those who were recognized by the old government as being of pure descent were accepted as such. See Schürer, *Geschichte* II, 211, n. 495.

224 Maimonides, in his commentary to the Mishnah, explains that whoever served as a witness in the *ʿarchei* of Sepphoris was of worthy lineage. Maimonides obviously had the word *ʿed* before him. Cf. the commentary of *Tosefot Yom Tov* on the passage. This commentator recognized the difference between the interpretations of Rashi and Bertinoro, on the one hand, and that of Maimonides. The latter sensed the difficulty of the words *ḥatum ʿed*, but his explanation does not indicate why one who testified in the *ʿarchei* of Sepphoris should be considered of worthy lineage.

225 Gulak, *Ḥeqer*, pp. 44ff. See note 204 above. The *Targum Jonathan* to the Prophets (Joshua 15:15, 16) has *Kiryat ʾArchei* (קרית ארכי) for *Kiryat Sefer* (קרית ספר = the city, Devir). The Septuagint has *polis grammaton* (πόλις γραμμάτων, "city of records").

To be sure, the archive could have been associated with a court. Tannaitic sources, however, use the phrase *bet-din* to refer to a court. Perhaps the archives were kept wherever the court met. In this regard the reference to the judges of Sepphoris (*dayyanei Ẓippori*) in M. *Babaʾ Batraʾ* 6:7 should be noted.

226 i.e. Israelites of suitable lineage whose daughters could marry priests. See *Tosefot Yom Tov* on M. *Sanhedrin* 4:2.

227 P. *Sanhedrin* 1, 19c (ed. Venice) reads:

תני אמר רבן שמעון בן גמליאל בראשונה לא היו חותמין על כתובת נשים כשירות אלא כהנים לויים וישראלי׳ משיאין לכהונה

> It was taught (in a *baraita*): R. Simeon ben Gamaliel said, "At first only priests (and) Levites and Israelites who may give their daughters in marriage into the priestly stock would sign the marriage document of suitable women."

The parallel in T. *Sanhedrin* 7:1 omits כשירות. Ms. Leiden has it. Gulak, *Ḥeqer*, *ibid.*, assumes that the passage refers to a woman who intends to marry a priest. Cf., however, A. Büchler, "Family Purity and Family Impurity in Jerusalem Before the Year 70 C.E." in *idem*, *Studies in Jewish History*, pp. 65f.

228 See L. Blau, *Die jüdische Ehescheidung und der jüdische Scheidebrief* (1911-12), II, 61.

229 Gulak (*Ḥeqer*, p. 46) postulates the existence of officials who examined genealogical documents. He claims that these registers could not be entrusted to gentiles and the archives of Sepphoris must have been Jewish. Cf. *Apion* I, 29.

the Alexandrians.[230] An inscription from Hierapolis (Asia Minor) specifically refers to an "archive of the Jews."[231] Josephus relates that the *sicarii*, at the outset of the revolution (ca. 66 C.E.), set fire to the archives (τὰ ἀρχεῖα) of Jerusalem in order to ingratiate themselves with the poor whose debts were recorded there.[232] These were probably Jewish archives as the terrorism of the *sicarii* was aimed particularly at the wealthy, aristocratic class who controlled the Temple and its offices.[233]

In rabbinic literature, on the other hand, there are frequent references to the "archives of the gentiles" (*ʿarchaʾot shel-goyim* or *nokhrim*), "the archives of the Samaritans" (*ʿarchaʾot shel-Kutim*), "the archives of Egypt" (*ʿarcheion shel-miẓrayim*) and "the archives in Syria" (*ʿarcha'ot she-be-suriya'*).[234] The various designations: ערכאים, ערכאות, ערכי, ארכי, ארכיים , ארכיון, ארכי also appear without any qualifications, but in most cases the context indicates that a non-Jewish institution is intended. Indeed, S. Krauss has suggested that the rabbis always perceived the *ʿarchei* as a non-Jewish institution, as the foreign term itself implies.[235] The frequent references to non-Jewish or foreign archives suggests that the exclusively Jewish registries had faded into history. The municipal rights of the Jews must have been severely restricted following the First Revolt (70 C.E.) undermining whatever authority their archives continued to possess.[236] Under the twofold political and religious persecution of Hadrian all such municipal institutions were abolished.[237] The report of the Tosefta that in the days of Rabbi Aqiba (ca. 110-135 C.E.) the *ḥakhamim* had already adopted a liberal at-

---

[230] *BGU* IV, 1131; 1151. Cf. *Ant.* XIX, 281. Also see V. Tcherikover, *Ha-Yehudim Be-Miẓrayim Bi-Tequfat Ha-Helenistit Ha-Romit Le-ʾOr Ha-Papirologyah* (1963), pp. 103f.

[231] *Corpus Inscriptionum Judaicarum* II, 775. Cf. W. Judeich *et al.*, *Altertümer von Hierapolis* (1898), ≠ 212. Also see V. A. Tcherikover and A. Fuks, *Corpus Papyrorum Judaicarum* (1957-64) II, 9f.

[232] *War* II, 427. On archives in general see S. Baron, *The Jewish Community* I, 93; J. Juster, *Les Juifs dans l'empire romain* (1914) I, 475f. and L. Fuchs, *Die Juden Aegyptens in ptolemäischer und römischer Zeit* (1924), pp. 93f.

[233] See D. M. Rhoads, *Israel in Revolution*, pp. 111ff. Tiberias also had an archives, but the Hellenistic complexion of the city (see Hoehner, *Herod Antipas*, pp. 97ff.) casts some doubt as to whether it was a strictly Jewish institution. See below, pp. 54f. Also cf. *Life* 6 and *Apion* I, 31. On the latter source, see J. Jeremias, *Jerusalem in the Time of Jesus*, trans. F. H. Cave and C. H. Cave (1969), p. 283.

[234] For ערכאות של גוים (נוכרים) see M. *Gittin* 1:5 and T. *Gittin* 1:4; for ערכאות של כותים see B. *Gittin* 19b and for ארכיון של מצרים see *Pesiqta' de R. Kahana* (ed. Buber) 27a, *Tanḥuma'* (ed. Buber) *Ki Teṣe'* 13, and *Yalqut* Deut. 938. The talmudic discussions concerning ערכאות שבסוריא (P. *Sanhedrin 3, 21a and B. Sanhedrin* 23a) imply that it was a place where *Jews* held *court* proceedings (cf. above, n. 225) in the time of R. Yoḥanan (third century). Gulak, (*Ḥeqer*, p. 57, n. 2) regards this usage of *ʿarcha'ot* as peculiar since the term is usually used in connection with the depositing of *shetarot* (documents). Thus this particular instance may not be relevant to our discussion. In any case, the *ʿarcha'ot she-be-suriya'* may have been Roman *administered.*

[235] This would include the *ʿarcha'ot she-be-suriya'* (see preceding note). Krauss goes so far as to claim that the *ʿarchei ha-yeshanah* of Sepphoris was also a gentile (Roman) institution. See S. Krauss, *Talmudische Archäologie* (1910-12) III, 196 and cf. the discussion below, pp. 50f.

[236] See Blau, *Ehescheidung* II, 58.

[237] See Avi-Yonah, *The Jews of Palestine*, pp. 46f. and Allon, *Toledot* II, 43ff.

titude concerning the validity of documents deposited in the archives of the gentiles is, therefore, not surprising.[238]

Returning to Mishnah *Qiddushin*, all of the offices ''beyond'' which examination of descent was deemed unnecessary were obviously Jewish institutions. In fact, the anonymous list of institutions with which our passage begins seems to have been composed with Jerusalem and the Temple in mind. The ''altar,'' or priestly cult, and the *dukhan* upon which the Levites sang could only refer to the Temple.[239] As for the Sanhedrin, elsewhere in the Mishnah it is explicitly stated that a *bet-din* empowered to try capital cases had to be composed of priests and Levites or Israelites who may give their daughters in marriage into the priestly stock.[240] This *bet-din* must have been the Sanhedrin of Jerusalem as capital cases were usually tried there.[241] While many cities may have had their own ''public clerks'' and ''managers of charity,'' only in Jerusalem were these lesser officials likely to have been of unquestionable ancestry.[242] The nucleus of our excerpt, therefore, depicts organs of the Jewish community which were extant prior to the destruction of the Temple and Jerusalem in 70 C.E. Accordingly, the appended statements of Rabbi Yose and Rabbi Ḥaninah must also refer to Jewish institutions of that particular era.[243] The king whose army is referred to by Rabbi Ḥaninah was probably of the Herodian line, perhaps Agrippa I or Agrippa II.[244] Ḥaninah's contemporary, Yose, also had a pre-70, Jewish institution in mind, the ''old'' (*ha-yeshanah*) archives of Sepphoris.[245]

---

[238] T. *Gittin* 1:4 (ed. Zuckermandel) reads:

אמ׳ ר׳ אלעזר בר׳ יוסי אמ׳ להן רבן שמעון בן גמל׳ לחכמ׳ בצידן לא נחלקו ר׳ עקיבא וחכמ׳ על השטרות העולין בערכאות של גוים שהן כשירין על מה נחלקו על שנעשו בהדיוט

> Eleazar ben R. Yose said, ''Simeon ben Gamaliel said to the *ḥakhamim* in Sidon, 'R. Aqiba and the *ḥakhamim* were not in disagreement over the validity of documents deposited in the archives of the gentiles. Over what did they disagree? Over those (documents) prepared by laymen.' ''

Simeon ben Gamaliel is probably a mistake for Simeon ben Yohai. See Lieberman, *Tosefta᾽ Ki-Feshutah* VIII, 785f. and cf. M. *Gittin* 1:5. Also see Halivni, *Nashim*, pp. 497ff. and M. Feldblum, *Perushim U-Meḥqarim Ba-Talmud* (1969), pp. 86ff. On the motivations for these rulings see S. Baron, *History* II² (1952), p. 265 and Blau, *Ehescheidung* II, 61f.

To be sure, it was probably not the intention of the *ḥakhamim* to give a blanket permission; they allowed the people to resort to gentile archives in cases involving gentiles and especially when a Jew could ''save'' (כמציל מידם , see B. *Gittin* 44a and B. ᶜ*Avodah Zarah* 13a) property from falling into non-Jewish hands.

[239] On the following, see A. Büchler, *Ha-Kohanim Va-ᶜAvodatam*, trans. N. Ginton (1966), p. 148 and G. Allon, *Meḥqarim* I, 97f.

[240] M. *Sanhedrin* 4:2.

[241] See S. Safrai, ''Jewish Self-Government,'' *The Jewish People in the First Century* I, 397f.

[242] Cf. the comment of Abaye on the public clerks, B. *Qiddushin* 76b.

[243] The purpose of these statements may have been to expand the Mishnah to institutions outside of Jerusalem. See Büchler, *Kohanim*, p. 148. Both R. Yose and R. Ḥaninah would still have had pre-70 institutions in mind.

[244] In the *gemara* (B. *Qiddushin* 76b) Rab Judah (d. 299) states in the name of Samuel (d. 254) that R. Ḥaninah's statement refers to armies of the House of David. Rab Joseph (d. 333) finds support for this in I Chron. 7:40. The *gemara*, however, indicates that this explanation is problematic.

The term *ha-yeshanah* (הישנה) differentiates this particular archive from the later, more prevalent "archives of the *goyim*" found in rabbinic literature. It now remains to be seen whether the term has the same connotation when it is used to describe the *castra* of Sepphoris.

Castra in Rabbinic Literature

Like *ᶜarchei*, the term *castra* appears very often in rabbinic sources and also, as far as can be determined, refers to a non-Jewish institution.[246] In the Midrashim, the various Semitic forms of *castra*[247] represent the non-Jewish camps or fortifications from which God does not desire or expect devotion.[248] The camp (מחנה) of Israel, which was pitched outside of the Tent of Meeting, seems to be contrasted with the *castra* (in plural sense) of the other nations:[249]

אמ׳ ר׳ יהושע בן לוי אילו היו אומות העולם יודעין מה אוהל מועד יפה להן היו אהליות וקסטריאות מקיפות אותו[250]

Rabbi Joshua ben Levi said, "If the nations of the world had known how beneficial the Tent of Meeting (could have been) for them, they would have surrounded it with groups of tents and camps (*castariot*)."

Another aggadic source mentions the "evil kingdom" (מלכות הרשעה) of Rome which instructed its *castra* situated at Bet Peor to locate the grave of Moses.[251] In *Megillat Taᶜanit* the seventeenth of *Elul* is declared a festival because the Romans vacated Jerusalem on that day. The scholion to the passage explains that the

---

The suggestion here that R. Ḥaninah had either Agrippa I or II in mind follows the interpretation of S. Klein ("*Zum jüdischen Heerwesen in der mischnischen Zeit*," *Jeschurun* 10 (1923), p. 88) who claims that the bodyguard of one of these kings is intended. A. Aptowitzer, however, takes Klein to task, contending that a Herodian was unlikely to be concerned about the genealogical purity of any of his soldiers. Aptowitzer prefers a Maccabean king, and argues in favor of John Hyrcanus I. See A. Aptowitzer, *Parteipolitik der Hasmonäerzeit in rabbinischem und pseudepigraphischem Schrifttum* (1927), pp. 230ff., 309f. John Hyrcanus, however, who had his troubles with the Pharisees, is not any more likely than Agrippa I or II. See Schürer, *History* I (ed. Vermes-Millar), pp. 211f.

245 Büchler claims (*Kohanim*, p. 148) that it was more difficult to maintain purity of descent after the First Revolt when there was a mass exodus from Judah to Galilee. On R. Ḥaninah, see Hyman, *Toledot* II, 479.

246 See S. Klein's article, "*Kastra*" in the German *Encyclopaedia Judaica* IX, cols. 1034ff. and cf. S. Krauss, *Paras Ve-Romi Ba-Talmud U-Va-Midrashim* (1938), pp. 221ff.

247 Above, p. 14.

248 See *Genesis Rab.* 28:2.

249 *Leviticus Rab.* 1:11 (ed. Margulies). This passage is repeated in many places. See, for example, *Numbers Rab.* 1:3, *Tanḥumaᵓ Terumah* (ed. Buber) 8 and *Yalqut*, Deut. 831. The camp (מחנה) of Israel is not explicitly mentioned here, but it is evident that a contrast is intended. For the location of the Tent of Meeting outside of the camp of Israel see Ex. 33:7.

250 Ed. Vilna of *Leviticus Rab.* 1:11. *Tanḥumaᵓ Terumah* 8 and *Yalqut* Deut. 831 all read:

היו מקיפין אותו אהליות וקסטריות.

251 See B. *Sotah* 14a and the sources noted by L. Ginzberg, *The Legends of the Jews* (reprinted, 1968) VI, 410, n. 60 who identifies the "evil kingdom" (מלכות הרשעה) as the Roman government.

soldiers of *castra* (in plural sense, קסטריאות) stationed in Jerusalem were responsible for the violation of Jewish women causing them to be undesirable as wives to Jewish men. The departure of the *castra* from Jerusalem was obviously a joyous occasion.[252]

The usage of the expression in halakhic contexts is even more instructive. The Tosefta expands the list in Mishnah ᵓ*Oholot* (18:10) which designates the areas that are not considered "gentile dwelling places" (מדורות הגוים).[253] Rabbi Judah contends that encampments and legionary stations (הקסטראות והלגיונות)[254] are unclean, i.e. are capable of rendering a person ritually unfit through contact. The *ḥakhamim* disagree with Rabbi Judah. The issue is whether the encampments and legionary stations are considered temporary settlements where burials were unlikely to occur. For the rabbis there is no question as to the composition of these places; they are *gentile* establishments whose provisional nature raises questions only insofar as their halakhic status is concerned.

Another legal account declares that *maᶜaser sheni* (second tithe)[255] cannot be redeemed with money hidden in a *castra* or in *Har Ha-Melekh.*[256] Earlier in the text it is stated that currency issued during the Bar Kokhba rebellion (מעות כזביות) also could not be used for redemption purposes.[257] Hence, S. Lieber-

---

[252] See H. Lichtenstein, "*Die Fastenrolle, eine Untersuchung zur jüdisch-hellenistischen Geschichte*," *HUCA* 8-9 (1931-2), 235. Lurie claims that the term *castra* in this passage is a later usage referring to Syrian camps in the days of the Hasmonean uprisings. See B. Z. Lurie, *Megillat Taᶜanit* (1964), pp. 142f. Cf., however, S. Applebaum, "Judea as a Roman Province," in *Aufstieg und Niedergang der römischen Welt*, pt. 2, vol. 8 (1977), 395. Applebaum places the event in the Bar Kokhba period.

The following *midrash*, which appears in *Lamentations Rab.* 1:17 and *Song of Songs Rab.* 2:2, is particularly interesting. The *Lamentations Rab.* source (ed. Buber) is quoted here.

צוה ה׳ ליעקב סביביו צריו כגון חלמיש לנוה סוסיתה לטבריה קסטרא לחופה (!) יריחו לנוערן לוד לאונו

> The Lord has summoned against Jacob His enemies all about him (Lamentations 1:17): For example, Ḥalamish (an enemy) to Naveh, Sussita to Tiberias, Castra to Ḥaifa, Jericho to Naᶜaram (and) Lydda to Ono.

For each Jewish city mentioned, a hostile city is juxtaposed. The first city mentioned in each pair is the antagonistic city. Castra is clearly opposed to Ḥaifa, a Jewish city. Sussita and Lydda were well known Hellenistic centers. Castra too must have been non-Jewish. Some scholars identify this place with a *Castra Samaritanorum* mentioned in a sixth-century source. See Allon, *Toledot* II, 249, Klein, ᵓ*Ereẓ Ha-Galil*, p. 129 and Avi-Yonah, *Map*, p. 7. Even if this identification is correct and this *castra* was held by Samaritans, it would most likely have been perceived as non-Jewish by the author of the *midrash*.

[253] i.e. which render a person ritually impure because people are likely to have been buried there. The gentiles were assumed not to have taken the precautions necessary to render their land clean. (See M. ᵓ*Oholot* 18:5). The Tosefta (18:12) expands the list of M. ᵓ*Oholot* (18:10) of gentile places where burials were unlikely to have occurred.

[254] The Mishnah has מקום לגיונות for לגיונות.

[255] This tithe of harvested produce had to be consumed in Jerusalem. If a person preferred, he could redeem this part of his produce by setting aside coins of the value of the second tithe plus one-fifth. The produce could then be eaten, but the coins had to be used to purchase food in Jerusalem which was to be consumed in a state of purity.

[256] See T. *Maᶜaser Sheni* 1:6. Cf. B. *Babaᵓ Qammaᵓ* 98a and P. *Maᶜaser Sheni* 1, 52d.

[257] See T. *Maᶜaser Sheni* 1:6.

man has suggested that the particular *castra* under discussion was a fortress held by the Romans after the rebellion, when it became difficult for Jews to retrieve money hidden in it.[258] Similarly, *Har Ha-Melekh* had been resettled with gentiles (Romans) and was dangerous for Jews to approach.[259]

Thus the *castra*, like the *ʿarchei*, was generally perceived of as a non-Jewish institution.[260] It has been shown, however, that the *tannaim* of the mid-second century who referred to the *castra ha-yeshanah shel-Ẓippori* in Mishnah *ʿArakhin* had a specifically Jewish (pre-70 C.E.) institution in mind. On the other hand, the ben Simai account, which also emanates from the mid-second century,[261] refers to a gentile *castra* at Sepphoris. As in the case of the *ʿarchei*, the term *ha-yeshanah* was implemented to distinguish between an older, defunct Jewish institution and the *castra* with which the second century rabbis were familiar. In sum, *ha-yeshanah* referred not only to the antiquity of both the archives and encampment of Sepphoris, but also to the former Jewish jurisdiction over these institutions.

The ʿArchei and the Castra

The question naturally arises as to the historical events which resulted in the transition of the *ʿarchei ha-yeshanah* and the *castra ha-yeshanah* to non-Jewish auspices.[262] Several scholars understood that the term *ha-yeshanah* was an indication of changed historical circumstances.[263] Büchler, in fact, assumed that the functions and histories of the *ʿarchei ha-yeshanah* and the *castra ha-yeshanah* were interrelated.[264] He, furthermore, posited a connection between the *ʿarchei, castra*

---

258 Lieberman, *Tosefta' Ki-Feshutah* II, 718.

259 The people of *Har Ha-Melekh* were hostile to Jews. Thus its wine and oil were not permitted. On the traditions and location of the place see Sperber, *The Land*, p. 168, n. 29.

260 A clear reference to a Jewish *castra* comes from outside of rabbinic sources. *Notitia dignitatum Orientis*, 25 refers to a *castra Judaeorum* located in Egypt in the Byzantine period. See Tcherikover, *Ha-Yehudim Be-Miẓrayim*, p. 23. This, of course, has no bearing on the discussion of the rabbinic sources presented here. Another *castra*, the nature of which cannot be determined, is mentioned in connection with Tiberias. See P. *ʿEruvin* 5, 22b where the term *kaẓrin* (קצרין) seems to refer to a *castra*. Cf. Klein, *ʾEreẓ Ha-Galil*, p. 96. On a place called *castra de-Galil*, see H. Hildesheimer, "*Geografyah Shel ʾEreẓ Yisrael*," in H. Bar Daroma, trans., *Gevulot Ha-ʾAreẓ* (1965), pp. 41ff. This place also appears to have been gentile in nature as it appears in a list of gentile locations which mark the boundaries of *Ereẓ Yisrael*. See *Sifre Deut.* 51, T. *Sheviʿit* 4:10, P. *Sheviʿit* 6, 36c. Cf. Klein, *Sefer Ha-Yishuv*, I, 159ff.

261 Above, pp. 34f.

262 Of course, these institutions did not necessarily continue in existence but may have reappeared at a later date under non-Jewish jurisdiction.

263 S. Krauss has suggested that the "old" *castra* and "old" *ʿarchei* were establishments which were destroyed during the "Third Jewish-Roman War" in the days of Antoninus Pius (137-161 C.E., Krauss misses the point concerning the Jewish-gentile implications of *ha-yeshanah*. Cf. n. 235). Unfortunately, aside from an oblique reference in the *Historia Augusta* (*Ant. Pius* 5, 4-5) to rebellious Jews (*Judaeos rebellantes*) who were subdued under Antoninus Pius, there is no evidence for anything resembling a full-scale revolt. See S. Krauss, *Antoninus und Rabbi* (1910), p. 117. On the supposed revolt under Pius see Smallwood, *The Jews Under Roman Rule*, pp. 467f., Avi-Yonah, *The Jews of Palestine*, p. 77 and G. Allon, *Toledot* II, 63.

264 Büchler, *Kohanim*, p. 148.

and those who in the words of Rabbi Ḥaninah were "registered in the army of the king."[265] According to Büchler, the statement of Rabbi Ḥaninah, like that of Rabbi Yose preceding it in the Mishnah, refers to Sepphoris.[266] Büchler claims that those who were "registered in the army of the king" were the soldiers encamped in the *castra* of Sepphoris.[267] The Mishnah, however, gives no indication that Ḥaninah's comment refers to Sepphoris. Nor is there any reason to suppose that Ḥaninah had Sepphoris in mind, as he is not known to have been a resident of that city. Büchler further contends that Sepphoris received a "new" archives when the city reverted to Roman jurisdiction after the death of Agrippa II. This view is hardly tenable since, as was demonstrated earlier, there is no evidence for the inclusion of Sepphoris among Agrippa's domains.[268]

Klein, more convincingly, has postulated that *ha-yeshanah* referred to the pre-70 period when both the *ᶜarchei* and *castra* came into existence as Jewish institutions. Since *castra*, a Latin term, can only reflect a period of Roman domination, Klein proposes that the encampment was established by Herod and remained in existence until the First Revolt spread to Galilee ca. 67 C.E.[269] Similarly, Klein suggests that the term *ha-yeshanah* was applied to Jotapata, the walled city of Mishnah *ᶜArakhin,*[270] because its original settlement had come to an end when Vespasian razed the city to the ground in 67 C.E.[271] As for the *ᶜarchei ha-yeshanah*, Klein believes that the establishment of that institution is documented by Josephus, who reports that Nero, during the governorship of Felix (ca. 52-60 C.E.), transferred the Jewish archives (τὰ ἀρχεῖα) of Tiberias to Sepphoris. This *ᶜarchei ha-yeshanah* would then have come to an end after the Bar Kokhba revolt when it was replaced by a "new," Roman archives.[272] The text of Josephus reads:[273]

> νῦν δὲ ἔλεγεν αὐτοὺς ἠτυχηκέναι τῷ νεωτέρῳ δωρεὰν Ἀγρίππᾳ δοθέντας ὑπὸ Νέρωνος ἄρξαι γὰρ εὐθὺς τὴν μὲν Σέπφωριν ἐπειδὴ Ῥωμαίοις ὑπήκουσεν τῆς Γαλιλαίας καταλυθῆναι δὲ παρ' αὐτοῖς τήν τε βασιλικὴν τράπεζαν καὶ τὰ ἀρχεῖα
> And now he (Justus of Tiberias) said that they (the Tiberians) have been unfortunate in being given by Nero as a present to Agrippa the younger (Agrippa II). For Sepphoris at once became the capital of Galilee when it submitted to the Romans and their (the Tiberians') royal bank and (their) archives were dissolved (*katalythenai*).

It is clear from this passage that Sepphoris replaced Tiberias as the administrative capital of Galilee. Josephus, however, does not explicitly state that

---

265 See the Mishnah text, above, p. 46.
266 As opposed to Jerusalem. See Büchler, *Kohanim*, p. 148.
267 Cf. the views of Jeremias, *Jerusalem*, pp. 299f.
268 Above, pp. 39f.
269 S. Klein, "*Ẓippori,*" p. 52. For Herod's fortification of Sepphoris see above, p. 2.
270 See the mishnaic passage reproduced on p. 15.
271 *War* III, 338. Cf. S. Klein, "*Neue Beiträge zur Geschichte und Geographie Galiläas,*" *Jeschurun* 10 (1923), 131f.
272 Klein, "*Ẓippori,*" p. 54. Cf. Cohen, *Josephus*, p. 244, n. 4.
273 *Life* 38. Translation is the writer's.

the royal bank and archives *of Tiberias* were reestablished at Sepphoris.[274] On the contrary, he asserts that these institutions were terminated, *katalythenai* (καταλῦθηναι).[275] The text merely states that Tiberias lost its administrative rights. Sepphoris, on the other hand, must have maintained its own indigenous bureaucratic machinery as early as the days of Gabinius (57-55 B.C.E.) when the city was recognized as the administrative center of Galilee.[276] Once Tiberias lost the primacy which it had gained under Herod Antipas,[277] the administrative offices of Sepphoris, which had been functioning all along, were given jurisdiction over the entire Galilee. The archives of Sepphoris, furthermore, had a reputation as an "old" establishment which maintained documents containing signatures of reliable witnesses. This reputation could not have developed, as suggested by Klein, between the time of Nero and the Bar Kokhba revolt (ca. 132), a period when the establishment of Jewish administrative offices must have been severely limited.

---

[274] Cf., however, the translation of H. St. J. Thackeray in the Loeb Classical Library: "Sepphoris, by submission to Rome, had forthwith become the capital of Galilee and the seat of the royal bank and the archives."

[275] This word connotes "breaking up" or coming to an end, especially of political systems. See Liddel and Scott, *Lexicon*, p. 899.

[276] See above, p. 2. Cf. Smallwood, *The Jews Under Roman Rule*, pp. 31f. and Schürer, *History* (ed. Vermes-Millar), p. 268. Cities were known to have placed clerks and other magistrates in charge of all types of written records which were kept in archives. Treasurers were responsible for the city's financial books. In Egypt, village scribes (*komogrammateis*) were appointed and royal banks were established in the administrative capitals. A similar arrangement existed in Herodian Palestine. See Jones, *The Greek City*, pp. 79; 239 and G. M. Harper Jr., "Village Administration in the Roman Province of Syria," *Yale Classical Studies* 1 (1928), 121f. Apparently, even villages kept archives or, at the very least, records as indicated by the title "*komogrammateis*." The role of the city treasurers (*tamai*) is described by Jones, p. 241. On the operation of local banks, see M. Rostovtzeff, *History* I, 180.

[277] See *Life*, 37.

CHAPTER FOUR

CONCLUSION

The term "*ha-yeshanah*" was applied to both, the *ʿarchei* and the *castra* of Sepphoris, to indicate that they were once Jewish institutions. The rabbis of the second century knew that the archives and fortifications of their own day could only be Roman establishments. For this reason, they employed the expression *ha-yeshanah* to refer to an earlier era when Jewish jurisdiction over these (or similar) institutions was a reality. Both phrases, *ʿarchei ha-yeshanah shel-Ẓippori* and *castra ha-yeshanah shel-Ẓippori*, appear in contexts which suggest that the period preceding the First Revolt was intended. The *ʿarchei ha-yeshanah shel-Ẓippori* is included among other pre-70 institutions, most, if not all, belonging to Jerusalem.[278] Similarly, *castra ha-yeshanah shel-Ẓippori* is enumerated along with Jerusalem as a walled city in a list composed with pre-70 cities in mind.[279]

The history of the archives of Sepphoris is somewhat difficult to piece together. This institution must have gone back several generations for it to have gained a reputation in the second century as a repository for Jewish marriage documents of unimpeachable validity. It is difficult to determine whether the archives continued to function after the First Revolt. Rabbi Yose's reference to the *ʿarchei ha-yeshanah*, however, clearly indicates that Jewish archives were long extinct. Whatever archives were functioning in second-century Sepphoris were gentile establishments.[280] The contemporary tannaitic discussion concerning the validity of documents deposited in the archives of the gentiles corroborates this point.[281]

The history of the *castra* is somewhat less fragmentary than that of the *ʿarchei*. Because the acropolis of Sepphoris was a natural site for a fortification,[282] the city was known for its stronghold capabilities. A city which was reputed to have repulsed an attack by Ptolemy Lathyrus in the days of Alexander Yannai,[283] must have possessed formidable fortifications. Herod, who captured Sepphoris after the garrisons (τῶν φυλάκων) of the Maccabean Antigonus had been withdrawn,[284] seems to have further fortified Sepphoris. When Judas, the son of Ezekias, and his band revolted after the death of Herod (4 B.C.E.), they specifically attacked the royal palace (τῷ Βασιλείῳ) at Sepphoris in order to pro-

---

[278] Above, p. 50.

[279] Above, pp. 18, 24f.

[280] To which Jews, on occasion, resorted.

[281] See above, pp. 49f. and n. 238.

[282] Above, p. 29.

[283] *Ant.* XIII, 338.

[284] *War* I, 304.

cure munitions. Varus, the governor of Syria, subdued the insurrectionists and burned the city.[285] It remained for Herod Antipas to rebuild Sepphoris and restore its fortifications. Josephus relates that Sepphoris now became the "ornament" of all Galilee (πρόσχημα τοῦ Γαλιλαίου παντὸς), a description which is used by other Greek writers to describe once impregnable cities.[286]

Up to this point Sepphoris had to have maintained a standing corps of Jewish troops. Schürer claims that Antipas' reconstructed city could not have been exclusively Jewish and must have already included a considerable pro-Roman element.[287] Accordingly, the reluctance of Sepphoris to get involved in the First Revolt was due to the well-established cosmopolitan atmosphere of the city. If this were so, one would expect the Romans to have counted on the support of Sepphoris and to have provided a garrison long before the city requested one at the outset of the revolt. When Sepphoris finally did declare for Rome in 67, it was provided with its first foreign garrison.[288] There is no mention of non-Jewish units before then. Josephus boasts that it was he who was responsible for the fortification of the city before it had abandoned the Galilean cause.[289] Thus the earliest possible date for the "new" *castra* is 67. If Josephus' report is accurate,

---

[285] *War* II, 56; *Ant.* XVII, 271.

[286] *Ant.* XVIII, 27. Strabo (*Geography* 10, 2,3) speaks of the cities of the Aetolians, Calydon and Pleuron, as having been the "ornament" (πρόσχημα) of Greece before their subjugation. Plutarch (*Lives, Alexander* 17) reports that Alexander had even received the submission of Sardis, the "ornament" of the barbarian seacoast. According to Herodotus (Bk. V, 28), Miletus was once the "ornament" of Ionia. For other examples, see Liddel and Scott, *Lexicon*, p. 1531.

[287] Schürer admits (*Geschichte* II, 210f., n. 494) that Sepphoris continued to be a *primarily* Jewish city. The pro-Roman element, however, had changed the character of the city enough for the Mishnah to refer to the "ancient government (ἄρχη) of Sepphoris." (On Schürer's understanding of *ʿarchei*, see n. 223.) Thus, according to Schürer, Sepphoris received a new *ʿarchei* under Herod Antipas.

[288] Above, p. 41. There are other reasons for doubting Schürer's contention that Sepphoris was a cosmopolitan city. Cohen and Freyne note that Josephus speaks of the residents of Sepphoris as "kinsmen" (ὁμόφυλοι, *War* 3,32 and *Life* 376-377), a fact whose importance is minimized by Schürer (cf. previous note). See Cohen, *Josephus*, p. 244, n. 4 and Freyne, *Galilee*, p. 123. Freyne further claims (pp. 144 and 151, n. 89) that Greek influences in first-century Sepphoris appear to have been rather limited. Although the coins issued at Sepphoris in 68 C.E. have Greek inscriptions they lack human images, a fact which Freyne believes is indicative of the Jewish "ethos" which prevailed (with few exceptions) in Galilee at large. It must also be remembered that Sepphoris seems to have vascillated before turning to the Romans for aid. Besides the problematic evidence cited earlier (p. 2, n. 10), attention should be drawn to *Life* 31 where Josephus says he permitted the residents of Sepphoris to communicate with their fellow citizens who had been taken hostage by Cestius Gallus at the start of the war. Anti-Roman activity at Sepphoris, however limited, would appear to have been the likely reason for the taking of hostages. Even if this report is discounted (see *War* II, 511 where Josephus says that Sepphoris welcomed Gallus and cf. Cohen's discussion of the revolutionary tendencies of Sepphoris in *Galilee*, pp. 216 and 246ff.), it must be admitted that there still is no evidence for Roman troops at Sepphoris before 67 C.E. In Freyne's words (p. 76): "At that time [the period of the Revolt] Sepphoris was the capital of Roman Galilee (*Life* 37ff.) and everything we know about its situation then suggests that it did not have an official Roman presence, no matter how Romanophile its tendencies were."

[289] *Life* 395. Cf. above, p. 2, n. 10.

Sepphoris soon after admitted six thousand infantry which had been provided by Vespasian.[290]

With its long military history, it is no wonder that the *tannaim* anachronistically referred to the earlier, Jewish city of Sepphoris by the Latin term *castra*. The rabbis, evidently, were familiar with a Roman *castra* of their own day which was contrasted with the *castra ha-yeshanah shel-Ẓippori* to which the *halakhot* of houses in cities "encompassed by a wall since the days of Joshua bin Nun" applied. As with the gentile *ʿarchei*, it is difficult to ascertain whether the new *castra* continued to function after the First Revolt. It may have only been garrisoned periodically. It is unlikely however, that pro-Roman Sepphoris was deprived of all of its forces immediately after the war. A reduction of strength, however, would certainly have been in order. At the very least, the city would have required a municipal police force to maintain order and patrol the countryside.[291] A *hipparchos* and a small contingent of mounted constables would have been sufficient. In times of exceptional trouble, Sepphoris, with its natural defense capabilities and geographical importance, would have been the logical choice for a more elaborate military unit. With the VI Ferrata stationed at Kefar ʿOtnay, the force at Sepphoris could have easily been upgraded to keep a watchful eye on Galilee after the Bar Kokhba revolt.[292] Indeed, some promotion in status is implied by the new name, *Diocaesarea*, which Sepphoris received already before the outbreak of the revolt.[293] Hopefully, further excavations will someday reveal epigraphic

[290] The fact that Vespasian's name appears on coins issued in Sepphoris in 67-68 C.E. suggests that Josephus' report concerning the provisioning of Sepphoris is reliable. Cf. above, p. 3, n. 12. Seyrig contends that Vespasian had received the authority of a governor. See Seyrig, "Irenopolis-Neronias-Sepphoris," pp. 284ff. and his "Additional Note" in *Numismatic Chronicle* 15 (1955), 157ff.

[291] On the garrisoning of post-First Revolt Palestine, see Schürer, *History* I (ed. Vermes-Millar), p. 367 and Smallwood, *The Jews Under Roman Rule*, pp. 33f.

[292] It is possible that the Romans placed units in Galilee as a response to the Bar Kokhba revolt. Attempts have been made to portray the involvement of Galilee in the revolt, but conclusive evidence is so far lacking. The paucity of references to Galilean involvement suggests that the participation of that region, at most, was restricted. See the articles ed. by A. Oppenheimer in "*Ha-Yishuv Ha-Yehudi Ba-Galil Bi-Tequfat Yavneh U-Mered Bar-Kokhba*," *Cathedra* 4 (1977), pp. 53-83. Cf. Freyne, *Galilee*, p. 97, n. 65. It seems likely, however, that Galilee would have been included in the post-Revolt military precautions taken by the Romans. The latter would certainly have wanted to prevent any resurgence of anti-Roman activity in an area which had actively participated in the First Revolt. Curiously, traces of the legion VI Ferrata have been found at Har Ḥazon in Upper Galilee and at Tel Shalem in the Jordan Valley (south of Bet Shean). Both places are a considerable distance from Kefar ʿOtnay, the permanent base of the sixth legion. See, in the same issue of *Cathedra*, G. Foerster, "*Ha-Galil ʿErev Mered Bar-Kokhba: Ha-ʿEdut Ha-ʾArkiʾologit*," p. 80. It should also be noted that inscriptions on milestones found along the ancient Legio-Sepphoris road mention emperors of the second, third and fourth centuries. Apparently, the Romans maintained the road right on up to the last days of Constantine (d. 337) who is mentioned along with the sons who shared in his rule toward the end of his reign. Perhaps the continued preoccupation with the roadway is some indication of the strategic importance of the area. See Hecker, "*Kevish Romaʾi*," pp. 175ff. *Avi-Yonah* assumes that the *castra* was still in existence during the revolt against Gallus ca. 351 C.E. See *The Jews of Palestine*, p. 178.

[293] See above, p. 3, n. 13. Meshorer suggests that Sepphoris, as a Jewish city, was regarded by the Romans as "representative of the Jewish people" and therefore was punished for the revolt at

evidence which will enlighten us as to the size and type of unit stationed at the *castra shel-Ẓippori* during its various Roman phases.

the end of Trajan's reign (117-118 C.E.). The "punishment" was completed with the loss of the right to mint coins and the renaming of the city. While Meshorer's suggestion cannot be proven, it does seem probable that the new name represented a change of attitude on the part of the Romans towards Sepphoris. Meshorer draws on numismatic evidence to show that, for the most part, Sepphoris enjoyed unusually good relations with Rome. The only exception seems to have been the Hadrianic period. The inscriptions from the period of Caracalla (ca. 206-217) are particularly interesting. These speak of an alliance between the "holy council" of the city and the senate of Rome. See Y. Meshorer, "Sepphoris and Rome," pp. 159-171 and *idem*, "*Matbeᶜot Ẓippori*," pp. 185-200. If Meshorer's assessment of the numismatic evidence is correct, the suggestion put forward here that only a small force was maintained in the *castra* during peaceful times would seem even more cogent. Rome would certainly have taken advantage of its peaceful alliance with Sepphoris by maintaining a limited amount of forces in the city. During more troubled times the unit could have been bolstered. The one difficulty with Meshorer's proposal is the turn of events during the fourth century. Why would Sepphoris, a city supposedly allied with Rome, become the center of the revolt (however limited) under Gallus? Perhaps the periods of Hadrian and Gallus were times in which some troublesome factions in Sepphoris got the upper hand. More study of these periods is obviously warranted in view of Meshorer's findings.

PART TWO

THE PRIESTS

FOREWORD

According to the so called "*Baraita* of Twenty-Four *Mishmarot*," which lists the priestly courses (*mishmarot*) and their places of residence, the *mishmar* of *Yedaᶜyah* was located at Sepphoris.[1] The fact that all of the places mentioned in the list were in Galilee, led S. Klein to conclude that the "*Baraita*" reflects the historical situation following the Bar-Kokhba revolt (ca. 135 C.E.), when the Jewish population relocated in that area of the country.[2] Several scholars have noted, however, that priests are reported to have been living in Sepphoris even during the days of the Second Temple.[3] In fact, of all the towns and cities included in the "*Baraita*," only Sepphoris is reported to have had priestly residents who actually served at the Temple. The rabbinic sources also mention specific incidents which apparently occurred in the priestly community of Sepphoris during the amoraic period.[4] Indeed, it would seem as though there was a settlement of priests at Sepphoris throughout most of the tannaitic and amoraic periods. An investigation of the rabbinic traditions must, however, precede the drawing of historical conclusions. The present study evaluates these traditions in order to elucidate the history of the priests of Sepphoris.

---

[1] According to T. *Taᶜanit* 2:1, the priests were divided into twenty-four *mishmarot*. These "courses" were designated by the names of the heads of the priestly families enumerated in I Chronicles 24:7-18. The division into courses enabled all the priests to participate in the Temple service as each *mishmar* would take its weekly turn officiating. For details concerning this arrangement, see J. Liver, *Peraqim Be-Toledot Ha-Kehunah Ve-Ha-Leviyyah* (1969), pp. 33-52 and the more general article of D. Sperber, "*Mishmarot and Maᶜamadot*" in *Encyclopaedia Judaica*, 12 (1971) cols. 89-93.

The "*Baraita*," which has been reconstructed by S. Klein from a talmudic report (P. *Taᶜanit* 4, 68d; see below, p. 123) and medieval *piyyutim*, contains a list of the *mishmarot* and their places of residence. See the various works of S. Klein on the subject: *Beiträge*, pp. 94f; "*Baraitaᵓ Shel-ᵓArbaᶜah Ve-ᶜEsrim Mishmarot*," *Maᵓamarim Shonim La-Ḥaqirat ᵓEreẓ Yisrael* (1924), pp. 3-29; *Sefer Ha-Yishuv* I, 162ff. and *ᵓEreẓ Ha-Galil*, pp. 63ff. Archeological discoveries later substantiated the existence of such a list. See M. Avi-Yonah, "The Caesarea Inscription of the Twenty-Four Priestly Courses," in *The Teacher's Yoke*: *Studies in Memory of Henry Trantham*, eds. E. J. Vardaman and J. L. Garrett (1964), pp. 46-57 and T. Kahana, "*Ha-Kohanim Le-Mishmeroteihem U-Le-Meqomot Hityashvutam, Tarbiz*, 48 (1978-79), 19f. Also below, pp. 125, 131 and n. 360.

[2] *Beiträge*, pp. 94f. and "*Baraitaᵓ*," p. 26. In Temple times, priests would naturally have preferred to live in Judea from where they could easily proceed to Jerusalem when needed. The sources indicate that this was in fact the general rule. See B. Z. Lurie, "*ᶜArei Ha-Kohanim Bi-Yemei Bayit Sheni*," *HUCA* 44 (1973), Hebrew section, 1-19.

[3] See Lurie, *ibid.*, p. 17, A. Büchler, *Kohanim*, pp. 146ff., and Klein, "*Ẓippori*," p. 55; "*Baraitaᵓ*," p. 6 and *ᵓEreẓ Ha-Galil*, pp. 72, 89.

[4] See below, pp. 116ff.

CHAPTER ONE

THE PRIESTS OF SEPPHORIS IN THE TIME OF THE SECOND TEMPLE

Joseph ben Elim in Rabbinic Sources

Tosefta *Yoma*ᵓ 1:4 reports the following:[5]

למה מפרישין כהן אחר תחתיו שמא יארע בו פסול ישמש תחתיו ר׳ חנניה סגן הכהנים[6] אומ׳ לכך היה סגן ממונה כהן שנמצא בו פסול ישמש תחתיו וכהן גדול חוזר לכהונה[7] וזה ששימש תחתיו כל מצות כהונה גדולה עליו דברי ר׳ מאיר ר׳ יוסה או׳ אע״פ שאמרו כל מצות כהונה[8] עליו אינו כשר לא לכהן גדול ולא לכהן הדיוט אמ׳ ר׳ יוסה מעשה היה ביוסף בן אילים[9] מציפורי[10] ששימש תחת כהן גדול שעה אחת ולא היה כשר לא לכהן גדול ולא לכהן הדיוט כיצא[11] אמר למלך פר ושעיר שקרבו היום משל מי היו משלי או משל כהן גדול ידע המלך על מה אמ׳ לו אמ׳ לו מה זה בן אילים[12] לא דייך ששימשת תחת כהן גדול שעה אחת לפני מי שאמר והיה העולם אלא שאתה מבקש ליטול לך כהונה גדולה באותה שעה ידע בן אילים[13] שהוסע מן הכהונה[14]

Why is another priest (*kohen* ᵓ*aḥer*) set aside in his (the regular High Priest's) stead? (Answer:) Should he (the regular High Priest) be disqualified, he will serve instead. Rabbi Ḥananiah, the *segan* of the priests (*kohanim*) says, "For this reason a *segan* was appointed; he was to serve instead of a (High) Priest who had been disqualified." (And afterwards) the (regular) High Priest returns to his position, and all the obligations of the high priesthood are incumbent upon the one who served in his stead, so, Rabbi Meir maintains. Rabbi Yose says, "Even though they said[15] that all of the obligations of the (high) priesthood (*kehunah*) are incumbent upon him, he is not fit to be a High Priest or an ordinary priest (*kohen hedyot*)." Rabbi Yose says: "It happened that (*ma*ᶜ*aseh hayah*) Joseph ben Elim[16] of Sepphoris served instead of the High Priest

---

[5] Ms. Vienna (ed. Lieberman).

[6] Ms. Erfurt has חנניא בן גמליאל (Ḥanania ben Gamaliel), but the statement reappears elsewhere in the name of Ḥananiah *Segan Ha-Kohanim*. See below, p. 83. The *editio princeps* and Ms. London omit the statement altogether.

[7] Mss. London and Erfurt and the *editio princeps* all read לכהונה גדולה.

[8] Ms. London and the *editio princeps* have כהונה גדולה.

[9] Ms. London has אילם, Ms. Erfurt: אולם and the *editio princeps*: אלים.

[10] Ms. London and *editio princeps* read: מצפורי. Ms. Erfurt has בציפורי. The latter reading, of course, is impossible since the incident clearly took place at the Temple. See, however, p. 31, n. 106, on the interchange of ב and מ.

[11] Mss. London and Erfurt and the *editio princeps* have כשיצא.

[12] Mss. London and Erfurt again have אולם and אילם respectively. Cf. n. 9.

[13] *Editio princeps* reads אילי׳ Mss. London and Erfurt are consistent with their earlier readings. Cf. nn. 9 and 12.

[14] Ms. London has כהונה גדולה. *Editio princeps* reads: הכהונה גדולה.

[15] The term אמרו ("they said") is used here to refer to the view of earlier *tannaim*. See Epstein, *Mavo*ᵓ II, 726ff., where he presents instances where אמרו and אע״פ שאמרו refer to either the First Mishnah (*mishnah ri*ᵓ*shonah*) or to matters already taught in the Mishnah.

[16] The spelling Elim will be used throughout this study for the sake of consistency. For a summary of the variant forms of this name, see Rabbinovicz, *Diqduqei Soferim* on B. *Yoma*ᵓ 12b.

for one hour, and (afterwards) he was not fit to be a High Priest or an ordinary priest (*kohen hedyot*). Upon vacating (the position) he said to the king, 'To whom did the bullock and the goat which were sacrificed today belong, to me or to the (regular) High Priest?' The king understood his question and replied, 'What is this ben Elim? Is it not enough for you to have served instead of the High Priest for one hour before the One Who spoke and created the world? Rather you seek to obtain the high priesthood for yourself!' At that moment ben Elim understood that he had been deposed from the priesthood (*kehunah*)."

This passage elaborates upon the report of the Mishnah (*Yoma*ʾ 1:1) that a replacement for the officiating High Priest was designated before the Day of Atonement (*Yom Kippur*).[17] The reason provided in the Tosefta for this procedure is identical with that given in the Mishnah, i.e. lest some mishap render the High Priest unfit to bring the required sacrifice and to carry out the rest of his Day of Atonement duties. The Tosefta notes the view of Rabbi Ḥananiah, "the *segan* of the priests,"[18] that the substitute priest held an official position with the title *segan*. The post-Day of Atonement status of both, a disqualified High Priest and the substitute who replaced him, is then discussed. According to Rabbi Meir (ca. mid-second century), the disqualified priest returns to his position and the substitute, although no longer the High Priest, is obliged to observe the commandments pertaining to the holder of that office.[19] Rabbi Yose (a contemporary of Meir), however, denies the substitute priest any official capacity either as a High Priest or as an ordinary priest (*kohen hedyot*).[20]

The reason for the inclusion of the *maʿaseh* reported by Yose is not immediately apparent. Joseph ben Elim's question and the king's reply indicate that the

---

[17] ומתקינין לו כהן אחר תחתיו שמא יארע בו פסול The Mishnah uses the word *matqinin* (מתקינין) indicating that the priest was merely "designated" as a substitute. In contrast, the Tosefta has *mafrishin* (מפרישין) which would suggest that the substitute was also "set aside" in a special chamber, as was the regular High Priest, before the Day of Atonement. Cf. the discussion developed in P. *Yoma*ʾ 1, 38c-d (below, 67f.) which seems to be based on the understanding of the Tosefta. See the comments of Lieberman, *Tosefta*ʾ *Ki-Feshutah* IV, 720f. On the chamber, see n. 36.

[18] Ḥananiah (or Ḥanina) probably lived during the last years of the Temple and is known to have been at Yavneh later on. An analysis of the traditions attributed to him appears in Neusner, *Rabbinic Traditions* I, 400ff.

[19] According to M. *Horayot* 3:4, an incumbent High Priest and one who has "passed" from that office (*kohen she-ʿavar*) differ only in that the latter is no longer responsible for the bullock of the Day of Atonement or the daily meal offering (*ʿasirit ha-ʾeifah*). His participation in the Day of Atonement service is otherwise valid, and he is still obligated to observe the following laws pertaining to the high priesthood: (1) He must marry a virgin. (2) He is forbidden to marry a widow or a divorced woman. (3) He may not become unclean for his relatives by participating in their funerals. And (4) he may not bare his head or rend his clothes as signs of mourning. See Jeremias, *Jerusalem*, pp. 152ff. Like the death of the incumbent High Priest, that of the *kohen she-ʿavar* also allows a manslayer to return from the city of refuge.

[20] The two *tannaim* may not be in disagreement. The statement attributed to Yose may only be an elaboration of the view of Meir. Accordingly, Yose would concede that the deposed substitute High Priest remained *responsible* for the observance of the high priestly commandments, but he could no longer *officiate* as either a High Priest or an ordinary priest. Interestingly, the Palestinian Talmud (below, pp. 67f.) presents Yose's view anonymously and does not indicate any disagreement with it. Cf. Lieberman, *Tosefta*ʾ *Ki-Feshutah* IV, 723.

Sepphorean priest would have liked to continue as High Priest. Had the king decided that the sacrifices were ben Elim's monetary responsibility,[21] the latter would have known that the king's intention was to keep him in office following the Day of Atonement.[22] Ben Elim was hoping that the king would hold him responsible for the provision of the sacrificial animals.[23] He knew very well that the animals of the disqualified High Priest could still be used on the altar. Unfortunately, things did not work out as he would have liked. Indeed, ben Elim understood from the response of the king that he had been removed from the "*kehunah*" (priesthood). The terminology suggests that ben Elim was deposed from *all* priestly functions. This interpretation would then support the view of Yose. The term *kehunah*, however, was already used earlier by Yose himself to refer to the high priesthood.[24] Furthermore, the king's reply, "You seek to obtain the high priesthood for yourself," indicates that *kehunah* referred specifically to that office.[25] The *maᶜaseh* merely establishes that the original High Priest resumes his position to the disadvantage of the deposed substitute. It does not, however, specify whether the latter is fit to serve as either a High Priest or *kohen hedyot*.

Thus the *maᶜaseh* cannot have been used by Yose to substantiate his view. In fact, the ben Elim account does not appear to be relevant to his difference of opinion with Meir. It must be concluded that the *maᶜaseh* merely provides an example of an occasion when the High Priest could not fulfill his duties on the Day of Atonement.[26] As such, it establishes the need for the designation of a substitute priest. In the mid-second century, the status of a deposed High Priest was of academic interest to Meir and Yose. In the present context, however, the ben Elim story does not appear to have had any bearing upon their deliberations.

---

[21] The High Priest had to pay for the daily meal offering and the bullock offered on the Day of Atonement. See the sources referred to by Jeremias, *Jerusalem*, pp. 151f. The offerings were evidently purchased on credit. Lieberman notes that it was the custom not to pay until the offerings had been "accepted." See M. *Sheqalim* 4:9 and cf. Lieberman, *Toseftaᵓ Ki-Feshutah* IV, 726, n. 29. On the offerings brought by ben Elim, see below, n. 34.

[22] When the regular High Priest's impurity would have passed allowing him to resume the duties of his office. It should be noted that rabbinic sources attest to four different ways of designating a High Priest: (1) Inheritance. (2) Choice of the king. (3) Choice of the people. (4) Choice of the priests by means of a lottery. See Allon, *Meḥqarim* I, 74f., for a discussion of all of these methods.

[23] See n. 21. The interpretation presented here is one of two suggested by Lieberman for the *maᶜaseh*. See Lieberman, *Toseftaᵓ Ki-Feshutah* IV, 725ff.

[24] See his statement, "Even though they said ...," which follows R. Meir's clear reference to the high priesthood (כהונה גדולה). Cf. the variant in n. 8.

[25] On the use of the term *kehunah* to refer to the high priesthood, see Lieberman, *Toseftaᵓ Ki-Feshutah*, p. 726 and Allon, *Meḥqarim* I, 61. It should be noted that Ms. London and *editio princeps* have the word "gedolah" after (ha-) *kehunah* (see n. 14), but this may have been added by a copyist who sensed the difficulty with the text.

[26] The *maᶜaseh* does not specifically state that the incident occurred on the Day of Atonement. However, the prominence of the High Priest, the fact that a substitute was required, and the reference to the High Priest's bullock (פר) all confirm that this was a Day of Atonement incident. Furthermore, the version of the Palestinian Talmud (below, pp. 67f.) explicitly says so.

The *ma^caseh* itself tells us very little about Joseph ben Elim. The tradition preserved in the name of Yose, a resident of Sepphoris, indicates that ben Elim was also from that city. No reason is provided for the selection of a Sepphorean to substitute for the High Priest. The fact that ben Elim actually received this honor and even entertained the thought of usurping the position of the temporarily disqualified incumbent would seem to indicate that he was a high ranking priest in Jerusalem. Indeed, it has been suggested that Joseph held the office of *segan*, or deputy-High Priest, referred to earlier by Rabbi Ḥananiah.[27] This matter will be considered at length below.[28] For now it will suffice to note that the passage itself gives no indication that such was the case.[29] None of the particulars concerning ben Elim are disclosed other than that he was from Sepphoris and that he served on the Day of Atonement in place of the regular High Priest. The discourse between ben Elim and the unnamed king is clearly of a legendary character. Indeed, the two participants are not presented as historical figures. No indication is given as to when the *ma^caseh* was supposed to have happened. The conversation suggests that ben Elim was an ambitious priest who sought the position of High Priest. It is difficult to discern whether ben Elim felt he had a

---

[27] See, for instance, L. Greenwald, *Toledot Ha-Kohanim Ha-Gedolim* (1932), p. 122 and Jeremias, *Jerusalem*, pp. 162f.

[28] pp. 80ff.

[29] If anything, the context of the Tosefta passage suggests that ben Elim was an ordinary priest. Further on in the Tosefta (T. *Yoma*ᵓ 1:6) the rise of Phineas of Ḥabtah to the high priesthood is reported. One who held that office had to excel in beauty, strength, wealth, wisdom and appearance. Phineas, however, lacked the requirement of wealth when he was chosen by lot to be High Priest. Josephus, who also reports the selection of Phineas as High Priest (*War* IV, 156), states that he was "a man who not only was not descended from high priests, but was such a clown that he scarcely knew what the high priesthood meant" (trans. of Thackeray in the Loeb Classical Library). The Ms. Erfurt version of the Tosefta narrative continues:

משרבו המלכים התקינו שיהו מעמידים כהנים הדיוטות ומעבירין אותן בכל שנה ושנה

> When the kings multiplied, they established that ordinary priests (*kohanim hedyotot*) should be appointed (as High Priests) and that they should be replaced every year.

This statement would seem to be relevant to both Phineas and Joseph ben Elim. The reports concerning Phineas clearly indicate that he was a *kohen hedyot*, i.e. an ordinary priest who was not of high priestly lineage. The same may be said of ben Elim who, like Phineas, also served as High Priest by chance (if only temporarily) and was not considered worthy to continue in the position. The statement that the kings appointed ordinary priests every year to serve as High Priests would seem to be particularly relevant to the ben Elim story. After all, ben Elim was relying on the whim of a king for his promotion. To be sure, the editor of the Tosefta could have been responsible for this suggestive context. The Phineas narrative appears elsewhere (*Sifra*ᵓ ᵓ*Emor* 2:1, *Tanhuma*ᵓ ᵓ*Emor* 6 and the additions to *Leviticus Rab.*, 26, ed. Margulies, pp. 611f.) without the appended statement concerning the kings' appointment of ordinary priests. Josephus, on the other hand, may have wanted to portray the rebels who selected Phineas in the worst light possible. It should be remembered that Josephus was very proud of his own high priestly lineage (*Life* 2). The ben Elim account also appears in different contexts (presented below), and a parallel in Josephus indicates that ben Elim was related to the High Priest for whom he substituted. It would seem then that he was a member of a high priestly family. Finally, Tosefta *Yoma*ᵓ contains several stories which cast the High Priest in a poor light (e.g., 1:12 and 1:22). Thus the context suggesting that both Phineas of Ḥabtah and Joseph ben Elim were *kohanim hedyotot* may have been purely coincidental.

legitimate claim to the high priesthood or whether he was simply hoping to take advantage of the High Priest's disqualification. The words attributed to the king seem hyperbolic for a Jewish ruler. The kings of the Jews during the Second Temple period were seldom known for their piety.[30] At best, the pious response of the king to ben Elim's opportunism is an embellishment of an event whose details had become obscure with the passage of time.

The Joseph ben Elim story also appears in the Palestinian Talmud:[31]

> מתקינין לו כהן אחר תחתיו שמא יארע בו פסול מה מייחדין ליה עימיה אמ׳ ר׳ חגיי משם דאין[32] מייחדין ליה עימיה דו קטל ליה אותו אחד מושחין ואין מושחין שנים אמ׳ ר׳ יוחנן מפני איבה עבר זה ושימש זה הראשון כל קדושת כהונה עליו השיני אינו כשר לא לכהן גדול ולא לכהן הדיוט אמ׳ ר׳ יוחנן עבר ועבד עבודתו כשירה[33] עבודתו משלמי נשמעינה מן הדא מעשה כבן אילם מציפורין שאירע קרי לכהן גדול ביום הכיפורים ונכנס בן אילם ושימש תחתיו בכהונה גדולה וכשיצא אמ׳ למלך אדוני המלך פר ושעיר[34] שליום הכיפורים משלי הן קריבין או משלכהן גדול וידע המלך מה הוא שואלו אמ׳ לו בן אילם אילו לא דייך אלא ששימשתה שעה אחת לפני מי שאמר והיה העולם וידע בן אילם שהוסע מכהונה גדולה מעשה בשמעון בן קמחית שיצא לדבר עם המלך ערב[35] ונתזה צינורה שלרוק מפיו על בגדיו וטימתו ונכנס יהודה אחיו ושימש תחתיו בכהונה גדולה
>
> Another priest is prepared in his stead lest he (the regular High Priest) be disqualified. Is he (the substitute priest) set aside with him?[36] Rabbi Ḥaggai said, "By Moses![37] He is not set aside with him lest he kill him. '*ᵓOto*' (Leviticus 6:13)—One

---

[30] With the exception of Agrippa I, no Jewish king is portrayed in rabbinic literature as having earned the respect of the people in religious matters. The ben Elim episode will be shown to have belonged to an earlier period than that of Agrippa I (41-44 C.E.). On Agrippa I in rabbinic sources, see J. Klausner, *Historiyah Shel-Ha-Bayit Ha-Sheni* IV (1952), pp. 291f.

[31] P. *Yomaᵓ* 1, 38c-d. Ms. Leiden is presented here. The story also appears in parallel *sugyot* in P. *Horayot* 3, 47d and P. *Megillah* 1, 72a. However, the opening words of the *sugya* ("Another priest is prepared in his stead ...") indicate that it was originally a discussion of M. *Yomaᵓ* 1:1. Still, it is curious that the Babylonian Talmud also introduced the *maᶜaseh* into the *gemara* to *Horayot* and *Megillah*. See below, nn. 53 and 69. On the problem of parallel *sugyot* in the Palestinian Talmud, see above, p. 35, n. 130.

[32] The parallel *sugya* in Ms. Leiden P. *Horayot* 3, 47d reads: משה דינון. The last letter of the first word is difficult to discern in the other parallel in P. *Megillah* 1, 72a (Ms. Leiden).

[33] P. *Horayot* 3, 47d has פסולה but this has to be a mistake since the Mss. of the parallels have כשירה. Cf. also the remark of Rabbah bar bar Ḥannah in the name of Yoḥanan which appears in the Babylonian text presented below, p. 71.

[34] P. *Horayot, ibid.* has פר ואיל (a bullock and a ram). This reading makes better sense since the goat (שעיר) was brought by the High Priest *in behalf of* the people to whom it really belonged. A ram, however, could have been brought by the High Priest on his own volition. See Lieberman, *Toseftaᵓ Ki-Feshutah* IV, 724f. On the role of the High Priest in the Day of Atonement ritual see n. 79.

[35] Ms. Leiden to the parallels in *Yomaᵓ* and *Megillah* have יום הכפורים in the margin. Ms. Leiden to the *Horayot* parallel has שיצא לטייל עם המלך ערב יום הכיפורים עם חשיכה. This reading, however, appears to be a mistake. See below, n. 41.

[36] According to M. *Yomaᵓ* 1:1, the High Priest was "set aside" (*mafrishin*) in the Palhedrin Chamber (*lishkat palhedrin*) seven days before the Day of Atonement. On the identification of this chamber see Allon's article "*Parᵓirtin*," in his *Meḥqarim* I, 48-55.

[37] This translation follows the reading משה דינון (Cf. n. 32) and the understanding of *Penei Moshe* on P. *Horayot* 3, 47d and P. *Megillah* 1, 72a. Cf. B. Ratner, *ᵓAhavat Ẓiyyon Vi-Yerushalayim, Yomaᵓ*, p. 7.

priest is annointed and not two."[38] Rabbi Yoḥanan said, "Because of enmity (only one is set aside)."[39] If this one (the regular High Priest) is removed (from office) and the other serves (in his place), the sanctity of the (high) priesthood remains on the first; the second is not fit to be either a High Priest or an ordinary priest (*kohen hedyot*). Rabbi Yoḥanan said, "If he (the substitute, having already served as High Priest) is removed (from his position) and officiates (as a High Priest), his service is valid." To whom does his service belong (*ʿavodato mi-shel-mi*?) Let us derive it from this: It happened in the case of (*maʿaseh be*) ben Elim from Sepphoris that the High Priest suffered a seminal pollution[40] on the Day of Atonement, and ben Elim entered and served in his stead in the high priesthood. And when he vacated (the office) he said to the king, "My master the king, did the bullock and the goat which were sacrificed on Yom Kippur belong to me or to the High Priest?" (And) The king understood what he was asking. He replied, "Ben Elim, is it not enough for you to have served for an hour before the One Who spoke and created the world?" And ben Elim knew that he had been removed from the high priesthood (*kehunah gedolah*).

It happened that (*maʿaseh be*) Simeon ben Kimḥit went out to speak with an Arab[41] king, and a stream of spittle from his (the king's) mouth fell upon his clothes. And it rendered him unclean. Consequently, his brother Judah entered and served in the high priesthood in his stead.

This *gemara* analyzes the statement of the Mishnah (*Yomaʾ* 1:1): "Another priest is prepared in his stead lest he be disqualified."[42] The views of two third century *amoraim*, Rabbi Ḥaggai and Rabbi Yoḥanan, establish that the substitute was not set aside with the regular High Priest. The statement, "If this one is removed (from office) and the other serves (in his place), the sanctity of the (high) priesthood remains on the first; the second is not fit to be either a High Priest or an ordinary priest," appears anonymously despite the fact that the identical view is attributed to Rabbi Yose in the Tosefta. There is no further discussion here of this opinion. Rabbi Yoḥanan, however, takes the view for granted and explains that if indeed the *kohen she-ʿavar* (a former High Priest, in

[38] Lev. 6:13 reads: "This is the offering that Aaron and his sons shall offer to the Lord on the occasion of his anointment (*be-yom himashaḥ ʾoto*)." The singular "*ʾoto*" is understood by R. Ḥaggai to refer to the High Priest only.

[39] It might appear that R. Yoḥanan disagrees altogether with the idea of preparing a substitute in advance. However, Yoḥanan only objects to the actual setting aside of the substitute with the regular High Priest. He does not seem to object to the designation of a substitute. The reference to Leviticus 6:13 is misleading since it suggests that the actual designating of another High Priest through anointing was the issue and not simply his physical separation. Perhaps the biblical reference is an interpolation. Or else, R. Ḥaggai could have meant that only one person is set aside *and* anointed.

It should also be noted that Yoḥanan's statement could be understood in connection with the sentence following it. That is, a substitute who actually served temporarily as High Priest could no longer serve as either a High Priest or an ordinary priest *because of enmity*. Cf. the Babylonian version presented below (p. 71) where the two statements are in fact related. For the interpretation presented here, see *Penei Moshe* on P. *Megillah*, 1, 72a.

[40] On the impurity resulting from a seminal pollution, see *Deut*. 23:11-12 and B. *Pesaḥim* 78a. The impurity rendered the sufferer unclean until evening at which time he had to bathe himself.

[41] Most of the parallels to the Simeon ben Kimḥit narrative have ערבי (Arab) or הערבי (the Arab) instead of ערב (eve). See Lieberman, *Toseftaʾ Ki-Feshutah* IV, 806.

[42] See n. 17.

this case the substitute whose role ended with the reinstatement of the regular High Priest) were to serve again as a High Priest,[43] his service is valid.[44] The ben Elim account, which also appears anonymously,[45] answers the question *ʿavodato mi-shel-mi*?—who is responsible for the provision of the sacrifice(s) when the regular High Priest has been disqualified?[46] The answer to the query put by ben-Elim to the king is supposed to indicate the *halakhah*. The king did not hold ben Elim responsible for the sacrificed animals because he had no intention of allowing him to remain in office following the Day of Atonement. Evidently, the regular High Priest had to provide the animals even if he had been disqualified.

The Tosefta did not reveal the type of disqualification which resulted in the appointment of Joseph ben Elim. According to the Palestinian Talmud's version of the *maʿaseh*, ben Elim substituted for the regular High Priest because the latter had been rendered unclean by a seminal pollution. At first the words, "the High Priest suffered a seminal pollution," would appear to be an interpolation introduced to explain the reason for the disqualification. However, the relationship of the *gemara* to the Mishnah suggests otherwise. The Mishnah stipulates that the High Priest was to be "set aside" from his home and assigned to the Chamber of Palhedrin for the entire week preceding the Day of Atonement.[47] Despite this precaution, it was recognized that the High Priest could still be disqualified from serving. Thus the Mishnah states that a substitute is prepared in his stead "lest he (the High Priest) be disqualified (*pasul*)." The type of disqualification intended is not specified. It is perhaps for this reason that the ben Elim story is included in the *gemara* associated with this *mishnah*. The seminal pollution provides an example of how the High Priest could be rendered unfit.[48]

[43] That is, if he were to officiate in the full, eight garment dress of the High Priest. See Rashi on B. *Yomaʾ* 12b and *Qorban Ha-ʿEdah* on P. *Megillah* 1, 72a.

[44] It is assumed here that the passage means he served as a High Priest, not as an ordinary priest. Halivni has noted, however, that the words עבר ועבד עבודתו כשרה could just as well have referred to an ordinary priest (*kohen hedyot*). See D. Halivni, *Meqorot U-Mesorot, Moʿed* (1975), pp. 18 and 16, n. 1. This seems unlikely at least in the contexts of P. *Megillah* 1, 72a and P. *Horayot* 3, 47d where the discussion follows a similar statement by R. Yoḥanan: עבר והביא עשירית האיפה שלו כשר which could only have referred to a High Priest since he alone was responsible for the meal offering.

[45] The attribution to Yose has again been omitted. It is curious that both statements of Yose in the Tosefta appear in the accounts of the Palestinian Talmud anonymously. The redactor may have considered Yose's views to be the majority ruling.

[46] Responsibility for the monetary value of the offerings is intended here. See n. 21 and cf. Lieberman, *Toseftaʾ Ki-Feshutah* IV, 725.

[47] According to Maimonides, the precaution was intended to keep the High Priest away from a wife who was in a state of impurity. A man who had sexual relations with a woman having a discharge was rendered unclean for seven days. See Leviticus 15:24. Maimonides compares the quarantining of the High Priest before the Day of Atonement to that of Aaron and his sons during ordination (Leviticus 8:33). See Maimonides' comments on M. *Yomaʾ* 1:1. On the Chamber of Palhedrin see n. 36.

[48] It will be shown below that the High Priest was disqualified by a nocturnal pollution. The *gemara* here, however, gives no indication that such was the case. The term *qeri* can refer to any seminal pollution. See "*Baʿal Qeri*" in *Encyclopedia Talmudit* 4 (1952), cols. 130-131.

In fact, the *gemara* follows up the ben Elim story with a similar episode regarding the High Priest Simeon ben Kimḥit who had been rendered unfit by the spittle of a king during a conversation on the Day of Atonement.[49] The ben Kimḥit story is produced without any introduction or explanation. It merely provides another example of a High Priest who was disqualified on the Day of Atonement. The ben Elim and ben Kimḥit stories support the presumption of the Mishnah that the High Priest could be disqualified even though he had been quarantined during the entire week preceding the Day of Atonement. Although the ben Elim story is used to clarify who is responsible for the provision of the sacrifice once the High Priest is disqualified, the underlying connection with the Mishnah cannot be denied. The ben Elim and ben Kimḥit legends may have been regarded as "historical" premises for the appointment of a substitute High Priest.[50] Thus the seminal pollution was not introduced into the story to explain away the disqualification of the High Priest any more than the spittle was provided for a similar purpose in the ben Kimḥit account. Both forms of uncleanness were intrinsic to the stories in which they appear.[51]

Thus there is no reason to assume that the seminal pollution was interpolated to explain the disqualification of the regular High Priest for whom Joseph ben Elim substituted. On the contrary, it clarifies the importance and relevance of the ben Elim incident to the discussion of the Mishnah. As will be indicated, the seminal pollution is also alluded to in a report of Josephus. Even without the

---

[49] The text under discussion does not explicitly state that the ben Kimḥit episode occurred on the Day of Atonement. Cf. nn. 35 and 41. The contexts of several of the parallels, however, indicate that the incident happened on the Day of Atonement. See, for example, T. *Yoma*ᵓ 3:20 (ed. Lieberman) and *Aboth de Rabbi Nathan*, ed. Schechter, Version "A," chap. 35. Cf. the comments of Lieberman, *Toseftaᵓ Ki-Feshutah* IV, 805f.

[50] See Rabinowitz, *Shaᶜarei Torat ᵓEreẓ Yisrael*, p. 243. According to Schwarz, the ben Elim incident led to the staying awake of the High Priest on the Day of Atonement (M. *Yoma*ᵓ 1:4, 7), but the idea of a designated substitute did not arise until the time of Simeon ben Kimḥit. Schwarz accepts the identification of ben Kimḥit with Simeon the son of Kamithos of *Ant*. XVIII, 35 who served as High Priest ca. 17-18 C.E. See A. Schwarz "*Der Segan*," *MGWJ* 64 (1920), 349. On Simeon the son of Kamithos see Schürer, *Geschichte* II, 271. For a discussion of the ben Kimḥit family, see Margaliot, *Shemot Ve-Kinnuyim*, pp. 46f.

[51] This still leaves the difficulty of the omission of the seminal pollution in the Tosefta version. In the latter, however, the discussion of the *mishnah* centers on the designation of a substitute and not on the explanation "lest he be disqualified." The Tosefta uses the ben Elim story as an example of an instance when a substitute was needed. The reason such an occasion arose is irrelevant to its discussion.

The report in M. *ᵓAvot* (5:5) that the High Priest never experienced a seminal pollution on the Day of Atonement during Temple times should now be considered. Perhaps as early as the tannaitic period this "miracle" was found to be difficult. Thus a parallel in *Aboth de Rabbi Nathan* (ed. Schechter, Version "A," chap. 35) concedes that exceptions did occur. (The exception given in Version "A," however, is the Simeon ben Kimḥit story, which seems irrelevant. Version "B" omits the exception altogether.) The *amoraim* also found the report of *ᵓAvot* to be difficult since the precautions prescribed by M. *Yoma*ᵓ 1:4, 6, 7 (see n. 84) in order to avoid a seminal pollution would thereby be rendered superfluous. Thus R. Yose bar R. Bun (fourth century Palestinian *amora*) ascribed the miracle to the First Temple. See P. *Yoma*ᵓ 1, 39a. Cf. Lieberman, *Toseftaᵓ Ki-Feshutah* IV, 723 and *idem, Hellenism*, pp. 176f. and n. 120.

verification of Josephus, this important detail would have to be considered an original part of the ben Elim story.[52]

The Babylonian Talmud presents the ben Elim story in the following *baraita*:[53]

ת״ר אירע בו פסול ומינו אחר[54] תחתיו ראשון חוזר לעבודתו שני כל מצות כהונה
גדולה עליו דברי ר׳ מאיר ר׳ יוסי אומר ראשון חוזר לעבודתו שני אינו ראוי לא לכ״ג
ולא לכהן הדיוט אמר ר׳ יוסי מעשה ביוסף בן אלם בציפורי[55] שאירע בו פסול בכהן
גדול ומינוהו תחתיו ואמרו חכמים ראשון חוזר לעבודתו שני אינו ראוי לא לכהן גדול
ולא לכהן הדיוט כ״ג משום איבה כהן הדיוט משום מעלין בקודש ולא מורידין אמר
רבה בר בר חנה א״ר יוחנן הלכה כר׳ יוסי ומודה ר׳ יוסי שאם עבר ועבד עבודתו
כשרה אמר רב יהודה אמר רב הלכה כר׳ יוסי ומודה ר׳ יוסי שאם מת ראשון שחוזר[56]
לעבודתו פשיטא מהו דתימא הויא ליה צרה מחיים קמ״ל

The rabbis taught (*teno*ᵓ *rabbanan*): If he (the High Priest) was disqualified and another (priest) was appointed in his stead, the first returns to his service and the second is responsible for the obligations of the high priesthood, so Rabbi Meir maintains. Rabbi Yose says, "The first returns to his service, the second is not suited to be either a high priest or an ordinary priest (*kohen hedyot*)." Rabbi Yose said, "It happened in the case of (*ma*ᶜ*aseh be*) Joseph ben Elim of Sepphoris[57] that a disqualification befell the High Priest and they appointed him (Joseph) in his stead. And the sages (*ḥakhamim*) said, 'The first returns to his service, the second is not suited to be either a High Priest or an ordinary priest.' " He is not suited to be a High Priest because of enmity. He is not (suited to be) an ordinary priest because (the degree of) holiness can be raised but not lowered. Rabbah bar bar Ḥannah said in the name of Rabbi Yoḥanan, "The *halakhah* is in accord with Rabbi Yose, and Rabbi Yose agrees that if he (the substitute having already served as High Priest) is removed (from his position) and officiates (as a High Priest), his service is valid." Rabbi Judah says in the name of Rav, "The *halakhah* is in accord with Rabbi Yose, and Rabbi Yose agrees that should the first (the High Priest) die, he (the substitute who has already served as High Priest) returns to his service." Is this not obvious? You might have thought that this would cause distress to him during his lifetime.[58] He (Rabbi Judah, in the name of Rav) informs us (otherwise).

---

[52] Interestingly, the *Yoma*ᵓ *sugya* concludes with a discussion of the statement of Rabbi Judah in the Mishnah that another wife is readied for the regular High Priest lest his present wife die. The *ḥakhamim* reject Judah's opinion since "there would be no end to the matter." In the *gemara*, R. Mana (fourth century) notes that this objection could also be raised vis-à-vis the earlier ruling of the Mishnah that another priest was readied in case the regular High Priest is disqualified. In this case there would also be "no end to the matter" as both the High Priest and his substitute could become unfit as a result of seminal pollutions. It is curious that a fourth century sage, Mana, specifically refers to a seminal pollution when other types of impurities would have also disqualified the High Priest.

[53] B. *Yoma*ᵓ 12b-13a, ed. Vilna. Parallels appear in B. *Megillah* 12b and B. *Horayot* 9b. On these see n. 69 below.

[54] Ms. Munich has ומינו כהן אחר.

[55] Ms. Munich has ביוסף בן אול׳ מצפרי which makes better sense since the incident could not have happened in Sepphoris. Cf., however, p. 31, n. 106, on the interchange of ב and מ.

[56] Ms. Munich has שני חוזר לעבודתו.

[57] Following the reading of Ms. Munich above, n. 55.

[58] The substitute would be anxious for the High Priest's demise so that he could replace him. This would arouse enmity between the two. See the commentary of Rashi on the passage.

Once again, the ben Elim account is introduced in the course of a discussion of Mishnah *Yomaʾ* 1:1.[59] Like the Tosefta, the *baraita* of the *gemara* presents the views of Meir and Yose concerning the post-Day of Atonement status of a disqualified High Priest and his substitute. Again, the *maʿaseh* is reported in the name of Yose, suggesting that it supports his view.[60] Here, however, the story has been abbreviated. The reader is simply informed that a High Priest was once disqualified and Joseph ben Elim of Sepphoris replaced him. No mention is made of a seminal pollution or of any conversation with a king. Instead, the ruling of the *ḥakhamim* has been appended giving the impression that the ben Elim episode resulted in their ruling that the regular High Priest returns to his post and his substitute no longer serves in the priesthood.[61] By omitting the details and appending the decision of the *ḥakhamim*, the *baraita* has made the story relevant to its discussion of the status of the substitute who has fulfilled the role of High Priest. Rabbi Yose appears to be invoking the *ḥakhamim* to support his view. Indeed, the wording of the latter's decision is identical to the original comment of Yose!

The reasoning of the *ḥakhamim* is elaborated upon: The substitute priest could no longer serve as High Priest because of the ill-feeling that might result between him and the regular holder of that office. He could no longer officiate as an ordinary priest because of the rule that the degree of holiness could only be raised. To return to the status of a *kohen hedyot* would have meant a demotion in sanctity. Like the view of the *ḥakhamim*, this explanation also does not appear in the Tosefta or the Palestinian Talmud. As D. Halivni has noted, it is apparent from the ensuing discussion that Rav (first half of third century) was not familiar with this explanation. Otherwise, he would not have stated[62] that should the High Priest die the substitute could assume the position of the former. This would have been obvious as enmity would no longer be a factor preventing him from serving.[63] It would seem then that the ben Elim account was reworked into a *baraita* in the Babylonian schools, long after the time of Yose. The *baraita* could not have been transmitted in its present form from Palestine otherwise Rav would certainly have been familiar with it.

There are other indications that this version cannot be considered original and is actually later than the other parallels discussed. In the Palestinian *gemara*, it

---

[59] The discussion commences (B. *Yomaʾ* 12a) with the initiation of the substitute priest, i.e. how he assumes the responsibility of officiating High Priest. One *amora* suggests that the donning of the High Priest's girdle (*ʾavnet*) signifies the installation of the new priest. A long digression deals with the composition of the girdle and the High Priest's garments (12b). The *gemara* returns to its elaboration of the Mishnah by presenting, in the form of a *baraita*, the views of Yose and Meir concerning a substitute who has served as High Priest and the ben Elim account.

[60] Cf. the Tosefta version above, pp. 63f.

[61] The version in B. *Megillah* 9b suggests that such a case did indeed come before the *ḥakhamim*. There the text reads ובא מעשה לפני חכמים ("a *maʿaseh* came before the *ḥakhamim*").

[62] The view of Rav is actually presented by R. Judah, his disciple.

[63] Halivni, *Moʿed*, pp. 16f.

was Yoḥanan who stated that the service of a deposed substitute who violated the *halakhah* and officiated again as a High Priest is valid.[64] Here the view is presented in the name of Yoḥanan by his student, Rabbah bar bar Ḥannah.[65] The latter actually combines the views of Yoḥanan and Yose. As far as Yose was concerned, the substitute no longer had any priestly responsibilities once he served in place of the High Priest. Yose did not seem to have anything to say about a substitute who continued to officiate after the regular High Priest returned to work. Rabbah, however, expands Yose's view by including that of Yoḥanan in it. Accordingly, Yose would agree ("The *halakhah* is in accord with Rabbi Yose, and Rabbi Yose agrees ...") with Yoḥanan that the service of a substitute who had already served as High Priest is valid *once it has been completed*, but was unacceptable *a priori.*[66]

The details of the ben Elim story were not pertinent to this elaboration of the position of Yose. As mentioned in our discussion of the Tosefta, the king's removal of ben Elim from the high priesthood only meant that the latter was no longer considered a High Priest. It did not indicate whether ben Elim could continue to serve as an ordinary priest.[67] Thus the *maᶜaseh* does not clarify Yose's contention that the substitute lost all of his priestly responsibilities. Yose could not have used the *maᶜaseh* to substantiate his view even though it seems that that was his intention. This ambiguity remains in the Tosefta. In the version of the Palestinian Talmud, the *maᶜaseh* is not used to substantiate the view of Yose, but rather to indicate who was responsible for the provision of the sacrificial animals.[68] The editors of the Babylonian Talmud made the *maᶜaseh* relevant by abbreviating it and appending the view of the *ḥakhamim*. The decision of the *ḥakhamim* regarding the status of a substitute who has served as High Priest is invoked by Yose to support his view. Indeed, Yose merely seems to repeat the words of the *ḥakhamim*. The dialogue between the king and ben Elim does not appear precisely because it is irrelevant to the discussion. That it has been omitted should not, therefore, be understood as an indication that it was not part of the original *maᶜaseh*. Although the significance of the dialogue cannot be determined from the rabbinic sources, there is no reason to assume that it was not included in the *maᶜaseh* originally attributed to Yose.[69]

---

[64] Above, pp. 67f.

[65] On Rabbah bar bar Ḥannah see A. Hyman, *Toledot* III, 1076.

[66] Meir would maintain that his service *was* acceptable *a priori*. See Lieberman, *Toseftaʾ Ki-Feshutah* IV, 722f. and n. 19 above.

It should be noted that the editor's hand is apparent here as the statements of both Rabbah and Judah (in the name of Rav) are phrased exactly the same ("The *halakhah* is in accord with Rabbi Yose, and Rabbi Yose agrees ...").

[67] See above, p. 65.

[68] Yose's view is presented anonymously in the Palestinian version. See above, p. 68.

[69] The other narratives of the Babylonian Talmud in which the ben Elim story appears (B. *Megillah* 12b and B. *Horayot* 9b) also omit the details of the *maᶜaseh* and concentrate upon the harmonization of the views of Meir and Yosi/*ḥakhamim*. These discussions concern the differences

In sum, the rabbinic evidence portrays Joseph ben Elim as an opportunist who once substituted for an unnamed High Priest on the Day of Atonement. No reason is given for the selection of a Sepphorean for this honor. Although he was a valid replacement, his ambitions were not taken seriously and he was not permitted to continue as High Priest once the holiday was over. It is not clear whether ben Elim actually believed that he had a legitimate claim to succeed the incumbent High Priest. He may simply have been depending on the whim of the king. The version presented in the Palestinian Talmud adds that the High Priest for whom ben Elim substituted had been disqualified by a seminal pollution. This detail has been shown to belong to the legend despite the fact that it does not appear in the versions of the Tosefta or Babylonian Talmud. The legend was recast as a *baraita* in the Babylonian Talmud where it was used to substantiate the view of Rabbi Yose concerning the status of a former High Priest. The fact that only part of the story was reproduced in the *baraita* is inconsequential; the details were omitted because they did not shed any light on Yose's view.

Josephus on Joseph ben Elim

Fortunately, Josephus provides information which may help to elucidate the historical context behind the ben Elim legend. In his *Antiquities* (XVII, 165f.), the historian writes:

> ἐπὶ δὲ τοῦ Ματθίου τούτου ἱερωμένου συμβαίνει καὶ ἕτερον ἀρχιερέα καταστῆναι πρὸς μίαν ἡμέραν ἣν Ἰουδαῖοι νηστείαν ἄγουσιν αἰτία δ' ἐστὶν ἥδε· ὁ Ματθίας ἱερώμενος ἐν νυκτὶ τῇ φερούσῃ εἰς ἡμέραν ᾗ ἡ νηστεία ἐνίστατο ἔδοξεν ἐν ὀνείρατι ὡμιληκέναι γυναικί καὶ διὰ τόδε οὐ δυναμένου ἱερουργεῖν Ἰώσηπος ὁ τοῦ Ἐλλήμου συνιεράσατο αὐτῷ συγγενὴς ὤν Ἡρώδης δὲ τόν τε Ματθίαν ἐπεπαύκει τῆς ἀρχιερωσύνης
>
> Now it happened in the time of this Matthias who was serving as (High) Priest that another High Priest was appointed for a single day, the one (day) which the Jews observe as a fast (*mian hemeran hen ioudaioi nesteian agousin*). The reason was the following (*aitia d'estin hede*): Matthias, who was the priest on the night bringing forth the day on which the fast occurred, seemed in a dream to have consorted with a woman, and since he could not perform the sacred rites because of this occurrence, a relative, Joseph the son of Ellem, assisted as (High) Priest.[70] And Herod deposed Matthias from the high priesthood ...

---

outlined in M. *Megillah* (1:9) and M. *Horayot* (3:4) between the incumbent High Priest and a priest who has "passed" from that office (*kohen she-ʿavar*). Ben Elim is mentioned in passing merely to introduce the view of the *ḥakhamim* in support of Yose. The *gemara* attempts to establish whether the Mishnah is in accordance with Yose or Meir. The dates of the *amoraim* (Rav Ḥisda and Rav Yosef) whose views on this matter have been appended to the ben Elim account indicate that these discussions emanate from the late third- early fourth centuries.

[70] The intention, of course, is that Joseph took over his responsibilities. A ritually impure High Priest could not have taken part in the Temple proceedings in any way. Josephus uses the word συνιεράομαι which is translated by Liddel and Scott (*Lexicon*, p. 1717) as "join in performing holy rites." Apparently Josephus meant that Joseph assisted Matthias by substituting for him. R. Marcus, in the Loeb Classical Library, translates: "served as priest in his stead."

Josephus includes this account in his reporting of the events following the destruction of the golden eagle erected by Herod over the Temple gate.[71] The dying king held two rabbis,[72] Judas son of Sariphaeus and Matthias son of Margalothus, and their youthful followers responsible for the insurrection. Despite his illness, Herod brought some forty of those taken captive before a public assembly where he rebuked them at great length. At this point, the spectators, who feared that Herod in his wrath would include them in the impending executions, pleaded with the king to confine the punishment to the perpetrators. In the parallel version in *The Jewish War*, Josephus concludes at this point by indicating that Herod acquiesced and limited the punishment to those directly involved in the eagle incident. The main instigators, including the two rabbis, were burned alive. The other accomplices were given over to the executioners.[73]

In *Antiquities*, Josephus states that Herod "dealt mildly" with the spectators but held the High Priest, Matthias, partially responsible for the eagle incident.[74] Josephus interrupts the narrative to inform his readers of the circumstances surrounding Herod's replacement of the High Priest. It is here that Joseph ben "Ellem" is introduced into the narrative.[75] Only later does Josephus mention the fate of Matthias son of Margalothus and his gang.[76]

The person whom Josephus refers to as Joseph the son of Ellem (Ἰώσηπος ὁ τοῦ Ἐλλήμου) is undoubtedly the Joseph ben Elim of the rabbinic sources. Josephus and the rabbis seem to be describing an identical incident albeit from their individual perspectives. The High Priest whose place was taken by Joseph ben Elim was, according to Josephus, Matthias the son of Theophilus. This High Priest held office ca. 5-4 B.C.E.[77] Josephus informs his readers that ben Elim

---

[71] *Ant.* XVII, 149ff. A somewhat different treatment of the sedition and its consequences appears in *War* I, 648ff.

[72] Josephus actually refers to them as *sophistai*. See *Ant.* XVII, 152 and *War* I, 648, 650.

[73] For an unspecified execution. See *War* I, 655.

[74] *Ant.* XVII, 164.

[75] H. G. M. Williamson has shown that Josephus uses the phrase "The reason was the following" (*aitia d'estin hede*) to introduce material from outside sources. Although the actual source used here is unknown, Williamson concludes that Josephus was probably quoting one. See H. G. M. Williamson, "The Historical Value of Josephus' Jewish Antiquities XI 297-301," *JTS* n.s. 28 (1977), 50f. According to G. Hölscher, the report concerning Matthias and ben Elim was derived from a list of High Priests composed by an unknown author. See Hölscher's article, "*Die Hohenpriesterliste bei Josephus und die evangelische Chronologie*," in *Sitzungsberichte der Heidelberger Akademie der Wissenschaft* (1940), pp. 11f. Cf. H. Bloch, *Die Quellen des Flavius Josephus in seiner Archäologie* (1879), pp. 147ff. Bloch also makes a case for the use by Josephus of a High Priest list.

[76] *Ant.* XVII, 167. No mention is made of the fate of Judas son of Sariphaeus.

[77] See Schürer, *Geschichte* II, 270. According to Büchler, the Matthias ben Theophilus intended in the rabbinic sources is not the one who held office ca. 4 B.C.E. but rather another person by that name who was High Priest ca. 65 C.E. during the reign of Agrippa II. Büchler, however, places most of the rabbinic reports concerning Galileans in Jerusalem in this pre-First Revolt period. He forces the data concerning ben Elim into agreement with his theory that many Galileans were in Jerusalem when the war broke out. See Büchler, "*Schauplätze*," pp. 198f. Curiously, Büchler did not make the same assumption in his earlier work, *Kohanim*. The views in this work will be discussed

was Matthias' relative. Unlike ben Elim, who according to the rabbinic accounts emanated from Sepphoris, Matthias was a native of Jerusalem.[78] Josephus does not explicitly state that the day on which ben Elim substituted for Matthias was the Day of Atonement, using instead the words "the one (day) which the Jews observe as a fast" (*mian hemeran hen ioudaioi nesteian agousin*). That the fast intended was the Day of Atonement cannot be doubted. The High Priest was the central figure in the Temple proceedings of the Day of Atonement. Indeed his service was indispensable to the proper observance of that holiday.[79] Only on the Day of Atonement would it have been necessary to appoint another High Priest if the regular holder of that office could not fulfill his duties.[80]

---

below. J. Derenbourg, *Essai sur l'histoire et la geographie de la Palestine* (1867), p. 160, n. 1, notes that the words attributed to the king in the rabbinic sources do not seem appropriate coming from the Idumean, Herod. Thus it could be maintained (although not suggested by Derenbourg) that one of the Agrippas, perhaps Agrippa I, who is portrayed by the rabbis in a better light than Herod (above, n. 30), was intended. There is no reason, however, to assume that Josephus confused the High Priests and that an Agrippa and not Herod was meant. Yose ben Ḥalafta, who reported the incident (in the Tosefta and Babylonian Talmud) may merely have been familiar with it because it involved a native of his hometown, Sepphoris (see below, p. 78). Yose, or the rabbis who preserved his report, were probably not interested in the political background of the incident. In fact, they may not have known which king was actually involved. To the rabbis, the *maᶜaseh* was clearly of halakhic interest. As such, the king's response may merely be an embellishment (as argued above, pp. 66f.). This seems more reasonable than Josephus' misuse or misunderstanding of his source, especially in view of the fact that the historian's version is older than that preserved in the name of Yose.

[78] *Ant.* XVII, 78. Stern has suggested that Matthias, like his relative ben Elim, was a Galilean. Stern maintains that the report of Josephus that Matthias was of a Jerusalem family (*genos*) only indicates that he lived there for some time before becoming High Priest. See M. Stern, "The Reign of Herod and the Herodian Dynasty," *The Jewish People in the First Century* I, 272, n. 2. Cf. H. Graetz, "*Zur Geschichte der nachexilischen Hohenpriester*," *MGWJ* 30 (1880), 52f. In a different study, Stern points out that Josephus calls another High Priest, Simeon ben Boethus, a Jerusalemite even though the historian also refers to his Alexandrian origins. See M. Stern, "*Mediniyuto shel-Hordos Ve-Ha-Ḥevrah Ha-Yehudit Be-Sof Yemei Bayit Sheni*," *Tarbiz* 35 (1966), 238, n. 22. Cf. *Ant.* XV, 320. While Matthias may not have been a Jerusalemite originally, the suggestion that he emanated from Galilee (or Sepphoris itself, as Graetz maintains) seems a bit forced. There is no reason to assume that Joseph ben Elim's relatives all emanated from the same city or region of the country.

[79] On the Day of Atonement, the High Priest brought a bull as an expiatory sacrifice for himself and the priesthood. He also offered a goat as an atonement for the sins of the people. The duties of the High Priest were highlighted by his entrance into the Holy of Holies where he burned the incense and sprinkled the blood of the sacrifice on the curtain. See M. *Yomaʾ* 4:3 and 5:1, 3, 4. On the day-to-day responsibilities of the High Priest, see Jeremias, *Jerusalem*, pp. 151f.

[80] A. Wikgren, in his notes to *Ant.* XVII, 166 (Loeb Classical Library), claims that the fast day referred to by Josephus was the Fast of Esther which occurred on the thirteenth of March (*Adar*). Wikgren seems to have been misled by Josephus' statement at the end of the passage (*Ant.* XVII, 167) that an eclipse occurred "on that same night." This eclipse has been thought by many to be the one which took place on March 13, 4 B.C. See Wikgren, *ad loc.* Cf. W. E. Filmer, "The Chronology of the Reign of Herod the Great," *JTS* n.s. 17 (1966), 284f. and E. M. Smallwood, "High Priests and Politics in Roman Palestine," *JTS* n.s. 13 (1962), 17. There are several problems with Wikgren's suggestion. First of all, the Fast of Esther was not observed until the post-talmudic period. During the time of Josephus the 13th of *Adar* (the date of the supposed fast) was celebrated as the day of the Maccabean victory over Nicanor. See H. Lichtenstein, "*Die Fastenrolle*," pp. 280f. and 321. Second, other eclipses are known to have occurred including one on September 15/16, 5 B.C.E. See T. D. Barnes, "The Date of Herod's Death," *JTS* n.s. 19 (1968), 209. Cf. Filmer's

The essence of the ben Elim story presented by Josephus resembles that of the rabbinic narratives: Ben Elim substituted for a High Priest who had been disqualified by some sort of impurity. According to Josephus, Matthias, the High Priest, could not complete his duties on the Day of Atonement because he had dreamt on the night of the fast that he had consorted with a woman.[81] At first it would appear as though this version is not that which is provided in the account of the Palestinian Talmud. According to the latter, the High Priest suffered a seminal pollution. It seems likely, however, that Josephus and the Talmud were referring to the same thing. The Mishnah specifically considers a person who suffers impure thoughts in his sleep to be unclean.[82] The reason for this was because of the suspicion of a nocturnal pollution.[83] Thus it is no wonder that Matthias was disqualified because of the impure thoughts he experienced in his vision. Although the Talmud does not explicitly state that the impurity occurred on the eve of the Day of Atonement, it seems reasonable to assume that a nocturnal pollution was intended.[84] In any case, the similarity of the reasons provided by Josephus and the Talmud for the disqualification of the High Priest is evident.

---

discussion and E. M. Smallwood, *The Jews Under Roman Rule*, p. 104, n. 158. Finally, the assumption that the eclipse establishes the date of the occasion on which ben Elim substituted for Matthias is questionable. The eclipse may very well have happened "on the same night" as the executions of the insurgents involved in the eagle incident. However, the fast could have been on a different day completely. The use by Josephus of distinctly different sources for the ben Elim account and the eagle incident may also have resulted in a confused chronology. See n. 75. Josephus uses the phrase *he nesteia* ("the fast day") in other contexts which suggest that he meant the Day of Atonement. Curiously, these passages also contain chronological problems. See the notes of R. Marcus on *Ant.* XIV, 66 and 487 in the Loeb Classical Library. The Day of Atonement is also referred to as "the fast day" (*yom ẓom*) in the Commentary on Ḥabakkuk (11:8) from Qumran.

[81] Lieberman (*Tosefta᾿ Ki-Feshutah* IV, 723, n. 22 and 724, n. 23) understands Josephus to mean that Matthias only *remembered* the dream on the night of the Day of Atonement, but the vision actually occurred the night before the holiday. In this way, Lieberman is able to reconcile the Mishnah (*Yoma᾿* 1:4, 6, 7, see n. 84), which states that the High Priest did not sleep the night of the holiday, with the ben Elim account. As mentioned earlier (n. 26), however, the Palestinian Talmud clearly indicates that the High Priest was disqualified *on* the Day of Atonement. Josephus appears to be saying that Matthias "seemed in a dream to have consorted with a woman" on the very night of the fast day on which he was officiating.

[82] See M. *Miqva᾿ot* 8:3. The comments in this Mishnah are attributed to *tannaim* of the Yavnean period.

[83] This is not expressly stated in the Mishnah but is strongly suggested by the context, which speaks of impurities caused by the discharge of semen. Cf. the comments of R. Ovadiah Bertinoro on the passage.

[84] Admittedly, the Mishnah stipulates precautions which were taken to avoid a nocturnal pollution. According to M. *Yoma᾿* 1:4, the High Priest was not permitted to eat much on the eve of the Day of Atonement because such indulgence could bring sleep upon him. M. *Yoma᾿* 1:6-7 indicates that the High Priest was to stay awake reading from the Bible and the young priests were to see to it that he did not succumb to his desire to sleep. These precautions would certainly have rendered a nocturnal pollution impossible. It is not known, however, when or for what reason these precautions were implemented. It is possible that they were not yet in effect when the ben Elim incident was supposed to have happened. The measures taken to prevent the High Priest from sleeping may have been formulated by later *tannaim* as a result of incidents such as the one reported to have occurred in ben Elim's day. See n. 50. It is equally possible that the precautions were ineffective.

One thing that Josephus fails to report is that ben Elim was from Sepphoris. This should not, however, cast any doubt upon the rabbinic report. First of all, Yose ben Ḥalafta, who reported the incident, was himself a resident of Sepphoris, which may have been the reason he was familiar with the episode.[85] Second, Josephus and Yose were interested in two diametrically opposed aspects of the story. For Josephus, Matthias is the central figure; it is his fate and the resulting change of High Priests which is of concern to the historian. Ben Elim is merely an accessory to the events which enabled Herod to depose Matthias and replace him with someone more to his liking. Josephus does not say much concerning ben Elim because he (or his source) was not interested in him. In the rabbinic version, however, ben Elim is the central figure. The *maᶜaseh* itself is presented to support the need specified in the Mishnah for the designation of a substitute High Priest.[86] Ben Elim is an example of someone who served in that capacity. Josephus is more interested in Herod's removal of Matthias from the high priesthood than in ben Elim. Thus he does not reproduce any discussion which might have taken place between ben Elim and the king. In contrast, such a discussion is given a prominent place in the accounts of the Tosefta and Palestinian Talmud. Since ben Elim is the protagonist in the rabbinic version, it is not surprising that his origin is mentioned.

Still, Josephus and the rabbis seem to be describing different aspects of the same event. Each account has its difficulties. The rabbis present the story as a legend without historical detail. Josephus, on the other hand, does not elaborate upon the significance of Matthias' removal from office. Herod could certainly have deposed the High Priest as soon as his complicity in the eagle incident became known. Why did the king have to wait for Matthias to be disqualified on the Day of Atonement? Josephus is certainly not revealing the full story.

The Herodian attitude towards the high priesthood warrants special attention. It stands to reason that Herod, especially in the state of mind he was in before his death, would have suspected the involvement of the High Priest in any insurrection having to do with the Temple. After the removal of Matthias, Herod would certainly have wanted to appoint a more loyal High Priest. M. Stern has shown that the Herodians favored the priestly house of Boethus whenever a change in the high priesthood was desired.[87] Following the Day of Atonement, Herod chose Joazar, of the house of Boethus, to be the successor of Matthias.[88] Joazar

---

[85] It could, of course, be maintained that since the ben Elim story appears anonymously in the Palestinian Talmud, the ascription to Yose is questionable. Yose does, however, appear to have had a historical interest in his hometown. See the list of references to Sepphoris in the *halakhot* of Yose in Bacher, *Tannaiten* II, 152, n. 2.

[86] At least in the versions of the Tosefta and the Palestinian Talmud. See above pp. 65 and 69f.

[87] See Stern's discussion in "Aspects of Jewish Society: The Priesthood and Other Classes," *The Jewish People in the First Century* II (1976), 604ff. and *idem*, "*Mediniyuto*," pp. 247ff.

[88] *Ant.* XVII, 164. Matthias may have been connected in some way with the house of Ḥanan. See Stern, "*Mediniyuto*," p. 239.

himself was later deposed by Archelaus (4 B.C.E.-6 C.E.), the son of Herod. By removing Joazar, Archelaus gained the support of the people who undoubtedly associated the High Priest with Herod's wicked punishment of the rebels involved in the eagle incident.[89] Still, it was another priest of the house of Boethus, Eleazer, the brother of Joazar, who was appointed.[90] Only when this priest proved to be unpopular with the people did Archelaus turn to Jesus, the son of See, who belonged to a different priestly house.[91] Before the end of his reign, however, Archelaus reappointed Joazar.[92] Although the house of Boethus did not produce any High Priests under the Roman procurators (6-41 C.E.), when Herod's grandson Agrippa (I) ascended the throne in 41, he too turned to the house of Boethus to fill the high priesthood.[93]

The Herodian preference for the House of Boethus may help to elucidate an obscure episode in the history of the high priesthood. The rabbinic account of Joseph ben Elim's attempt to usurp the high priesthood may have a historical foundation. It is possible that ben Elim knew that Matthias' days as High Priest were numbered as a result of his cooperation with the rebels. Knowing that the king was about to make a change in the high priesthood, ben Elim could very well have been waiting for an opportune moment to assert himself. Thus when Matthias was disqualified from participation in the Day of Atonement proceedings, ben Elim's ambitions came to the fore. His bid for the high priesthood was certainly not as casual as the rabbinic legend would have it. It must be remembered that ben Elim was not only substitute High Priest but also a relative of Matthias. It is possible, therefore, that he was relying upon the support of the people who no doubt would have preferred a relative of the ex-High Priest over the choice of the king. Herod, of course, was hardly in any frame of mind to appoint a relative of Matthias who was also a favorite of the people. Perhaps, for this reason, Joseph ben Elim was passed over for a member of the house of Boethus.

---

[89] See *Ant.* XVII, 207-208, where Josephus says that the people demanded the removal of those honored by Herod, in particular, Joazar who did not serve as High Priest in accordance with the law. According to XVII, 339, however, Archelaus, upon returning from a visit to Rome, replaced Joazar because the latter had supported a revolt while he was away. This contradicts the assumption that Joazar was a friend of the Herodians and their Roman protectors. Smallwood eliminates this difficulty by postulating a consistently pro-Herodian and pro-Roman stance on the part of Joazar. Archelaus acquiesced to the demands of the people to remove Joazar but explained his action to the Romans as a result of the High Priest's participation in the recent revolt. This was merely an excuse fabricated, as Smallwood says, "for Roman consumption." Joazar could not really have been a true rebel otherwise he would not have been reappointed in 6 A.D. See Smallwood, "High Priests," pp. 20f. and *The Jews Under Roman Rule*, pp. 105f. and 116.

[90] *Ant.* XVII, 339.

[91] *Ant.* XVII, 341. He appears to have been a member of the house of Ḥanan. See Stern, "Aspects," p. 606 and *idem*, "*Mediniyuto*," p. 250.

[92] In *Ant.* XVIII, 3, Joazar is found functioning as High Priest once again. Smallwood, "High Priests," p. 21, assumes that it was Archelaus who reappointed him.

[93] *Ant.* XIX, 297. See Stern, "*Mediniyuto*," p. 251.

Joseph ben Elim: Segan Ha-Kohanim?

The fact that Joseph ben Elim officiated in place of the High Priest, Matthias son of Theophilus, suggests that he belonged to the upper echelons of the Jerusalem priesthood. In the Tosefta account, Rabbi Ḥananiah "*Segan Ha-Kohanim*" (*segan* of the priests), states that the *segan* was appointed precisely in order to serve in place of a disqualified High Priest.[94] Thus it could be maintained that Joseph ben Elim substituted for Matthias in the capacity of a *segan*.[95] If so, a priest from Sepphoris would have attained a prestigious position among the Temple personnel. Before examining this possibility, the role of the *segan* must be investigated.

In rabbinic literature, the *segan* appears as an assistant to the High Priest. His role appears to have been primarily ceremonial. Mishnah *Tamid* (7:3) relates that the *segan* ascends the ramp of the altar to the right of the High Priest whenever the latter wishes to burn an offering.[96] The *segan* helps the High Priest up the ramp and signals (by waving a cloth) to the cymbal clasher and the Levites that the drink offering has been poured.[97] Other priests help the High Priest with the sacrifice itself. In Mishnah *Yomaʾ* (3:9, 4:1), the *segan* again appears to the right of the High Priest on the Day of Atonement for the drawing of the lots to determine which goat was to be designated "for the Lord" and which "for Azazel."[98] If the High Priest drew the lot bearing the words "for the Lord" with his right hand, the *segan* would say to him "My lord, High Priest, raise your right hand!"[99] Mishnah *Yomaʾ* (7:1) also indicates that when it was time for the High Priest to read from the Torah on the Day of Atonement, the *segan* would hand the scroll to him.[100] In the Tosefta (*Sanhedrin* 4:1), the *segan* appears once again to the right of the High Priest when the latter accepts condolences or gives them to others.

A *baraita* in the Palestinian Talmud summarizes the role of the *segan*:[101]

חמשה דברים היה הסגן משמש הסגן אומר לו אישי כהן גדול הגבה ימינך סגן מימינו
וראש בית אב משמאלו הניף הסגן בסודרין אחז הסגן בימינו והעלהו לא היה כהן גדול
מתמנה להיות כהן גדול עד שהוא נעשה סגן

---

[94] See above, p. 63.

[95] See n. 27 for writers who hold this view.

[96] The High Priest could offer a sacrifice whenever he desired. See M. *Yomaʾ* 1:2.

[97] After the cymbals were clashed, the Levites would sing.

[98] See Leviticus 16:8-10, 20-22 on this ceremony. The Mishnah also notes that the head of the priestly subdivision (*roʾsh bet ʾav*) stood to the left of the High Priest.

[99] If the lot was drawn by the High Priest's left hand, the *roʾsh bet ʾav* (see previous note) would say to him "My lord, High Priest, raise your left hand!"

[100] Similarly, when the king read the Torah scroll in the year following a sabbatical year, the *segan* handed the Torah to the High Priest who in turn passed it to the king. See M. *Sotah* 7:8.

[101] P. *Yomaʾ* 3, 41a, Ms. Leiden. Although the passage is not introduced as a *baraita* it clearly represents a reformulation of *tannaitic* (mishnaic) material. The Palestinian Talmud often produces a *baraita* without an introductory formula. See Bokser, "Bibliographical Guide," p. 175.

> The *segan* served five purposes: The *segan* said to him, "My lord, High Priest, raise your right hand!" The *segan* (stood) to his right and the head of the (priestly) subdivision (*rosh bet ᵓav*) to his left.[102] The *segan* waved the cloth.[103] The *segan* held his (the High Priest's) right hand and raised him up. No High Priest was appointed unless he had been a *segan*.

This passage was obviously formulated with M. *Yomaᵓ* 3:9, 4:1 and M. *Tamid* 7:3 in mind. In fact, the first four "purposes" are quoted verbatim from these sources. The last statement of the passage would seem to represent the fifth purpose, yet it does not really assign a specific role to the *segan*. It also does not appear in the tannaitic sources. Of course, the statement could have been a deduction from the remark of Ḥananiah in the Tosefta to the effect that the *segan* served as the replacement for a disqualified High Priest. In this case, the fifth role, that of substitute High Priest, would have to be read into the statement. That this was the intention seems unlikely since none of the phraseology of the Tosefta appears in the statement.[104] Furthermore, it can just as cogently be maintained that a fifth purpose can be found in the Mishnah but has been omitted from the list presented in the Talmud. Thus A. Epstein has suggested that the handing over of the Torah scroll by the *segan* (M. *Yomaᵓ* 7:1) constituted the omitted role.[105] In this case, the words "No High Priest was appointed unless he had been a *segan*" would have been intended as a summary statement indicating that a person who had filled all the roles of the *segan* gained the necessary knowledge and experience to become High Priest.[106] If this interpretation is correct, the view of Ḥananiah that the *segan* replaced the High Priest when the latter

---

[102] The lot drawing of the Day of Atonement was probably intended here although according to T. *Sanhedrin* 4:1 the *segan* and the *rosh bet ᵓav* also stood in this formation when the High Priest accepted condolences. Cf. B. *Sanhedrin* 19a. Perhaps the formation at both of these ceremonies was intended. Cf., however, n. 105 below.

[103] The term used for "cloth" is *sudarin* (סודרין) which is a loan word from Latin *sudarium*. The word appears in Greek as σουδάριον. It refers to a type of face-cloth or handkerchief. See Krauss, *Lehnwörter* II, 373 and W. F. Arndt and F. W. Gingrich, *A Greek English Lexicon of the New Testament* (1979), p. 759.

[104] The author of the passage would not have hesitated to utilize the language of the Tosefta as he had earlier made use of the wording of the Mishnah. Perhaps he was not familiar with the view of Ḥananiah.

[105] See Epstein's review of Büchler's *Die Priester und der Cultus* in *MGWJ* 40 (1896), 141. Cf. *Shirei Qorban* on P. *Yomaᵓ* 3, 41a. It could also be maintained that T. *Sanhedrin* 4:1 provides the fifth purpose of the *segan*. That is, the stationing of the *segan* to the right of the High Priest when the latter accepts condolences could be the fifth role. This possibility seems less likely, however, since the summary list of the *segan*'s purposes is clearly based upon Mishnah *Tamid* and Mishnah *Yomaᵓ*—not on the Tosefta. In any case, the fact that both M. *Yomaᵓ* 4:1 and M. *Tamid* 7:3 were inverted when they were incorporated into the talmudic passage (see the respective *mishnayot*) suggests that the editor(s) worked in a haphazard fashion. That something was left out should not, therefore, be surprising.

[106] That this is the intention of the statement would be even more probable if Brandt's assumption that the word *segan* is related to Mandaic אשגאנדא meaning "candidate for the priesthood" is correct. Here, the *segan* could have been thought of as a candidate for the *high* priesthood. See W. Brandt, *Mandäische Schriften* (1893), p. 169, n. 1.

became unfit does not even appear among the duties delineated in the Talmud! To be sure, the role of substitute High Priest could have been the omitted fifth item in the list. It is unlikely though that this function would have been overlooked by either the *amoraim* or the editor(s) of the text.[107]

The view originally proposed by Schürer that the "captain (*strategos*) of the Temple" mentioned by Josephus and the New Testament is identical to the *segan* of the rabbinic sources has been widely accepted.[108] The *strategos* appears in the writings of Josephus as the overseer of all officiating priests. The historian mentions a *strategos* named Ananus who, along with the High Priest Ananias, was sent to Rome in chains for alleged involvement in a revolt ca. 51 C.E.[109] In another report, Josephus relates that on the Passover preceding the First Revolt, the watchmen of the Temple informed the *strategos* of the spontaneous opening of the brass gate, a portent of the impending destruction of the sanctuary.[110] Finally, Josephus describes how a *strategos*, Eleazar, son of the High Priest Ananias, sparked the First Revolt by persuading the officiating priests not to accept the sacrifices and gifts of foreigners.[111] The New Testament presents the *strategos* as an official who is responsible for maintaining order at the Temple. In Acts, the *strategos*, together with the other priests and Sadducees, has Peter and John arrested for teaching the people and proclaiming the resurrection of the dead in

---

[107] B. Ratner presumes that the role of substitute High Priest has been omitted. See his *ʾAhavat Ẓiyyon Vi-Yerushalayim, Yomaʾ*, p. 39. It is possible that the role was omitted because it was only a potential function which few *seganim* actually fulfilled. However, the role would still seem noteworthy, and its inclusion would certainly have emphasized the importance of the *segan*. Epstein's suggestion, therefore, seems most reasonable particularly since the passage is based upon M. *Yomaʾ* and M. *Tamid*. (See n. 105) If, however, the last statement of the passage is somehow taken as the fifth purpose, it still cannot be identified with the role of substitute High Priest. Cf. n. 104.

[108] Schürer, *Geschichte* II, 320f. Cf. Jeremias, *Jerusalem*, p. 161; S. Safrai, "The Temple," *The Jewish People in the First Century* II, 875f.; *idem*, "The Temple and the Divine Service," *The World History of the Jewish People* VII, 299; W. Otto, *Herodes* (1913), col. 116; and M. Buttenwieser, "Priest," *The Jewish Encyclopedia* 10 (1905), 196. For a dissenting point of view see Schwarz, "*Der Segan*," pp. 45f. It should be noted that Schürer identifies functionaries of a lower rank having the title *segan/strategos* with the officials known in rabbinic literature as *ʾish har ha-bayit* (M. *Middot* 1:2) and *ʾish ha-birah* (M. *ʿOrlah* 2:12). See Schürer, *Geschichte* II, 331. Cf. the discussion of all of these offices in H. L. Strack and P. Billerbeck, *Kommentar zum neuen Testament aus Talmud und Midrash* (1922-28) II, 628ff. The *strategos* discussed here should not be confused with the *strategos* who appears in rabbinic literature as אסטרטיג. The latter is a municipal official. See Allon, "*Ha-ʾIstartegim Be-ʿArei ʾEreẓ Yisrael Bi-Tequfat Ha-Romit*," *Meḥqarim* II, 74-92.

[109] *Ant.* XX, 131. In *War* II, 243, Ananus is referred to as the son of Ananias. According to Büchler, *Antiquities* may have incorrectly reported the name of the *strategos* who was sent to Rome in chains with the High Priest, Ananias. This *strategos* would not have been the son of Ananias otherwise Ananias would have been the father of two *seganim*, Ananus and Eleazar. (The latter will be discussed shortly.) See Büchler, *Kohanim*, p. 87, n. 39.

[110] *War* VI, 293. Cf. the rabbinic account of this miracle in B. *Yomaʾ* 39b and see J. Neusner, *A Life of Yoḥanan ben Zakkai* (1970), pp. 64f.

[111] *War* II, 408. Cf. B. *Gittin* 56a where a similar act is attributed to Zechariah ben Avkilus. Eleazar is also referred to in *Ant.* XX, 208. The cessation of sacrifices in behalf of foreigners made the offering for the Emperor impossible. For the political and religious implications of this revolutionary act, see D. M. Rhoads, *Israel in Revolution*, pp. 99f.

Jesus.[112] This occurred sometime during the term of Caiaphas who was High Priest from ca. 18 to 36 C.E.[113] Thus the Greek sources attest to the office of *segan/strategos* perhaps as early as 18 C.E.[114] They do not indicate, however, that this official participated directly in the cult or for that matter was ever considered a substitute for the High Priest. According to Josephus and the New Testament, the *segan/strategos* was an administrative official of the Temple who possessed authority in procedural matters.[115]

Nevertheless, the view that the *segan* served as substitute High Priest is repeated several times in the Babylonian Talmud. Curiously, the view is almost always expressed in the name of Ḥananiah *Segan Ha-Kohanim*, and we can reasonably assume that the exceptions were derived from the saying originally attributed to him.[116] In contrast, both the Tosefta and the Mishnah report that

---

[112] See *Acts* 4:1 and 5:24, 26. The term *strategos* appears in the plural (*strategoi*) in the account of the Last Supper in Luke 22:4, 52. According to Schürer (*Geschichte* II, 322), the plural form refers to *seganim* of a lower rank. Cf. n. 108. Büchler, however, points out that the parallel account of the Last Supper in Mark 14:43 does not have the term. Cf. Matthew 26:47 and see Büchler, *Kohanim*, p. 86, n. 38.

[113] Schürer, *Geschichte* II, 271. According to Acts 4:6, the council before which Peter and John were brought included "Annas the High Priest and Caiaphas and John and Alexander and all who were of high priestly family." Annas, however, was High Priest from 6 to 15 C.E., well before the incident could have occurred. The identification of John and Alexander is uncertain, but it is generally accepted that the arrest and council meeting took place during the high priesthood of Caiaphas. See E. Haenchen, *The Acts of the Apostles: A Commentary* (1971), p. 216 and Jeremias, *Jerusalem*, p. 197.

[114] Assuming that Acts is not using the term *strategos* anachronistically and that the office was already in existence at the beginning of Caiaphas' high priesthood.

[115] Cf., however, Epstein ("Review," 141f.) who denies that the *segan* was the overseer of the officiating priests. Epstein does not seem to have taken the Greek sources into account. If the *segan* and *strategos* are *identical*, then there is reason to assign the role of overseer to that official. After all, Eleazar does seem to have control over the lower priests when he convinces them not to sacrifice in behalf of foreigners. This control over the priests, however, should not be construed as actual participation in the sacrificial cult. Neither the tannaitic nor the Greek sources discussed indicate that the *segan/strategos* was directly involved in the bringing of offerings. Cf. the end of n. 117 on the *segan* and the preparation of the Red Heifer. According to Rashi (B. *Yoma*ʾ 39a), the only time the *segan* was involved in the sacrificial service was when he substituted for the High Priest. Rashi, of course, assumes that the *segan* was the substitute, something which the sources just presented do not indicate. Cf. Rashi's comments on Jeremiah 52:24 ("*Kohen Mishneh*"). Curiously, *segen/segan* is used in biblical sources to refer to a prefect, ruler or other official. (e.g. Ezekiel 23:6, Nehemiah 2:16. See BDB, pp., 688 and 1104.) Similarly, the word appears in cuneiform records of Babylon and in Aramaic documents where it designates native chiefs of deported groups. See E. Bickerman, *From Ezra to the Last of the Maccabees* (1962), p. 5. That Josephus and the New Testament render *segan* as *strategos* is, therefore, not surprising. (Especially in view of the fact that the Septuagint usually has *strategoi* for *seganim*.) This understanding of the term *segan* would again point to an administrative rather than a cultic figure. It is often presumed that the "priest(s) of the second rank" mentioned in the Bible (II Kings 23:4, 25:18 and Jeremiah 52:24) and in the *War Scroll* from Qumran (2:1) is a reference to the *segan*. (Cf. Targum Jonathan on the biblical passages.) See *Büchler, Kohanim*, p. 79 and Y. Yadin, *The Scroll of the War of the Sons of Light Against the Sons of Darkness* (1962), p. 207, n. 6. This identification, even if correct, does not provide any insight into the duties of the office.

[116] See B. *Sotah* 42a and B. *Yoma*ʾ 39a. In B. *Horayot* 13a, Mar Zutra son of R. Naḥman, a fourth century Babylonian *amora*, presents an anonymous *baraita* containing language similar to that attributed to Ḥananiah in the other sources (שאם יארע בו פסול בכהן גדול נכנס הסגן ומשמש תחתיו.). In fact, the parallel discussion in B. *Nazir* 47b has Mar Zutra ascribe the view to Ḥanina ben Antigonus, which is almost certainly a mistake for Ḥananiah *Segan Ha-Kohanim*.

"another priest" (*kohen ʾaḥer*)—not the *segan*—was designated seven days before the Day of Atonement as the person to replace the High Priest should he be disqualified.[117] If Ḥananiah had been correct, there would have been no need for the designation of a *kohen ʾaḥer*; the *segan*, a regular official of the Temple, would have been readied each year before the holiday. While Ḥananiah presumably served as a *segan* and was familiar with the responsibilities of that office, he may at times have presented a subjective view of the cult. Neusner has noted that Ḥananiah's views on cultic matters were at times challenged by authorities at Yavneh despite the fact that he was supposed to have possessed first hand knowledge.[118] Thus some of Ḥananiah's views may not have been drawn from personal observation. Those that were may not have been considered by the Yavneans to have been indicative of the norm.[119]

Ḥananiah's understanding of the role of the *segan* may serve as a case in point. Ḥananiah could have been expressing his own opinion concerning the role of the *segan*. The fact that he does not say that he himself served as a substitute High

---

[117] Cf. the text of the Tosefta, above, p. 63. On the Mishnah, see p. 64 and n. 17. Schürer denies altogether that the *segan* served as a substitute High Priest. He seems, however, to have overlooked the Tosefta which juxtaposes the view of Ḥananiah *Segan Ha-Kohanim* with that of the Mishnah concerning a *kohen ʾaḥer*. See Schürer, *Geschichte* II, 320f. and cf. the remarks of Schwarz ("*Der Segan*," pp. 44f.) who believes that the reports of the Tosefta and Mishnah emanate from different periods. Buttenwieser, "Priest," p. 196, supports Schürer, contending that the Talmud (B. *Sanhedrin* 19a) explicitly differentiates between a *segan* and a *mashuaḥ she-ʿavar*, i.e. an anointed one who has served as High Priest. (Cf. *kohen she-ʿavar* in M. *Megillah* 1:9). Buttenwieser suggests that ben Elim was a *mashuah she-ʿavar* in that once he substituted he no longer served again. It could be argued, however, that the *segan* himself became a *mashuaḥ she-ʿavar* after he substituted for the High Priest. Buttenwieser also argues that the *memunneh* (appointed one) of M. *Tamid* (3, 5, 6, 7) and the *segan* were identical. Consequently, the *segan* would also have been responsible for the duties associated with the *memunneh*. These duties in effect made him the "superintendent" of the Temple service. While it is not clear whether the *memunneh* and the *segan* were identical (See *Tosafot* on B. *Sotah* 42a and cf. *Tosafot* on B. *Yomaʾ* 15b and on B. *Menaḥot* 100a. Also see Büchler, *Kohanim*, p. 88, n. 44), Buttenwieser's conclusion that the participation of the *segan* in the proceedings of the Day of Atonement precluded the possibility of his functioning as a substitute High Priest seems reasonable.

Other possible roles of the *segan* should at least be considered in brief. *Sifre* on Numbers 19:3 states that Eleazar, the son of Aaron, was responsible for the preparation of the Red Heifer because this was a duty of the *segan*. Presumably Eleazar was a *segan*. The reference to *segan* here is merely intended to emphasize that Aaron's son prepared the Red Heifer and not the High Priest *par excellence* himself. (Aaron's sons are constantly referred to as *seganim*. See, for example, B. *Sanhedrin* 110a and *Leviticus Rab.* 20:2.) It is noteworthy that a High Priest of the end of the Second Temple period, Ishmael ben Phiabi, is credited with the preparation of a Red Heifer. (See M. *Parah* 3:5.) Thus this duty was not necessarily a responsibility of the *segan*. According to Büchler (p. 88), the *segan* was also responsible for dressing the High Priest when the latter officiated at the Temple. This suggestion, however, depends on midrashic sources that reflect upon the relationship between Moses and Aaron. See *Sifraʾ Mekhiltaʾ De-Milluʾim, parashah* 1:6.

[118] Neusner, *Rabbinic Traditions* I, 403f. Ḥananiah's title, *Segan Ha-Kohanim*, would lead one to believe that he had witnessed Temple proceedings at one time. Neusner, however, notes (p. 411) that Ḥananiah never refers to his own participation in the cult. Cf. Büchler (*Kohanim*, p. 87) who claims that had Ḥananiah actually substituted for a High Priest some record of the experience would have been preserved in his testimonies. Cf. M. *ʿEduyot* 2:1,2.

[119] Neusner, *Rabbinic Traditions* I, 404, suggests that the Yavneans may not have accepted some of Ḥananiah's personal observations as "authoritative precedent."

Priest or witnessed other *seganim* in this role is suggestive in this regard. On the other hand, if he had served as substitute High Priest, the *tannaim* disregarded his experience when they decided the *halakhah*. Otherwise they would have said that the *segan*, not the *kohen ʾaḥer*, was readied before the Day of Atonement.[120] Since the rabbinic and Greek sources do not indicate that the *segan* held the position ascribed to him by Ḥananiah, it would seem that the decision of the *tannaim* was historically correct. Evidently, Ḥananiah's personal experience was considered exceptional and, consequently, was dismissed as an unreliable precedent for the *halakhah*.[121]

According to Büchler, the role of substitute was originally delegated to a relative of the High Priest but was later assumed by the *segan*. Accordingly, both Joseph ben Elim and Judah ben Kimḥit were selected as substitutes because they were related to the High Priest.[122] Büchler claims that the *segan* only acquired the additional role of substitute High Priest during the last decade of the Temple's existence. During that period, the Pharisees became increasingly more involved in Temple matters and managed to gain control of the office of *segan*.[123] Because of his position at the side of the High Priest, the *segan* was able to ensure that the former officiated in accordance with Pharisaic principles.[124] Büchler maintains

---

[120] The reference to a *kohen ʾaḥer* would have been superfluous. It is assumed here that the anonymous statement found in the Tosefta and the Mishnah concerning the role of the *kohen ʾaḥer* was the *halakhah*, at least as far as the *tannaim* were concerned. Interestingly, the Babylonian *amoraim* and later authorities seem to have accepted Ḥananiah's explanation that the *kohen ʾaḥer* and the *segan* were one and the same. Thus his statement to that effect appears frequently in the Babylonian Talmud. See n. 116. Also, cf. the discussion in B. *Nazir* 47b and especially the comments of *Tosafot* on *meshuaḥ milḥamah*. For the view of Rashi, see n. 115. Cf. the remarks of the Vilna Gaon on *Sifraʾ ʾAḥarei Mot, pereq* 8:4. The important point for our inquiry is that the *segan* and the *kohen ʾaḥer* were not identical in the time of Joseph ben Elim.

[121] Cf. n. 119. The only other possibility is that Ḥananiah was correct with regard to the rest of the year whereas a person other than the *segan* was specially selected as substitute for Yom Kippur. After all, M. *Yomaʾ* 1:1 is only concerned with that holiday. This possibility would sit well with the supposition that the *segan*, who was the High Priest's right hand man so to speak, would have been the most likely one to fill in for the latter on the spur of the moment. Yom Kippur would have been the exception. The problem, however, is that the one time the High Priest's service was indispensable was on Yom Kippur. It would seem reasonable to expect the *segan* to substitute for the High Priest on that day in particular, if indeed filling in for the latter was one of his usual responsibilities. Furthermore, the Greek and tannaitic sources (with the exception of Ḥananiah's statement) do not indicate that the *segan* held the position of substitute High Priest. For the perspective of the Babylonian *amoraim* and later authorities, see previous note.

[122] Büchler, *Kohanim*, pp. 80ff. On Judah ben Kimḥit, see above, pp. 67f.

[123] Actually, Büchler believes that the *segan* could have assumed the role as early as 17-18 C.E. after Judah ben Kimḥit served as substitute. (Büchler identifies Simeon ben Kimḥit with Simeon son of Kamithos. See n. 50.) Büchler, however, prefers a date after 62 since in that year, so he claims, there was a major Pharisaic revolution in the cultic affairs of the Temple. There is no historical reason to place the takeover of the role of substitute between 17-18 C.E. and 62 C.E.

Büchler also suggests that the other roles of the *segan* developed gradually and were not assumed all at once. See Büchler, *Kohanim*, pp. 82ff. and especially p. 84, n. 35.

[124] It is generally presumed that the religious orientation of the high priesthood was that of the Sadducean party. See Stern's discussion of this matter in "Aspects," pp. 609ff.

that the assumption of the responsibility of substitute High Priest by the *segan* assured the Pharisees that the high priesthood would fall into the proper hands in the event of a disqualification.[125] Although Büchler goes beyond the evidence in suggesting that the Pharisees actually gained control of the office of *segan*,[126] his suggestion that a particular interest group *promoted* the *segan* as the substitute High Priest during the final years before the Destruction is attractive. Neusner

[125] *Kohanim*, p. 85. Cf. Schwarz, "*Der Segan*," p. 45.

[126] Büchler's hypothesis depends heavily upon his assumption that there was a Pharisaic revolution in 62 C.E. This premise has been questioned by other scholars. See Jeremias, *Jerusalem*, p. 148, n. 1 and especially Epstein, "Review," pp. 139f. Much of the evidence adduced by Büchler to show that the Pharisees took over the office of *segan* is also suspect. Büchler notes that in the description of the annual water libation in M. *Sukkah* 4:9, the attending priest is said to have raised his hand in such a way as to indicate that the water was poured into the proper bowl on the altar. The crowd would say to him "Raise your hand!" The Mishnah explains that a priest once poured the water onto his feet and aroused the anger of the people, who pelted him with citrons. Josephus (*Ant.* XIII, 372) describes a similar incident involving the High Priest Alexander Yannai (ca. 126-76 B.C.E.). The Talmud (B. *Sukkah* 48b) preserves a *baraita* which states that the irresponsible priest was a Sadducee. (Cf. T. *Sukkah* 3:16 which has "Boethusian.") Büchler concludes that the procedure in M. *Sukkah* was intended to guard against the Sadducean practice of pouring the water on the ground in defiance of Pharisaic law. Similarly, the lot drawing ceremony in M. *Yoma*ʾ 4:1, in which the *segan* says to the High Priest, "Raise your right hand!" was intended to protect against the Sadducean practice of shifting the lot "for the Lord" to the right hand once it was drawn by the left. (The left was considered inauspicious as its use was common in chthonian rites. See Lieberman, *Hellenism*, pp. 166ff., especially n. 21.) Thus Aqiba is reported to have said that the Sadducees should not be permitted to rule in this matter (T. *Yoma*ʾ 3:2 and B. *Yoma*ʾ 40b). There are several problems with this interpretation. First of all, the Tosefta version of Aqiba's statement has *minim* and not *Ẓedukim* (Sadducees). The printed editions of the Talmud have *Ẓedukim* but this is a corruption. See Rabbinovicz, *Diqduqei Soferim* on B. *Yoma*ʾ 40b and cf. Lieberman, *Tosefta*ʾ *Ki-Feshutah* IV, 766. Second, assuming that both Josephus and the rabbis describe the same water libation incident, there still is no reference to the Pharisees or Sadducees in the former's account. It is not at all clear in *Ant.* XIII, 372 that it was the Pharisees who threw the citrons at Yannai. (Cf. Neusner, *Rabbinic Traditions* I, 137f.) Furthermore, if M. *Sukkah* is based upon a Pharisaic-Sadducean rivalry in the time of Yannai, why did it take the Pharisees until the 60's of the following century to implement similar safeguards with regard to the lot drawing ceremony? Finally, even if the testimony of Aqiba does refer to the anti-Sadducean nature of the lot drawing ceremony, it cannot be regarded as actual evidence. After all, his remarks could betray a Pharisaic *Tendenz*. For Büchler's views, see *Kohanim*, p. 83. On the water libation ceremony see A. Guttmann, *Rabbinic Judaism in the Making*, pp. 134 and 146f. Also, E. Schürer, *History* I (ed. Vermes-Millar), 223, n. 16.

Perhaps the most serious difficulty with Büchler's argument concerns the one *segan/strategos* whom we know served during the last decades before the Destruction, Eleazar son of Ananias. This priest was responsible for the cessation of the sacrifices of aliens (above, p. 82). Josephus does not say that Eleazar was a Pharisee. On the contrary, the historian informs his readers that the notable Pharisees (τοῖς τῶν Φαρισαίων γνωρίμοις) opposed Eleazar, insisting that the forefathers had not forbidden the offerings of foreigners (*War* II, 411f.). Even if Eleazar was a conservative Pharisee of the school of Shammai (Safrai suggests that he is to be identified with Eleazar ben Ḥananiah, a *tanna* of the school of Shammai. See Safrai, "The Temple," p. 876 and *idem*, "The Temple and the Divine Service," p. 300.) who was opposed by the more liberal sector of the party, it is unlikely that the Pharisees could have afforded such differences if in fact they were in the midst of a cultic revolution.

Despite these obvious difficulties, Büchler's theory has gained wide acceptance. Besides Safrai's articles, see H. Mantel, "The High Priesthood and the Sanhedrin in the Time of the Second Temple," *The World History of the Jewish People* VII, 273 and cf. Rhoads, *Israel in Revolution*, p. 100. Ḥananiah *Segan Ha-Kohanim*, who may also have served during the years before the Destruction, has also been considered a Pharisee. This matter will be dealt with shortly.

has observed that the supposition that the Pharisees ran the Temple is apparent throughout the sayings of Ḥananiah. It is at least possible that Ḥananiah, who may have served as *segan* in the 60's,[127] espoused a prevalent Pharisaic conception of his responsibilities. Ḥananiah could have adopted the position of the Pharisees[128] on this and other cultic matters despite the fact that it contradicted what he knew to be the actual practice of the Temple.[129] In any event, the notion that the *segan*, and not a specially designated priest (*kohen ʾaḥer*) should serve in place of the High Priest would only have developed towards the end of the Second Commonwealth.[130] There simply is no evidence that the role of substitute High Priest was considered one of the responsibilities of the *segan* before then.

Conclusion

Joseph ben Elim could not have substituted for Matthias ben Theophilus in the capacity of a *segan/strategos* in the year 4 B.C.E. At that time the duties of the *segan/strategos* certainly did not include filling in for the High Priest. Ben Elim must be considered a *kohen ʾaḥer*—a priest designated seven days before the Day of Atonement to serve in place of the High Priest in the event he is disqualified. Ben Elim was most likely chosen as Matthias' replacement because he happened to have been the closest relative of the High Priest participating in the Temple service during the week preceding the Day of Atonement of 4 B.C.E. There is no evidence that ben Elim was a regular official at the Temple.[131] His belief that he was entitled to continue as High Priest probably depended on the fact that he was related to the soon-to-be deposed Matthias. For Herod, however, the choosing of a High Priest was a political matter. The fact that ben Elim was related to Matthias certainly did not influence the king in his favor.[132] After ben Elim's

[127] Büchler, *Kohanim*, pp. 87f., claims that Ḥananiah could have become *segan* after Eleazar (above, p. 82) was appointed general over Idumea in 66. (see *War* II, 566 and cf. Smallwood, *The Jews Under Roman Rule*, p. 300, n. 25.) Büchler concedes though that Ḥananiah could just as well have served as *segan* before Eleazar. Neusner notes that Ḥananiah's sayings are found alongside of remarks by Aqiba, Ishmael, Dosa ben Harkinas and Aqaviah, suggesting that he was at Yavneh for a considerable time. Ḥananiah's sayings may also have been redacted there. See Neusner, *Rabbinic Traditions* I, 412. If Ḥananiah was at Yavneh throughout most of its existence as an academic center (ca. 70-125 C.E.), he could only have served at the Temple during the last decades before the Destruction.

[128] He could even have done so later, at Yavneh.

[129] So Neusner contends in his assessment of Ḥananiah. He also suggests that Ḥananiah could have been "a creature of the Pharisees" who in reality did not fill the position assigned to him. See Neusner, *Rabbinic Traditions* I, 412f.

[130] It would still only have been a *viewpoint* held by some and not, as Büchler would have it, a new policy concerning the role of the *segan*.

[131] It could be maintained that ben Elim was officiating during the week of the Day of Atonement as a member of a *mishmar* located at Sepphoris. The *mishmar* of *Yedaʿyah* does not, however, appear to have settled at Sepphoris during Temple times. See below, p. 93.

[132] If anything it worked against him. See above, p. 79.

brief stint as High Priest, he disappears from history. The fact that he substituted for the regular High Priest reveals nothing concerning the status of priests from Sepphoris in Jerusalem during Temple times. Joseph ben Elim received that honor because he happened to have been related to Matthias son of Theophilus and not by virtue of any special social, religious or political standing among the priests of Jerusalem.[133]

''*Ben Ḥamsan*''

Another Temple incident concerning a priest from Sepphoris is reported in rabbinic sources. It has been suggested that, like ben Elim, a Sepphorean known as ''ben Ḥamsan'' was somehow connected with a high priestly family.[134] A discussion of this possibility must, however, await an analysis of the sources. Tosefta *Sotah* 13:7 reads as follows:[135]

כל זמן שהיה שמעון קיים ברכה נכנסת בשתי הלחם ובלחם הפנים שתי הלחם מתחלקות בעצרת לכהנים ולחם הפנים ברגל לכל המשמרות לאנשי משמר[136] יש מהן שאוכלין ושובעין ויש מהן שאוכלין ומותירין ולא עלה ביד[137] כל אחד ואחד אלא כזית משמת שמעון הצדיק לא היתה ברכה נכנסת לא בשתי הלחם ולא בלחם הפנים[138] הצנועין מושכין ידיהם והגרגרנין חולקין ביניהן ולא עלה ביד כל אחד ואחד אלא כפול[139] מעשה בכהן אחד מצפורי[140] שנטל חלקו וחלק חבירו ואע"פ כן לא עלה בידו [אלא כפול][141] והיו קורין אותו בן החמסן[142] עד היום

[133] Cf. Freyne, *Galilee*, pp. 165 and 285, who suggests that Joseph ben Elim is an example of the ''priestly aristocratic landowners'' who resided in Sepphoris during Second Temple times. This suggestion, although possible, is not supported by the understanding of the sources proposed here.

[134] This theory is elaborated upon below, pp. 100ff.

[135] Ms. Vienna (ed. Lieberman).

[136] Ms. Erfurt reads: שתי הלחם מתחלק בעצרת ולחם הפנים מתחלק ברגל לכל משמרות.

[137] Ms. Erfurt has ולא היה מגיע.

[138] Ms. Erfurt has simply משמת שמעון הצדיק נסתלקה הברכה. Cf. the parallel in the Babylonian Talmud, below p. 96.

[139] Ms. Erfurt: ואין מגיע לכל אחד מהם אלא כפול.

[140] Ms. Erfurt: מעשה בצפורי. Cf. below, n. 180.

[141] Lieberman adds these words on the basis of Ms. Erfurt and the printed editions of the Tosefta. See his *Toseftaʾ Nashim*, p. 234.

[142] Ms. Erfurt and *editio princeps* have חמסן instead of החמסן. The definite form may be a corruption based on the appellation ''ben Ha-ʾAfun'' which appears in the Palestinian version of the *maʿaseh* (see below, p. 93). The indefinite form, ''ben Ḥamsan,'' will be used in the discussion here. It should be noted that the word ''ben'' is used in the various appellations discussed here to indicate that the person intended possessed a particular attribute. For this usage, see Kautzsch, E., ed., *Gesenius' Hebrew Grammar*, trans. A. E. Cowley (1910), p. 417. Cf. Büchler, *Kohanim*, p. 127, n. 16.

Lieberman, *Toseftaʾ Nashim*, p. 233, notes that Ms. Erfurt has a dot above the ס in חמסן and a צ in the margin. This gloss was probably introduced by someone familiar with the Babylonian parallel produced below, p. 96. The reading קמצן, which appears in ed. Zuckermandel (p. 319), is, according to Lieberman, a mistake. See his *Toseftaʾ Ki-Feshutah* VIII, 745, n. 29. Curiously, קמצן means ''miser,'' which would make sense in the present context. This term, however, seems to belong to later Hebrew usage. Still, the erroneous reading in ed. Zuckermandel is sometimes referred to for the origins of this usage. See, for example, E. Ben Yehuda, *Millon Ha-Lashon Ha-ʿIvrit*

For the entire time that Simeon the Righteous lived, a blessing settled upon the Two Loaves and on the Shewbread. The Two Loaves are divided on the ʿ*Azeret*[143] among the priests and the Shewbread (is divided) on a festival among all the priestly divisions (*mishmarot*).[144] There were those who would eat and be satisfied and those who would eat and leave (some) over. And each one received no more than the size of an olive. Since Simeon the Righteous died, a blessing has not settled upon the Two Loaves or on the Shewbread. The discreet (priests) would withdraw their hands, and the gluttonous (*gargeranin*) would divide (the breads) amongst themselves. And each one received no more than the size of a bean (*ke-pol*).[145] It happened that (*maʿaseh be*) a priest from Sepphoris took his share and that of his fellow priest. Nevertheless, he received no more than the size of a bean (*ke-pol*). And they called him "ben (Ha-) Ḥamsan" until today.

The latter part of Tosefta *Sotah* (chapters 10-15) contains traditions pertaining to the discontinuance of sundry miracles, practices and institutions. In chapter thirteen, the loss of some of these things is attributed to the deaths of various individuals. Thus it is stated (13:3) that *ruaḥ ha-qodesh* (prophetic inspiration) was discontinued following the deaths of the prophets, Ḥaggai, Zechariah and Malachi. The Tosefta reports, however, that the "*bat qol*" (heavenly echo) remained in effect.[146] Two instances of *bat qol* are presented. One announced at Yavneh that Hillel (ca. end of first century B.C.E.—beginning of first century C.E.) deserved to have been endowed with *ruaḥ ha-qodesh*. The other, which also occurred at Yavneh, announced that Samuel the Small (a Yavnean) should have also been a recipient of that form of prophecy. Samuel's dying words, which in fact are a vision of the impending doom of the Bar Kokhba period, are then reported.[147] This is followed by the statement that Judah ben Baba, a student of Samuel, deserved the same eulogy received by his teacher and by Hillel but "the hour was troubled."[148] The Tosefta returns to its theme with reports that Yoḥanan the High Priest and Simeon the Righteous[149] each heard messages while officiating in the Holy of Holies on the Day of Atonement.[150] According to

Ha-Yeshanah Ve-Ha-Ḥadashah VII (1960), 5999. It is likely, however, that קמצן was introduced into the passage because its root means "to grasp" and has cultic associations. See BDB, p. 888 and Jastrow, *Sefer Millim*, p. 1386.

143 The Feast of Weeks, or Pentecost, is intended here.

144 The phrase לאנשי משמר ("to the members of a *mishmar*") has not been translated here because it appears to be a scribal error. See Lieberman, *Tosefta*ʾ *Ki-Feshutah* VIII, 742.

145 Actually, a *pol* was a broad bean (*Vicia faba*) having large seeds. See J. Feliks, "Beans," in *Encyclopaedia Judaica* 4 (1972), col. 355.

146 On the *bat qol* see S. Lieberman, *Hellenism*, pp. 194ff.

147 T. *Sotah* 13:4. Samuel refers to the impending death by the sword of the scholars Simeon and Ishmael and their companions and to the despoilment of the people. Cf. Neusner, *Rabbinic Traditions* I, 239.

148 Cf. T. *Sotah* 13:3, 4. Both Hillel and Samuel were eulogized as "the humble and pious."

149 Simeon was also a High Priest. He has been identified as either Simeon I (ca. 300 B.C.E.) son of Onias I or Simeon II (ca. 200 B.C.E.) son of Onias II. See G. F. Moore, "Simeon the Righteous," *Jewish Studies in Memory of Israel Abrahams* (1927), pp. 348ff., A. Guttmann, *Rabbinic Judaism in the Making*, pp. 8ff. and Neusner, *Rabbinic Traditions* I, 58.

150 It is presumed that the messages were heard on the Day of Atonement since that was the only time the High Priest entered the Holy of Holies. Curiously, the messages are in Aramaic. See Neusner, *ibid.*, pp. 27f., 162 and 171f.

Neusner, these "heavenly-message" stories were compiled after the Bar Kokhba Revolt. Neusner notes the allusion of Samuel the Small to the disaster and the reference to the death of Judah ben Baba in "troubled" times and concludes that the latter's disciples produced the entire pericope at Usha, ca. 150.[151]

The message heard by Simeon the Righteous is followed by a listing of the miracles which were discontinued following his death. These are: (1) The westernmost light of the Temple *menorah* remained constantly lit. (2) The wood on the altar burned continuously. And (3) the Two Loaves and the Shewbread were blessed so that an olive's worth of the breads would satiate each priest. Neusner's assumption that this list cannot be any earlier than the preceding heavenly-message pericope seems reasonable.[152] It could, of course, be argued that a later redactor combined earlier traditions with the materials which emanated from Judah ben Baba's disciples. The emphasis, however, on Simeon's greatness and on the fame which accrued to him after his death is very much in keeping with the theme struck earlier concerning the eminence of Hillel, Samuel the Small, and Judah ben Baba. Indeed, it seems likely that Judah's circle, or some group shortly thereafter, was also responsible for the formulation of these Simeon traditions.[153]

The miracle pertaining to the Two Loaves and the Shewbread introduces an account concerning a priest from Sepphoris. The Two Loaves (*shetei ha-leḥem*) were two leavened loaves of wheat which were presented to the priests as a wave offering by those who worshipped at the Temple on Pentecost. The Shewbread (*leḥem ha-panim*) consisted of twelve cakes of unleavened flour which were set out each Sabbath upon a table standing before the Holy of Holies.[154] Both of these offerings were, according to our passage, endowed with a blessing during the time of Simeon the Righteous. The Tosefta explains: "The Two Loaves are divided on the *ʿAẓeret* (Pentecost) among the priests and the Shewbread (is divided) on a festival among all the priestly divisions." This statement emphasizes that the wonder occurred on the Pentecost and other festivals when the

---

[151] *Ibid.*, p. 239.

[152] *Ibid.*, pp. 27f. Neusner assigns the list to those pericopae lacking verification before 200 C.E. He uses the dates of "Mishnah-Tosefta" as his *terminus ante quem.* The *bat qol* narratives, however, are verified earlier at Usha. See Neusner, *Rabbinic Traditions* III, 186, 209 and 307f.

[153] Cf. previous note. Neusner, *Rabbinic Traditions* I, 57, notes that the rabbinic materials referring to Simeon do not concern legal matters. Neusner also asserts (p. 59) that the forms of these materials are late. He concludes that the stories concerning the life of Simeon were shaped in the second century and later. This would include Simeon's prophetic prediction of his death which appears following the *maʿaseh* concerning the priest from Sepphoris. (See T. *Sotah* 13:8. At this point, the Tosefta also notes that following Simeon's death his fellow priests no longer pronounced the ineffable name of God.) The argument made here is that the list of miracles emanates from the second century. Cf. the expanded list of the Palestinian Talmud which also appears in the context of second century discussions. See below, p. 94 and n. 176.

[154] On the Two Loaves see *Lev.* 23:17. For the Shewbread, see *Lev.* 24:5-9.

breads in question were to be distributed to a great number of priests.[155] The blessing ensured that despite the limited olive-size portion (*ke-zayit*) allotted to each priest, there were those who were satiated and still others who found less than a *ke-zayit* filling.[156] No matter how many priests came to Jerusalem on the Pentecost or festivals there would be enough leavened or unleavened bread to go around, and then some! The blessing, however, no longer settled upon the Two Loaves and Shewbread following the death of Simeon the Righteous. The discreet priests would "withdraw their hands" once they realized that the portions were limited. Their gluttonous colleagues, however, would divide the breads amongst themselves. Still, the blessing only applied to the olive-size portions and not to the smaller, bean-size amounts which the gluttonous group now obtained.

Unlike the other supernatural events connected with Simeon, a *maʿaseh* is provided to substantiate that this particular miracle had indeed been terminated. The incident pertaining to "ben Ḥamsan," who is reported to have been from Sepphoris, dramatizes the change effected after the death of the illustrious Simeon. The priest from Sepphoris did not wait for his gluttonous colleagues to divide the portions into equal bean-size shares. Instead, he took an extra portion, depriving a fellow priest of his share. Ben Ḥamsan was no ordinary *gargeran*. His excessive greed, however, did not pay, as he too only wound up with a bean-size portion.

This *maʿaseh* is not presented as a precedent for a *halakhic* ruling, but rather as a confirmation that the blessing had been removed from the Two Loaves and the Shewbread. As such, it may have been appended to the list of Simeon related miracles when the latter was composed in the mid to late second century.[157] The *tannaim* of the second century could have been referring to their own times when they noted that the greedy priest from Sepphoris was known as ben Ḥamsan "until today" (*ʿad ha-yom*).[158]

---

[155] Cf. T. *Sukkah* 4:20-21 (Ms. Vienna, ed. Lieberman):

שתי הלחם עבודתן ואכילתן בכל המשמרות מפני שהן באות חובות הרגל לחם הפנים עבודתו במשמר הקבוע ואכילתו בכל המשמרות

The preparation and eating of the Two Loaves is done by all of the *mishmarot* because they are an obligation of the festival. The *mishmar* on duty is responsible for the preparation of the Shewbread, but all the *mishmarot* eat of it.

[156] For this interpretation see Lieberman, *Toseftaʾ Ki-Feshutah* VIII, 743, especially n. 22.

[157] In his *Development of a Legend*, p. 198, Neusner explains that the phrase *maʿaseh be* is sometimes used as an editorial device for connecting a pre-existing story to the context. Cf. Neusner, *Purities* III, 196. It seems unlikely that the *maʿaseh* under discussion was appended after the second century by scribes familiar with the versions appearing in the *talmudim*. As will be shown, the talmudic versions presuppose the Tosefta's account and distort its intention. The *maʿaseh* and the list of miracles of the Tosefta seem original. The two circulated together and seperately in talmudic circles. See below, pp. 93ff. On the relationship of the Tosefta to the *talmudim* in general, see B. de Vries, "*Beʿayat Ha-Yaḥas bein Ha-Toseftaʾ U-Vein Ha-Talmudim*," *Tarbiz* 27 (1958), 148ff.

[158] See below, n. 167.

The sobriquet "ben Ḥamsan" emphasizes the folkloristic nature of the account. The person intended is not referred to by his real name. The word *ḥamsan* is obviously a reference to the priest's behavior. In the Bible, *ḥamas* means "violence."[159] It is used to refer to a lawless person, *ʾish ḥamas* (איש חמס),[160] or to a commodity such as wine (*yein ḥamasim*) gained by illegal means.[161] In rabbinic literature a "*ḥamsan*" is compared to a *gazlan* (גזלן), who is considered to be a worse character. Unlike the latter who does not reimburse the person from whom he steals, the *ḥamsan* at least offers to compensate his victim.[162] The *ḥamsan* obtains his goods by "snatching" or "stretching" out his hands.[163] Rav Huna (mid-fourth century Palestinian *amora*) explains that although the *ḥamsan* is willing to pay for the merchandise taken by force, his victim is not a willing partner in the transaction.[164] The *ḥamsan* is also described as one who snatches less than a *perutah*, an amount too insignificant to establish a liability for stealing.[165] Many of these elements are found in the *maʿaseh* under discussion. The priest from Sepphoris was greedy and took (perhaps by snatching) the portion of his fellow priest. The latter became an unwilling victim. The bean-size amount which the greedy priest ended up with was too little for him to fulfill the *mitzvah* of partaking of the breads (which required an olive's worth)[166] or for that matter to be liable for stealing. That which he does receive can certainly be compared to the wine obtained through lawlessness of which the Bible speaks. The characterization of the priest from Sepphoris as "ben Ḥamsan" is, therefore, a fitting description of his behavior.[167]

We are told virtually nothing concerning ben Ḥamsan other than that he was from Sepphoris and had a greedy manner.[168] No further biographical informa-

[159] See BDB, p. 329.

[160] Ps. 18:49. JPS (1972) translates "lawless man." Cf. II Samuel 22:49.

[161] Pr. 4:17.

[162] See B. *Babaʾ Qammaʾ* 62a. (In the name of the fourth century *amora*, Rav Ashi.)

[163] B. *Sanhedrin* 25b, and on 108a in the name of R. Yoḥanan (third century Palestinian *amora*). Also cf. B.*Qiddushin* 53a, presented below, p. 99.

[164] B. *Babaʾ Qammaʾ* 62a.

[165] P. *Babaʾ Meziaʾ* 4, 9c (In the name of the fourth Palestinian *amora*, R. Aḥa.) Cf. *Genesis Rab.* 31:5 and Lieberman, *Toseftaʾ Ki-Feshutah* VIII, 745.

[166] See Lieberman, *ibid.*, pp. 744f. It could be maintained that since the other greedy priests also did not receive more than bean-size portions they too should have been called *ḥamsanim*. After all, they could not fulfill the *mitzvah* either. Ben Ḥamsan, however, deserved his appellation because he received the bean-size amount *despite the fact* that he attempted to obtain more. The point is that ben Ḥamsan tried to obtain a fellow priest's share and still wound up with a negligible amount. The others did not engage in such *ḥamsan*-like behavior.

[167] Büchler has collected second and third century references to *ḥamsanim*. The rabbis of this period seem to have been especially concerned about the lawlessness of the *ḥamsanim*. Büchler's claim that the residents of Sepphoris in particular were distressed by the presence of *ḥamsanim* within their midst cannot be substantiated as it is based on general remarks made by Sepphorean rabbis. (Cf. above pp. 6f. on Büchler's methodology.) Büchler's evidence, however, does help to explain why ben Ḥamsan would be remembered "until today" by *tannaim* of the second century. See Büchler, *Political and Social Leaders*, pp. 43ff.

[168] The passage does not even say when the incident occurred. It could have happened on the Pentecost, on a festival which fell on a Sabbath (when the Shewbread would normally be eaten) or

tion is provided let alone any indication of his priestly origins. The reference, however, to *mishmarot* earlier in the narrative would seem to indicate that he was a member of a particular priestly division which was located at Sepphoris. Indeed, S. Lieberman has suggested that ben Ḥamsan belonged to the *mishmar* known as *Yedaʿyah* which is believed to have settled at Sepphoris.[169] Unfortunately, the passage does not connect ben Ḥamsan with any *mishmar*. *Yedaʿyah* is not explicitly mentioned, and it is not known whether that particular *mishmar* settled at Sepphoris as early as the Temple period.[170] Furthermore, the *maʿaseh*, as mentioned earlier, may have been appended to the list of supernatural events connected with Simeon. If so, the link between the elaborative statement mentioning the *mishmarot* and ben Ḥamsan would have been coincidental. Of course, the passage could have been edited during a later period when the *mishmar* of *Yedaʿyah* had settled at Sepphoris. The *mishmar* (if any) to which the legendary ben Ḥamsan belonged must, however, remain in doubt.

The ben Ḥamsan story is also reproduced in tractate *Yomaʾ* of the Palestinian Talmud.[171]

> כל ימים שהיה שמעון הצדיק קיים היתה ברכה משולחת בשתי הלחם ובלחם הפנים והיה נופל לכל אחד ואחד עד כזית ויש מהן שהיו אוכלין ושביעין ויש מהן שהיו אוכלין ומותירין משמת שמעון הצדיק ניטלה ברכה משתי הלחם ומלחם הפנים והיה נופל לכל אחד ואחד מהן עד כאפון הצנועים היו מושכין את ידיהן והגרגרנים היו פושטין את ידיהן מעשה בכהן אחד בציפורין שנטל חלקו וחלק חבירו והוא היה נקרא בן האפון עד היום הוא שדוד אמ׳ אלהי פלטיני מיד רשע מכף מעוול וחומץ

> All the days that Simeon the Righteous lived a blessing was sent onto the Two Loaves and the Shewbread, and to each one (priest) fell up to an olive's worth (*ʿad ke-zayit*). And there were those who used to eat and be satisfied and those who ate and left over. Since Simeon the Righteous died the blessing was removed from the Two Loaves and the Shewbread, and to each one would fall (only) up to (*ʿad*) the size of a chick-pea (*ke-ʾafun*).[172] The discreet (priests) would withdraw their hands, and the gluttonous ones would spread their hands. It happened that (*maʿaseh be*) one priest in (*sic*!) Sepphoris (*be-Ẓipporin*) took his share and that of his fellow priest, and he used to be called "ben Ha-ʾAfun" until today. It is what David said (Ps. 71:4): "My God, rescue me from the hand of the wicked, from the grasp of the unjust and the lawless (*ḥomeẓ*)."

---

on a Pentecost which fell on a Sabbath. (For the latter, see M. *Sukkah* 5:7.) On all of these occasions members from all of the *mishmarot* would presumably have been present at the Temple. Still, the intention of the Tosefta seems to be that both types of breads were involved, making the last possibility the most likely. Lieberman, *Toseftaʾ Ki-Feshutah* VIII, 742, notes that the miracle would not have been as great had it occurred on an occasion when only one *mishmar* was present.

[169] Lieberman, *ibid.*, p. 745.

[170] See below, pp. 128ff.

[171] P. *Yomaʾ* 6, 43c, Ms. Leiden. The passage is clearly a *baraita* as it repeats the tannaitic tradition. However, it is not introduced as a *baraita*. Cf. n. 101.

[172] On the chick-pea (*Cicer arietinum*) see J. Feliks, "Legumes" in *Encyclopaedia Judaica* 10 (1971), col. 1576.

As in the Tosefta, this version is part of a list of miracles which were discontinued with the death of Simeon the Righteous. Here, however, three additional miracles, all having to do with the Day of Atonement service, are included. The list follows a discussion concerning the dispatch of the scapegoat to the wilderness. Several questions are put to the second century *tanna*, Rabbi Eliezer ben Hyrcanus, who is reluctant to give definitive answers. The last question is what is to be done should the goat not die in its fall from the mountain.[173] The *ḥakhamim* reply that the messenger who accompanied the animal into the wilderness must descend the precipice and kill the goat. The Simeon related miracles are now introduced. The first of these continues the theme by declaring that in the days of Simeon the Righteous, the goat was killed by the time it fell halfway down the mountain. The other two Day of Atonement miracles also concern the scapegoat. They are: (1) The lot to determine which goat was to be dispatched to the wilderness always came up in the right hand.[174] And (2) the crimson thread tied to the door of the sanctuary would always turn white indicating that the goat had reached the wilderness.[175]

The list of miracles seems out of place in the present context. The discussion in the *gemara* began with the halakhic details concerning the scapegoat. To be sure, several of the miracles concern the goat, but the point of the list seems to be that miracles occurred during Simeon's high priesthood because he merited them. Unlike the context of the Tosefta which emphasizes the worthiness of prominent personalities, the *gemara* here makes no mention of other such persons.[176]

The extent of the miracle pertaining to the Two Loaves and the Shewbread is not elaborated upon. There is no explanatory statement like that found in the Tosefta stating that the miracle occurred on the Pentecost or other festivals when the breads were distributed to all of the *mishmarot.*[177] Without this information the magnitude of the miracle is unclear since it could be assumed that only the officiating *mishmar* (or, for that matter, a *bet ʾav*, a subdivision thereof) was entitled to the breads.

There are other differences with the Tosefta account. While the latter states that during the time of Simeon, each priest received an olive size portion (*ke-zayit*), this version has each priest acquiring "up to" (*ʿad*) a *ke-zayit*. Similarly, after Simeon's death the priests would receive only "up to" the size of a chick-

---

[173] The goat designated "for Azazel" was pushed over a precipice in the wilderness. The goat, which symbolically carried the sins of Israel, usually died instantly. See M. *Yomaʾ* 6:2-6.

[174] This was considered an auspicious sign. See n. 126.

[175] R. Ishmael reports in M. *Yomaʾ* 6:8 concerning this thread.

[176] Following the list is a *baraita* concerning miracles which occurred during the last forty years of the Temple. This in turn is followed by Simeon's prediction of his death but, unlike the report in the Tosefta (see n. 153), the focus here is upon the High Priest's appointment of a successor. R. Meir and R. Judah ben Ilai, both second century *tannaim*, comment on the succession story.

[177] See above, pp. 90f.

pea (*ʿad ke-ʾafun*).[178] In the Tosefta, the amount apportioned following Simeon's death was a bean's worth (*ke-pol*).[179] According to the Palestinian Talmud, the *maʿaseh* happened in Sepphoris itself (*be-Ẓipporin*).[180] Unlike the Tosefta version, this text does not state the amount of bread obtained by the greedy priest.[181] Thus there is no obvious connection between the *maʿaseh* and the previously reported loss of the blessing. The reason for the introduction of the *maʿaseh* is unclear. True, the account may indicate that after Simeon's death the priests had to resort to stealing from one another. The text, however, does not state this explicitly. None of the language of the preceding Simeon material is repeated. Indeed, one wonders if the *maʿaseh* really had anything to do with the Two Loaves and the Shewbread. Perhaps this really is a tradition concerning a priest from Sepphoris who was greedy concerning his priestly dues in Sepphoris itself.[182] In any case, the *maʿaseh* seems to be unrelated to the Simeon material, once again suggesting that it was appended to the list of miracles.[183]

The appellation, "ben Ha-ʾAfun" is derived from the fact that post-Simeon priests received up to a chick-pea's worth. The implication is that the greedy priest received that amount despite his efforts to obtain more, but this is nowhere stated. The term *Ha-ʾAfun* is not replete with the various meanings and nuances which connect the word *ḥamsan* with the *maʿaseh* in the Tosefta.[184] Perhaps the text originally read "ben Ḥamsan" but was changed to ben Ha-ʾAfun by an editor who sought to connect the *maʿaseh* with the preceding material which contains the word *ke-ʾafun*. The relevance of the proof text, Psalm 71:4, is not immediately clear. In a parallel to our passage in the Babylonian Talmud, the verse is produced in answer to a query by the fourth century *amoraʾ*, Rabbah bar bar Shela.[185] Apparently, the word *ḥomeẓ*

---

[178] See Lieberman, *Toseftaʾ Ki-Feshutah* VIII, 744.

[179] The *ʾafun* and the *pol* were distinctly different legumes. See Felik's description of both in "Legumes," cols. 1575-1576.

[180] Curiously, Ms. Erfurt of the Tosefta has a similar *maʿaseh be-Ẓippori.* While Lieberman (*Toseftaʾ Ki-Feshutah* VIII, 745) suggests that the Tosefta reading is an error for *be-Ẓipporai* (בציפוריי) meaning (it once happened) "to a Sepphorean," the fact that the Palestinian Talmud has a similar reading would suggest that this may not have been a mistake after all. It is at least possible that the *maʿaseh* may have been understood by some to refer to a priest in Sepphoris who was gluttonous with respect to his priestly dues. Cf. n. 212 below. The *maʿaseh* would only have referred to the breads after it was appended to the list of miracles. In the Tosefta, however, the connection between the *maʿaseh* and the list is clear. It should also be remembered that ב and מ may be interchangeable in post-biblical Hebrew. See above, p. 31, n. 106.

[181] As noted above (n. 141), Ms. Vienna of the Tosefta seems to be missing the amount, but Lieberman has corrected the text on the basis of Ms. Erfurt and other editions. It is clear that something is missing in Ms. Vienna. In any case, the Palestinian Talmud makes no reference to the amount received by the priest from Sepphoris.

[182] See n. 180 above.

[183] Cf. above, p. 91.

[184] Cf. above, p. 92.

[185] The passage is presented below, p. 96.

("lawless") is intended as a pun on biblical *ḥamiẓ* (חמיץ)[186] or, more probably on Aramaic *ḥimẓa*ᵓ (חמצא/חימצין) both of which mean "chick-pea."[187] However, the verse may just as well have been supplied by someone who confused *ḥamsan* (חמסן) of the Tosefta with *ḥamiẓ* or *ḥimẓa*.[188] Indeed, the word *ḥomeẓ* as used in Ps. 71:4 is similar in meaning to the form *ḥomes* (חומס, from the same root as חמסן) found elsewhere in the Bible.[189] Furthermore, the earlier reference to *ke-ᵓafun* (with the prefixed *ke*) betrays the confusion with the word *ke-pol* of the Tosefta. The entire text, therefore, appears to be a confused rewriting of the Tosefta tradition.

The story under discussion appears as part of a *baraita* in the Babylonian Talmud as follows:[190]

> ונשתלחה ברכה בעומר ובשתי הלחם ובלחם הפנים וכל כהן שמגיעו כזית יש אוכלו ושבע ויש אוכלו ומותיר מכאן ואילך נשתלחה מאירה בעומר ובשתי הלחם ובלחם הפנים וכל כהן מגיעו כפול[191] הצנועין מושכין את ידיהן והגרגרנין נוטלין ואוכלין ומעשה באחד שנטל חלקו וחלק חבירו והיו קורין אותו בן חמצן עד יום מותו אמר רבה בר (בר) שילא[192] מאי קרא אלהי פלטני מיד רשע מכף מעול וחומץ רבא אמר מהכא למדו היטב דרשו משפט אשרו חמוץ ואל תאשרו חומץ

> And a blessing was sent onto the ᶜ*omer*, the Two Loaves and the Shewbread. And each priest who received an olive's worth would eat and be satiated or eat and leave (some) over. From then on (after Simeon's death)[193] a curse was sent upon the ᶜ*omer*, the Two Loaves and the Shewbread and each priest would receive (an amount) the size of a bean (*ke-pol*). The discreet (priests) would withdraw their hands, and the gluttonous ones would take and eat.[194] And it happened that (*ma*ᶜ*aseh be*) one (priest) took his share and that of his fellow priest, and they used to call him ben-Ḥamẓan[195] until the day of his death (ᶜ*ad yom moto*). Rabbah bar bar Shela said, "What biblical verse (refers to this)? (Ps. 71:4): 'My God rescue me from the hand of the wicked, from the grasp of the unjust and the lawless (*ḥomeẓ*).' " Rava said, "From this (Isaiah 1:17): 'Learn to do good. Devote yourselves to justice; Aid the wronged.' Aid the wronged (*ḥamoẓ*) and do not aid the one who wrongs (*ḥomeẓ*)."

The elongated list of miracles which appears in the Palestinian Talmud is reproduced in the Babylonian *gemara* to Mishnah *Yoma*ᵓ 4:1. The discussion con-

---

[186] See Isaiah 30:24. The word *ḥamiẓ* in this verse is rendered by *JPS* as "salted." BDB, p. 330 has "seasoned." Feliks, however, explains that the word means chick-pea, and it was called *ḥamiẓ* because of the vinegary taste of its seeds and pod. See Feliks, "Legumes," col. 1576.

[187] See preceding note. Cf. Loew, *Die Flora der Juden* (1924-34) II, 431; J. Levy, *Wörterbuch*, s.v. חמצא and A. Kohut, ᶜ*Arukh Ha-Shalem* III, 431.

[188] ס and צ are sometimes confused in Palestinian Aramaic. See Dalman, *Grammatik*, p. 104.

[189] See Pr. 8:36. BDB (p. 329) translates חמס as "treat violently, wrong."

[190] B. *Yoma*ᵓ 39a-b, ed. Vilna.

[191] Ms. Munich and most of the Mss. have שמגיעו כפול instead of מגיע כפול. See Rabbinovicz, *Diqduqei Soferim* on this passage.

[192] Ms. Munich has רבה בר רב שילא instead of רבה בר בר שילא.

[193] That this refers to Simeon's death is understood from the context. See ensuing discussion.

[194] Or, according to most other Mss. (above n. 191), "Of those who received an amount the size of a bean, the discreet would withdraw ..."

[195] This variant form of ben Ḥamsan is discussed below, p. 98.

cerns the lottery procedure for determining which goat was to be sacrificed and which was to be sent to the wilderness. The list is introduced as a *baraita* (*teno rabbanan*) with the statement: "During the forty years in which Simeon the Righteous served ...". As the concern in the Palestinian *gemara* was the fate of the scapegoat, the first miracle mentioned there stated that during the days of Simeon the goat would be killed before its fall was completed. Here, however, the material preceding the list concerns the lottery. Thus the first miracle is that which states that during Simeon's lifetime the lot for the scapegoat always came up in the right hand.[196] The miracle concerning the fall of the scapegoat has been omitted, obviously because it did not serve as a relevant theme connector.[197] The list is otherwise similar to that of the Palestinian Talmud except that the order has been changed. Instead of confusing the items related to the scapegoat with those pertaining to the Temple, the Babylonian Talmud produces the former first.[198] It appears that the scapegoat elements were composed independently of those miracles pertaining to the Temple. The latter, it will be remembered, are presented alone in the Tosefta.[199]

The miracle pertaining to the Two Loaves and the Shewbread has been made even more comprehensive by the inclusion of the *ʿomer* which was offered on the sixteenth day of Nisan.[200] Here the miracle seems to be that each priest who received an olive's worth (*ke-zayit*) would have more than enough to satisfy him. After Simeon's death each priest would only receive the size of a bean (*ke-pol*).[201]

The *maʿaseh* does not indicate that the priest who took more than his share was from Sepphoris. His appellation, "ben Ḥamẓan," differs from the other names by which he is known in the parallels but is at least similar to "ben Ḥamsan" of the Tosefta. As in the Palestinian version, the relationship of the *maʿaseh* to the termination of the miracle is not clear. Here the gluttonous priest is said to be known by the name ben Ḥamẓan "until the day of his death" rather than "until

---

[196] Cf. above, p. 94.

[197] It was simply omitted from the beginning of the list.

[198] Cf. the Palestinian version discussed above, p. 94. For a comparison of the lists, see Neusner, *Rabbinic Traditions* I, 55f.

[199] Neusner (*ibid.*, p. 56) concludes that the list in T. *Sotah* 13:7 forms "a single, separate pericope."

As in the Tosefta, the Babylonian list is followed by Simeon's prophecy of his own death and the notice that after his demise the priests no longer pronounced the ineffable name of God. (See n. 153.) Finally, a statement similar to that of the Palestinian Talmud concerning the miracles which occurred during the last forty years of the Temple is produced. (See n. 176.)

[200] See Lev. 23:10-14. Apparently, the *ʿomer* was also distributed to all of the *mishmarot*. See Lieberman, *Toseftaʾ Ki-Feshutah* VIII, 743.

[201] Cf. the Tosefta version above, pp. 88f. The reading כל כהן שמגיעו כפול found in most of the Mss. (see n. 191) necessitates another explanation. According to Ritba, during the days of Simeon, the majority received a *ke-zayit* and found it to be more than enough. Those who received only a *ke-pol* still ate it and were satisfied. After Simeon's death some priests still received a *ke-zayit*. Of those, however, who obtained a *ke-pol* some would renounce their share by withdrawing, and others (the gluttonous ones) would attempt to obtain more. Apparently, a *ke-pol* was no longer satisfying. See Ritba on B. *Yomaʾ* 39a and cf. Rabbinovicz, *Diqduqei Soferim* on the same passage.

today'' as reported in the parallels. The Babylonian *amoraim* may have had little interest in the preservation of a local Palestinian legend. The fact that the event concerned a priest from Sepphoris who was remembered in Palestine ''to this day'' by a certain designation could have been irrelevant to them.

Ther verse included in the Palestinian text appears here in the name of the fourth century Babylonian *amora*, Rabbah bar bar Shela. Another proof-text, Isaiah 1:17, has been added in the name of Rava, a contemporary of Rabbah. Both verses indicate that ''ben Ḥamẓan'' (בן חמצן) was understood in the same sense as ben Ḥamsan (בן חמסן) in the Tosefta, i.e. a lawless person.[202] The verses were needed to explain the word *ḥamẓan* whose meaning was not obvious from the passage itself.[203] In fact, the root ḥ/m/ẓ usually means ''to sour''[204] so that the appellation warranted an explanation.

It is noteworthy that the Tosefta is the only version without proof texts. Had both the Palestinian and Babylonian *talmudim* read *ḥamsan* (חמסן), which was commonly understood as a lawless person, there would have been no need for the provision of the verses.[205] The confusing text of the Palestinian Talmud can hardly be considered reliable and, consequently, its reading, ben Ha-ʾAfun, must be rejected. Similarly, the Babylonian appellation, ben Ḥamẓan, is either a mistake for ben Ḥamsan of the Tosefta (ס and צ often interchange in Babylonian Aramaic)[206] or the result of confusion with the ''chick pea'' (*ḥamiẓ/ḥimẓaʾ*) tradition of the Palestinian Talmud.

The *maʿaseh* pertaining to ben Ḥamsan appears elsewhere in the Babylonian Talmud. It is not, however, reproduced as part of a list of miracles associated with Simeon the Righteous. Instead it appears in a context which confirms that at least in the Babylonian schools, it was an independent tradition. In B. *Qiddushin* (53a) there is a discussion of betrothal by means of the priestly portions. Rabbi Yoḥanan (third century Palestinian *amora*) maintains that the *tannaim* had decided that a priest could not use any of his priestly portions to betroth a woman. Rav (third century Babylonian *amora*) maintains, however, that the issue had never really been resolved. The subject was discussed anew in the time of the Babylonians Abaye and Rava (late third and early fourth centuries), the former supporting Rabbi Yoḥanan, and the latter, Rav. Rava

---

[202] R. Ḥananel on B. *Yomaʾ* 39a has: והיו קורין אותו חמסן.

[203] Cf. Loew, *Flora* II, 431 and S. Klein, ''*Ẓippori*,'' p. 76.

[204] BDB, p. 329. The usage of חומץ in Ps. 71:4 to mean ''lawless'' is difficult. See BDB, p. 330, where it is suggested that the root ח/מ/צ may have been confused with ח/מ/ס

[205] Actually, the verse provided by Rava (Isaiah 1:17) is missing in several Mss. (See Rabbinovicz, *Diqduqei Soferim* on B. *Yomaʾ* 39a.) According to Rashi (B. *Yomaʾ* 39b), the verse belongs in B. *Sanhedrin* 35a. (In B. *Qiddushin* 53a Rashi says the verse belongs in the discussion in B. *Babaʾ Qammaʾ* 46, but it does not appear there.) Interestingly, Rava provides a different interpretation in *Sanhedrin*. He uses the verse to indicate that a judge who postpones his verdict in a capital case is commendable. The interpretation attributed here to Rava is assigned to R. Ḥaninah in *Sanhedrin*. Ḥaninah understands the verse to mean that the plaintiff must be heard first.

[206] See J. N. Epstein, *Diqduq ʾAramit Bavlit*, p. 19.

attempts to use the *baraita* concerning the gluttonous priests to prove that Rav had been correct:[207]

אמר רבא וכרב מי לא תניא והתניא הצנועים מושכין את ידיהם והגרגרנים חולקים מאי חולקים חוטפים כדקתני סיפא מעשה באחד שחטף חלקו וחלק חברו והיו קוראין אותו בן חמצן עד יום מותו אמר רבה בר רב שילא מאי קראה אלהי פלטני מיד רשע מכף מעול וחומץ רבה אמר מהכא למדו היטב דרשו משפט אשרו חמוץ

> Rava said, "Has it not been taught (*tanya*ʾ) according to Rav? And it was taught (*ve-ha-tanya*ʾ): The discreet priests withdrew their hands, and the gluttonous ones divided." (No.) What is meant by "divided" (*ḥolekim*)?—"Snatched" (*ḥotefim*). As the last clause states: It happened that (*maʿaseh be*) one priest snatched (*ḥataf*) his portion and that of his fellow priest and they called him "ben Ḥamẓan" until the day of his death. Rabbah bar Rav Shela said, "What biblical verse (refers to this)? (Ps. 71:4): 'My God rescue me from the hand of the wicked, from the grasp of the unjust and the lawless.' " Rabbah (*sic*!)[208] said, "(Learn it) from the following (Isaiah 1:17): 'Learn to do good. Devote yourselves to justice; Aid the wronged.' "

Rava believed that the words, "the gluttonous ones divided" were proof that the priests had the right to apportion the shares amongst themselves. If the priests had the right to appropriate the shares, they obviously could do whatever they pleased with them, including betroth women. Thus Rav was correct; that is to say, the view that the priestly portions could not be used for betrothal continued to be disputed. The *gemara*, however, disproves this understanding. The *maʿaseh* at the end of the *baraita* indicates that the priests did not apportion their shares. On the contrary, just as ben Ḥamẓan snatched (*ḥataf*) his fellow priest's portion, so did his gluttonous colleagues. The word *ḥolekim* was to be understood as "snatched" (*ḥotefim*), not "divided." Thus the statement, "The discreet priests withdrew and the gluttonous ones divided," cannot be used as proof that the priests could betroth women with their portions.

The passage is interesting for several reasons. First of all, although cast in the form of a *baraita* with the introductory *tanya*ʾ (It was taught), the words, "The discreet ...," are quoted by Rava, a fourth century sage. The ben Ḥamsan incident which is used to discredit Rava's opinion must in its present form emanate from the same period.[209] The *maʿaseh* does not differ much from the version in B. *Yoma*ʾ except that it is not presented here as part of the Simeon the Righteous tradition. The usage of *ḥataf* (snatched) to describe ben Ḥamsan's misdeed is peculiar to this version and further illustrates that the *amoraim* understood *ḥamẓan* (חמצן) as a form of *ḥamsan* (חמסן) with its connotations of lawlessness.[210]

---

[207] What follows is from B. *Qiddushin* 53a, ed. Vilna.

[208] The text here has Rabbah (רבה) and not Rava as in B. *Yoma*ʾ 39b. Rabbah also appears in Ms. Munich on B. *Sanhedrin* 35a. It is possible that Rava was confused with Rabbah bar Rav Shela who also appears in the passage.

[209] According to Neusner (*Rabbinic Traditions* I, 31), the *maʿaseh* was also first appended to the Simeon material in B. *Yoma*ʾ 39a-b in the fourth century.

[210] Cf. above p. 92.

Thus it must be concluded that the Tosefta preserves the earliest (mid to late second century) and most reliable version of the *maʿaseh*. The Palestinian version has been shown to be a confused rewriting of the Tosefta tradition.[211] The *maʿaseh* was incorporated into the discussion in B. *Yomaʾ* 39a-b no earlier than the fourth century when the verses in the name of Rabbah bar bar Shela and Rava were added to explain the appellation "ben Ḥamẓan." The fact that the *maʿaseh* is used independently of the Simeon miracle list to settle a dispute between Abaye and Rava confirms that its meaning was discussed in the Babylonian schools in the late third-early fourth centuries.[212]

Ben Ḥamsan and the House of Phiabi

An ingenious attempt has been made to identify the legendary ben Ḥamsan as a member of the high priestly house of Phiabi.[213] J. Perles long ago noted that the Latin equivalent of *pol* is *faba* (bean).[214] The latter term is almost identical to the name Phiabi which appears in rabbinic literature as פאבי or פיאבי and in Josephus as φαβί.[215] Perles points to Tosefta *Kelim B.Q.* (1:6) which mentions a temple personality known as *baʿal ha-pol* (בעל הפול). This figure is reported to have been responsible for disciplining anybody who entered "between the porch and the altar" without washing his hands and feet. Simeon *Ha-Ẓanuaʿ*

---

[211] This version, however, may also emanate from the second century. See n. 176 where it is pointed out that R. Meir and R. Judah ben Ilai, two second century *tannaim*, comment on a Simeon tradition presented after the ben Ḥamsan *maʿaseh*. Note also the reference to R. Eliezer ben Hyrcanus earlier in the same narrative (above, p. 94).

[212] A further confirmation of this would be the discussion in B. *Ḥullin* 133a where the statement "The discreet withdrew their hands, and the gluttonous ones divided" is used by Abaye to explain his attitude towards acceptance of priestly dues. Abaye, who was a priest, explains that he originally snatched the priestly gifts (*mattanataʾ*) thinking that in so doing he expressed his love for the commandment to partake of the dues. When he heard the verse Deut. 18:3, which states that everyone offering a sacrifice "must give" certain parts of it to the priest, he decided it was improper to take the gifts himself. When Abaye heard that R. Meir interpreted the words, "they were bent on gain" (I Sam. 8:3) to mean that Samuel's sons *asked* for their portions, Abaye decided not even to request his dues. Finally, when he heard the words "the discreet withdrew their hands, and the gluttonous ones divided," Abaye decided never to accept the gifts except on the day preceding the Day of Atonement when he did so only to establish his priestly title. Although the *maʿaseh* concerning ben Ḥamsan is not repeated here, the fact that the words "the discreet withdrew ..." are used by Abaye to explain his attitude suggests that the incident was discussed in the fourth century. (In B. *Qiddushin* 53a, the *maʿaseh* was used to solve the dispute between Abaye and Rava, but it is not directly quoted by either sage. See above, pp. 99f.)

[213] At least three members of the house of Phiabi became High Priests. These were: (1) Jesus son of Phiabi who was appointed by Herod, (2) Ishmael son of Phiabi I, appointed by Valerius Gratus (15-26 C.E.), and (3) Ishmael son of Phiabi II, appointed by Agrippa II. See Stern, "Aspects," p. 607 and cf. Schürer, *Geschichte* II, 269, and 271f. It should be noted that it is not clear which Ishmael ben Phiabi is the one referred to in rabbinic sources.

[214] J. Perles, "*Baʿal Ha-Pol—Amtsnamen*," *MGWJ* 21 (1872), 256. Cf. Kohut, *ʿArukh Ha-Shalem* II, 148.

[215] For the rabbinic sources see S. Krauss, *Lehnwörter* II, 419. For Josephus, see *Ant.* XVIII, 34 and XX, 179. It should be noted that the name appears as Φιαβί, Φαβεῖ, Φαβί in the various Mss. of Josephus. See the critical apparatus in the Loeb Classical Library on the passages referred to.

("the Humble") was of the opinion that one was permitted to enter this sacred precinct without washing. R. Eliezer responded to Simeon as follows:[216]

העבודה אפילו כהן גדול פצעין את מוחו בגזירין מה תעשה שלא מצאך בעל הפול

By the worship! They would even split the head of a High Priest with clubs[217] (if he dared to enter the precinct without washing). What will you do to avoid the *ba^cal ha-pol* ("master of the bean")?

Perles further notes the similarity between this theme and a report concerning the house of Phiabi:[218]

אוי לי מבית ישמעאל בן פאבי אוי לי מאגרופן שהן כהנים גדולים ובניהם גבורים[219]
וחתניהם אמרכלין ועבדיהן חובטין את העם במקל

Woe to me because of the house of Ishmael ben Phiabi. Woe to me on account of their fists. For they are high priests, their sons are mighty ones, their sons-in-law are supervisors, and their servants beat the people with a staff.

The reference to the servants of the house of Phiabi beating the people certainly conjures up the notice in the Tosefta concerning the disciplinary action of the *baʿal ha-pol.*[220] The similarity of the terms "Phiabi" and *faba* would indeed seem to support Perles' view that *baʿal ha-pol* refers to Ishmael ben Phiabi. R. Margaliot has further noted the reference to *pol* in the Tosefta version of the ben Ḥamsan story and has suggested that here too is a reference to the Phiabi family. Margaliot contends that the confused titles, ben Ḥamẓan ("son of a chick-pea") and ben Ha-ʿAfun ("son of a bean") actually allude to the gluttonous founder of the House of Phiabi.[221]

Unfortunately, there are several difficulties with this theory. First of all, Margaliot assumes that all of the designations for ben Ḥamsan refer to the bean tradition. It has been shown, however, that the priest intended was probably called "ben Ḥamsan," an appellation which makes sense in the Tosefta without the chick-pea/bean overtones. Still, it could be maintained that the word *ḥamsan*, with its connotations of lawlessness, could also have been applied to the *baʿal ha-*

---

[216] Ed. Zuckermandel. Simeon *Ha-Ẓanuaʿ* seems to have been a priest who served at the Temple. See the entire passage in T. *Kelim.* If by R. Eliezer, Eliezer ben Hyrcanus (at Yavneh ca. 90-130 C.E.) is intended, then Simeon would have served towards the end of the Temple's existence.

[217] See Jastrow, *Sefer Millim*, p. 232, for this rendering of נזירין.

[218] B. *Pesaḥim* 57a, Ms. Munich. Cf. Perles, "*Baʿal Ha-Pol,*" p. 257. This passage is presented by Abba Saul ben Batnit (first century C.E.) in the name of Abba Joseph ben Ḥanan. For a discussion of this and other Ishmael ben Phiabi references, see Neusner, *Rabbinic Traditions* I, 397ff.

[219] Ed. Vilna has גיזברין ("treasurers"), but the reading presented here makes better sense in view of the context. Rabbinovicz does not record the reading גבורים in his *Diqduqei Soferim*, but it does appear in Codex Munich 95 (reprinted, 1971).

[220] Cf. Josephus' report (*Ant.* XX, 179-181) concerning the violence resorted to by members of the high priestly family of Phiabi against the lower priests and leaders in Jerusalem. Perles does not, however, use this source to support his view despite the fact that Ishmael ben Phiabi is explicitly mentioned.

[221] Margaliot, *Shemot Ve-Kinnuyim*, p. 45. Cf. Lieberman (*Toseftaʾ Ki-Feshutah* VIII, 745, n. 31) who contends that *baʿal ha-pol* may have been ben Ḥamsan but not Ishmael ben Phiabi.

pol who was said to have resorted to violence in order to protect the sanctity of the Temple. The word *ḥamsan*, however, does not have the more extreme sense of physical violence. Furthermore, the term *pol* may be derived from Greek *pyle* (πύλη) meaning "gate" and not from the Semitic word for bean. The *baᶜal ha-pol* would then refer to some type of guardian or inspector of the Temple gates.[222] Finally, an inscription from Tell el-Yehudeyeh (Leontopolis) bears the name Phiabi, strongly suggesting that the family name was Egyptian, and not Latin, in origin.[223]

Summary and Conclusion

The sources do not reveal much concerning ben Ḥamsan other than that he was a greedy priest from Sepphoris who lived during the Second Temple period. The ben Ḥamsan of rabbinic tradition is a legendary figure whose real identity cannot be established. It cannot be determined whether ben Ḥamsan was celebrating a festival in Jerusalem on his own or was a member of a particular *mishmar* emanating from Sepphoris.[224] Thus the *maᶜaseh* concerning ben Ḥamsan cannot be used to substantiate the presence of a *mishmar* at Sepphoris during the time of the Temple.

Nevertheless, the story is not without historical significance. It has been maintained that the *maᶜaseh* in its earliest form (Tosefta) dates from the latter half of the second century. The *maᶜaseh* pertaining to Joseph ben Elim, it will be remembered, was reported in the second century by Rabbi Yose.[225] The participation of priests from Sepphoris in the Temple service was evidently taken for granted in the second century. More significant perhaps is the way in which these priests were remembered. Both ben Ḥamsan and Joseph ben Elim are portrayed as aggressive, self-interested priests. Although the priests of Sepphoris who served at the Temple were remembered in the second century, they were not recalled favorably.

---

222 Kohut, *ᶜArukh Ha-Shalem* II, 148. A *yod* ending, however, would be expected to represent Greek η. Cf. Krauss, *Lehnwörter* I, 447.

223 See M. Stern, "The Reign of Herod," p. 274 and *idem*, "*Mediniyuto*," p. 246.

224 Cf. above, p. 93.

225 Klein ("*Ẓippori*," p. 55 and *ʾEreẓ Ha-Galil*, 71f.) also attributes the reporting of the ben Ḥamsan *maᶜaseh* to R. Yose. This, however, appears to be a mistake.

CHAPTER TWO

THE PRIESTS OF SEPPHORIS FOLLOWING THE DESTRUCTION

The following mishnaic report (M. *Taʿanit* 2:5) seems to indicate that priests resided in Sepphoris during the days of the *tanna* Rabbi Ḥalafta, who lived during the last half of the first and the beginning of the second centuries:[226]

מעשה בימי ר׳ חלפתה ובימי ר׳ חנניה בן תרדיון שעבר אחד לפני התיבה וגמר את כל הברכה וענו אחריו אמן[227] תקעו הכהנים תקעו מי שענה את אברהם בהר המוריה הוא יענה אתכם וישמע בקול צעקתכם היום הזה הריעו בני אהרון הריעו מי שענה את אבותיכם על ים סוף הוא יענה אתכם וישמע בקול צעקתכם היום הזה וכשבא דבר אצל חכמ׳ ואמרו לא היו נוהגים כן אלא בשערי מזרח

It happened (*maʿaseh be*) in the days of Rabbi Ḥalafta and in the days of Rabbi Ḥananiah[228] ben Teradyon that somebody went before the ark[229] and concluded the entire benediction. And they responded after him, "Amen."[230] "Sound (*tiqʿu*, the plain note), priests (*kohanim*), sound! May he who answered Abraham on Mt. Moriah answer you and hear the sound of your cry on this day." "Sound (*hariʿu*, the tremolo) sons of Aaron (*benei ʾaharon*), sound! May he who answered your fathers at the Sea of Reeds answer you and hear the sound of your cry this day." And when the matter came before the sages they said, "Such was the practice only at the Eastern Gates[231] (*shaʿarei mizraḥ*)."

The Mishnah in which this passage appears describes the fast day ritual instituted during periods of drought. If no rain had fallen by the first of Kislev, three fast days were observed. Were the drought to continue, three more fast days would be instituted. If rain still had not fallen by the end of the second set of

---

[226] Ḥalafta may also have been alive before the Destruction as he claims to remember Gamaliel the Elder (first half of first century). See T. *Shabbat* 13:2. He almost certainly lived into the second century as he appears in the company of Yoḥanan ben Nuri and Aqiba. See Hyman, *Toledot* II, 453 and A. Büchler, *ʿAm Ha-ʾAreẓ Ha-Galili*, trans. I. Eldad (1964), pp. 194f. It should be noted that Ḥalafta was the father of the Yose (ben Ḥalafta) so frequently mentioned in the studies presented here. The mishnaic text reproduced here is from Ms. Kaufmann A50.

[227] The printed editions have ולא ענו אחריו אמן. On this reading see below, n. 230.

[228] This name appears both as Ḥananiah and Ḥanina in rabbinic sources.

[229] The expression "went before the ark" (*ʿavar lifnei ha-tevah*) was used especially in reference to the recital of the *tefillah* by the public reader. See I. Elbogen, "Studies in Jewish Liturgy," reprinted in J. J. Petuchowski, *Contributions to the Scientific Study of Jewish Liturgy* (1970), pp. 39f.

[230] The printed editions have "they did *not* respond Amen after him," but this reading is not in agreement with Ms. Kaufmann or with the first edition published in Naples in 1492. According to Rabbenu Nissim and Ritba, this reading was introduced by Rashi. See the remarks of these commentators on B. *Taʿanit* 15b. Cf. Rabbinovicz, *Diqduqei Soferim* on the same passage. The Mishnah reproduced in the Palestinian Talmud (P. *Taʿanit* 2, 65a) also agrees with Ms. Kaufmann. See M. Schachter, *Ha-Mishnah Ba-Bavli U-Va-Yerushalmi: Hashvaʾat Nusḥaʾoteha* (1959), p. 110.

[231] The eastern gates of the Temple are meant. On these gates, see J. Morgenstern, "The Gates of Righteousness," *HUCA* 6 (1929), 1-37.

fast days, seven additional fast days were designated and on these the stores were closed and the *shofar* was sounded.[232] The material preceding our passage describes the procedure followed on these last seven days. The ark was brought into the city-square (*reḥovah shel-ʿir*)[233] where it was covered with wood-ashes. The *Nasi* and the *ʾav bet din* as well as all present would put ashes upon their heads. The eldest male present would then recite words of admonition. An elder[234] would be sent before the ark to pronounce twenty-four benedictions, the eighteen of the daily *tefillah* and six others to mark the fast. Each of the latter included biblical verses and an invocation of the God who had come to the aid of various figures (Abraham, the fathers at the Sea of Reeds, Joshua etc.) in the history of Israel. The *berakhah* formula (Blessed art thou ...) was then recited.

Although the passage does not indicate where the *maʿaseh* was supposed to have occurred, the parallels to the story note that Ḥalafta and Ḥananiah introduced fast day rituals in their respective hometowns of Sepphoris and Sikhnin.[235] In the case of Ḥalafta, the incident could have happened during the last years of the Temple. It seems more likely, however, that a post-Destruction date is intended since Ḥalafta probably did not become a mature scholar until well after 70.[236] Ḥananiah, furthermore, is reported to have suffered martyrdom during the Hadrianic persecution (ca. 135).[237] It seems reasonable to assume that the two scholars instituted similar ceremonies in response to the same drought and were remembered by later generations for their unusual practices. That the incident occurred sometime after the destruction of the Temple in 70 is further suggested by the comparison with the Temple ritual. Apparently, the rabbis attempted to introduce some aspect(s) of the Temple procedure into local fast day ceremonies, perhaps as a remembrance thereof.

The passage seems to indicate that following the conclusion of the benediction[238] and the audience's response of "Amen," the *shofar* was sounded by the

---

[232] M. *Taʿanit* 1:5-6. The Mishnah actually does not say that the *shofar* was sounded but rather "they sound the alarm" (*matriʿin*) which usually refers to the blowing of the *shofar*. In B. *Taʿanit* 14a the meaning of *matriʿin* is discussed, and it is concluded that it refers to the *shofar*. Also see S. B. Finesinger, "The *Shofar*," *HUCA* 8-9 (1931-32), 225f.

[233] According to S. Hoenig, the city-square preceded the synagogue as the Jewish place of worship. See S. Hoenig, "Historical Inquiries: I. Heber Ir II. City-Squares," *JQR* 48 (1957), 134ff. and *idem*, "The Ancient City-Square: The Forerunner of the Synagogue," *Aufstieg und Niedergang der römischen Welt*, pt. 2, vol. 19.1 (1979), 448-476. On the biblical *reḥov*, see Frick, *The City in Ancient Israel*, p. 84.

[234] It is not clear here whether the same person who recited the words of admonition is intended. In the Tosefta (*Taʿanit* 1:8-9), it is evident that the same person is intended. Cf. below, pp. 106f.

[235] The parallels to the Mishnah are presented below. According to Klein, Sikhnin is to be identified with Sogane. The latter, according to Josephus, was twenty furlongs from Gabara (Arabah). See *Life*, 265. Cf. S. Klein, "*Galiläa von der Makkabäerzeit bis* 67," in *Jüdische Studien Josef Wohlgemuth* (1928), pp. 70ff. Cf. *idem, Sefer Ha-Yishuv* I, 112. Romanoff, however, contests the view that Sikhnin and Sogane are the same. See his "Onomasticon," pp. 159-167.

[236] See n. 226.

[237] See B. *ʿAvodah Zarah* 17b.

[238] In the following discussion the word benediction will be used to refer to the individual prayers which composed the *tefillah*. The word "blessing" will refer only to the *berakhah* formula (Blessed art thou ...) with which each benediction concluded.

priests. If the references to *kohanim* and *benei ʾaharon* are accurate, there would be reason to believe that priests resided in Sepphoris and Sikhnin a short while after 70.[239] The reports discussed earlier dealt with individual priests from Sepphoris during Temple times. There is no reason to believe that these priests were connected with any larger group from Sepphoris.[240] The passage under discussion here, however, seems to represent the earliest reference to an *assemblage* of priests residing in Sepphoris.

Unfortunately, the passage leaves out important details such as who summoned the priests and recited the invocation ("May He who answered ..."). Most importantly, the mistake of Ḥalafta and Ḥananiah is not spelled out. Several possibilities exist. The sages may have taken exception to the manner in which the *shofar* was sounded, i.e. beginning with and emphasizing a different type of blast with each benediction. This elaborate system may have been reserved for the Temple Mount. The Mishnah, however, does not discuss the proper method of sounding the *shofar* in the material leading up to the *maʿaseh*. Thus there is no reason to assume that the mistake of the rabbis had anything to do with the soundings.[241] On the other hand, the Mishnah does discuss the invocations and clearly indicates that they were to be included *before* the conclusion of the benediction.[242] Consequently, the mistake of the rabbis may have been the pronouncement of the invocation *after* each benediction was completed. It is of course possible that Ḥalafta and Ḥananiah introduced *two* procedures which only applied to the Temple, the elaborate system of *shofar* soundings and the saying of the invocation *after* the *berakhah*. Again, the context suggests that the mistake of the rabbis was only the latter. The incorrect practice was formulated as a *maʿaseh* precisely in order to contrast it with the correct procedure described earlier in the Mishnah.[243] Presumably, the preceding material applied to areas outside of the Temple.[244] It is curious that the procedure followed at the Eastern Gates of the

---

[239] Klein uses the passage to document the presence of priests in both Sikhnin and Sepphoris after the Destruction. See his "*Galiläa*," p. 27; *ʾEreẓ Ha-Galil*, p. 57 and "*Baraitaʾ*," p. 8.

[240] See in particular the discussion concerning ben Ḥamsan above, pp. 92f.

[241] Cf., however, Maimonides (*Hilkhot Taʿaniyot* 4:14-17) who claims that the *ḥazoẓrot* (trumpets) were sounded after the recitation of the entire *tefillah* on fast days. In contrast, at the Temple both the *ḥazoẓrot* and the *shofar* were sounded after each of the additional benedictions. On this view see Rabbenu Nissim's comments on the Mishnah.

[242] The invocations are presented in M. *Taʿanit* 2:4.

[243] See p. 32, n. 116, where it is explained that a *maʿaseh* often presents a different understanding of a *halakhah*.

[244] As the usage of city-square (*rehovah shel ʿir*) would certainly suggest. See n. 233. It could be maintained, however, that the presence of the *Nasi* and *ʾav bet din* suggests that the city where the Sanhedrin was located, i.e. Jerusalem, was intended. On the contrary, the prominence of the *Nasi* in the ceremony suggests all the more that areas outside of Jerusalem were intended. In the later centuries after the Destruction we hear of several *Nesiʾim* participating in fast day ceremonies. The *Nesiʾim* in fact were responsible for declaring fast days. See L. I. Levine, "The Jewish Patriarch (Nasi) in Third Century Palestine," *Aufstieg und Niedergang der römischen Welt*, pt. 2, vol. 19.2 (1979), 663ff. and H. Mantel, *Studies in the History of the Sanhedrin* (1961), pp. 187f.

Temple is not expanded upon. Why the ordering of the invocation and the blessing are different at the Temple is not explained.

The account of the Tosefta may provide some insight into the perspective of the Mishnah:[245]

> עונין אמן על כל ברכה וברכה תוקעין ומריעין ותוקעין[246] כך היו נוהגין בגבולין במקדש מה הן או׳ ברוך ה׳ אלהי ישראל מן העולם ועד העולם ואין עונין אמן במקדש...
>
> על הראשונה הוא אומ׳ ברוך ה׳ אלהי ישראל מן העולם ועד העולם ברוך[247] גואל ישראל והן עונין אחריו ברוך שם כבוד מלכותו וגו[248] וחזן הכנסת או׳ להם תקעו הכהנים תקעו וחוזר ואו׳ להם מי שענה את אברהם בהר המוריה הוא יענה אתכם וישמע קול צעקתכם ביום הזה תוקעין ומריעין ותוקעין על השנייה הוא או׳ ברוך ה׳ אלהי ישראל מן העולם ועד העולם ברוך זוכר הנשכחות והן עונין אחריו ברוך שם כבוד מלכותו[249] וחזן הכנסת או׳ להן הריעו בני אהרון הריעו וחוזר ואו׳ להן מי שענה משה ואבותינו[250] על ים סוף הוא יענה אתכם וישמע קול צעקתכם ביום הזה תוקעין ומריעין[251] אחת תקיעה[252] ואחת הרעה[253] אחת תקיעה ואחת הרעה[254] עד שיגמור[255] את כולם וכך הנהיג ר׳ חלפתא בצפורי ור׳ חנניא[256] בן תרדיון בסיכני וכשבא דבר אצל חכמים אמרו לא היו נוהגין כן אלא בשערי מזרח[257] בלבד

They respond, "Amen" after each blessing (and) they sound the plain note, the tremolo and (again) the plain note. Such was the practice outside of the Temple (*bi-gevulin*).[258] What did they say at the Temple (*ba-miqdash*)?: Blessed is the Lord, God of Israel, for all eternity (Ps. 106:48). And they do not respond "Amen" in the Temple…

He (the elder) concludes the first (benediction) as follows: "Blessed is the Lord, God of Israel, for all eternity, Blessed is the Redeemer of Israel." And they respond to it: "Blessed be the name of the glory of His kingdom …" And the sexton (*ḥazan ha-keneset*) says to them: "Sound (*tiqʿu*, the plain note) priests, Sound!" And he (the

---

[245] T. *Taʿanit* 1:10-13, Ms. Vienna (ed. Lieberman).

[246] The words תוקעין ומריעין ותוקעין do not appear in Mss. Erfurt and London.

[247] ברוך is missing in Mss. Erfurt and London.

[248] Mss. Erfurt and London complete the sentence: לעולם ועד.

[249] Again Mss. Erfurt and London complete with לעולם ועד.

[250] Mss. Erfurt and London have אבותיכם. Cf. the version of the Mishnah.

[251] Mss. Erfurt and London and the first edition of the Tosefta read תוקעין ומריעין ותוקעין.

[252] Mss. Erfurt and London have the verbal form תקעו.

[253] Mss. Erfurt and London have the verbal form הריעו.

[254] Ms. Erfurt and the first edition omit the repeated phrase אחת...הרעה. Ms. London has the same readings as in nn. 252, 253.

[255] Mss. Erfurt and the first edition have גומר. Ms. London has גומרין evidently referring to the priests who did the sounding.

[256] Ms. London has חנינא.

[257] Ms. Erfurt has בשער המזרח.

[258] The term *gevulin* ("borders") is often rendered as outside of *Jerusalem*. See, for example, Kohut, *ʿArukh Ha-Shalem* II, 226. It is clear, however, that the term is used in contexts which contrast matters pertaining to the Temple itself with other areas of the country. Thus in P. *Ketubot* 2, 26d, the sacred things (*terumah* etc.) of the *gevul* are contrasted with the sacred things of the Altar. Of course, the practice of the Temple may very well have been the practice of Jerusalem. Thus Rashi on B. *Ketubot* 24b explains: בגבולין חוץ למקדש ולירושלים...

> elder) again says (*ḥozer ve-ʾomer*) to them, "May He who answered Abraham on Mt. Moriah answer you and hear the sound of your cry on this day." They sounded the plain note, the tremolo, and the plain note. On the second benediction he (the elder) says, "Blessed is the Lord, God of Israel, for all eternity, Blessed is He who remembers forgotten things." And they respond to it: "Blessed be the glory of His kingdom." And the sexton says to them: "Sound (*hariʿu*, the tremolo) sons of Aaron, Sound!" And he again says to them, "May He who answered Moses and our fathers at the Sea of Reeds answer you and hear the sound of your cry on this day." And they sounded the plain note and the tremolo (i.e.) first a plain note and then a tremolo, a plain note then a tremolo[259] until he completed all of them (the benedictions). Such was the procedure introduced by Rabbi Ḥalafta in Sepphoris and Rabbi Ḥananiah ben Teradion in Sikhnin. And when the matter came before the sages they said, "Such was the practice only at the Eastern Gates (*shaʿarei mizraḥ*)."

Two distinct ceremonies are described in the Tosefta, that of the areas outside of the Temple (*gevulin*) and that of the Temple itself. As in the Mishnah, the discussion in the Tosefta begins with the bringing of the ark into the city-square (*reḥovah shel-ʿir*). The Tosefta notes that after the ashes are placed on the ark, it is not to be left alone throughout the day. After an elaboration of the admonitions pronounced by the elder, the Tosefta states that he recites twenty four benedictions, the daily eighteen and six others specially included for the fast day. In an aside, it is noted that Symachus, a mid-second century *tanna*, disputes the substance of one of the closing blessings. The Tosefta then says that the additional benedictions were to be inserted between the sixth and seventh benedictions of the daily *tefillah*. At this point our passage is produced, the first statement of which indicates that the people were to respond "Amen" and the *shofar* was to be sounded, first with a plain note, followed by a tremolo and again a plain note. It should be noted that no indication is given as to who is responsible for the blowing of the *shofar*. The fast day procedure has now been outlined in its entirety and the Tosefta concludes, "Such was the practice outside of the Temple." The significance of the expression *reḥovah shel-ʿir* (city-square) now becomes apparent. Both the Mishnah and the Tosefta used the phrase in reference to the procedure which took place outside of the Temple Mount. The Tosefta specifically introduces the fast day ceremony of the Temple with the word *ba-miqdash*.

---

[259] According to the alternate reading of Mss. Erfurt and London (see n. 251) the order of the notes was not alternated after each benediction. This, of course, would not agree with the Mishnah. Lieberman, however, has noted that several commentators seem to have had the reading מריעין ותוקעין ומריעין. It is assumed in the forthcoming discussion that this was the intention of the Tosefta. The words immediately after this phrase, to wit אחת תקיעה ואחת הרעה seem to mean that the first benediction was followed by a plain note, a tremolo, and a plain note, the second by a tremolo, a plain note and a tremolo and so on. In the printed editions of B. *Taʿanit* 16b, a *baraita* is presented which also reverses the order of the soundings and uses the same language (תוקעין ומריעין ותוקעין) as the Tosefta. Maimonides (*Hilkhot Taʿanit* 4:16-17) seems to have had a similar text before him. Cf. H. Malter, *Massekhet Taʿanit min Talmud Bavli* (1930), p. 62. Also see the comments of Lieberman on our passage in *Toseftaʾ Moʿed*, p. 327 and *Toseftaʾ Ki-Feshutah* V, 1075.

How then did the procedure at the Eastern Gates of the Temple differ? The Tosefta explicitly notes two distinct differences. First, each of the additional blessings had to be preceded by the words, "Blessed is the Lord, God of Israel for all eternity."[260] Second, the appropriate response at the Temple was "Blessed be the name of the glory of His kingdom," and not "Amen." After providing biblical verses to indicate the proper response, the Tosefta outlines the complete Temple procedure using the first two fast day benedictions as examples. After the people respond "Blessed is the name ..." the sexton (*ḥazan ha-keneset*) summons the priests and repeats (*ḥozer ve-ʾomer*) the invocation, "May He who answered Abraham ..." which, as stated in the Mishnah,[261] was also recited earlier, before the conclusion of the benediction. Several medieval commentators suggest that the repetition of the invocation was necessary in order to separate the soundings of the *shofar* from the response, "Blessed is the name ..." The *shofar* had to be sounded in connection with the fast day prayer itself. If it was sounded immediately following "Blessed is the name ...," it would appear as though this *berakhah* was the reason for its use. In the *gevulin* where the people merely responded "Amen," the repetition of the invocation was unnecessary.[262]

The *shofar* was sounded after the reiteration of the invocation. As in the *maʿaseh* of the Mishnah, each benediction was followed by a different ordering of the notes.[263] Thus the sexton would address the priests differently depending upon which type of note was to be sounded first. Such at least was the procedure of the Temple.

The Tosefta closes its discussion of the fast day ritual with the comment concerning the incorrect procedure introduced by Ḥalafta and Ḥananiah. The reaction of the *ḥakhamim* to their actions is formulated in exactly the same language as that found in the Mishnah ("And when the matter came before the sages ..."). Here, however, a more detailed account of the fast day proceedings has been presented, and the material clearly differentiates between the Temple and the *gevulin*. The emphasis throughout has been upon the fact that Amen was not said in the Temple. The purpose in relating the particulars of the Temple ceremony was to illustrate how "Blessed is the name ..." was to be incorporated into the proceedings and to show the resulting liturgical changes. The soundings of the *shofar* seem to have been included merely to complete the picture.[264] True, the summary statement of the Tosefta concerning the practice in the *gevulin* ("They respond Amen ...") merely states that the plain note, the tremolo and (again)

---

[260] M. *Berakhot* 9:5 explains that when the *minim* began to claim that there was only one world it was ordained that the words "for all eternity" (see *Neh.* 9:5) should be added.

[261] M. *Taʿanit* 2:4.

[262] This interpretation follows that of Ritba and Rabbenu Nissim on B. *Taʿanit* 15a. Cf. also Lieberman, *Toseftaʾ Ki-Feshutah* V, 1074f.

[263] Following the understanding presented above, n. 259.

[264] Or perhaps to parallel the earlier description of the *gevulin* ceremony which, at least in Ms. Vienna (cf. above, n. 246), also includes a reference to the soundings.

the plain note were to be sounded. Since there is no indication that the order of the soundings was to be alternated after each benediction, the procedure of the *gevulin* may have been simpler in this respect also. Thus Ḥalafta and Ḥananiah could have also instituted the more elaborate method of the Temple for sounding the *shofar*.[265] When the context is taken into account, however, it is clear that the Tosefta stresses the difference which resulted from the saying of "Blessed is the name of the glory of His kingdom," i.e. the repetition of the invocation.[266] There is no reason to assume that Ḥalafta and Ḥananiah erred in any other way. In fact, they may even have known that Amen was the proper response but failed to understand that the invocation need not be repeated if "Blessed is the name ..." was not said.[267] In any case, the *shofar* soundings were certainly not the issue.

Thus the comment of the *ḥakhamim* referred to the repetition of the invocation. At least according to the Tosefta, Ḥalafta and Ḥananiah observed the proper procedure for the *gevulin* in all other respects. The elaborate picture painted by the Tosefta of the ceremony at the Eastern Gates could only have applied to the Temple Mount. The prominence of the priests, who are variously referred to as *kohanim* and *benei ʾaharon* (sons of Aaron) only underscores this point.[268] In contrast, the simple sketch of the *gevulin* ritual makes no reference to priests![269] The

---

[265] It is equally possible that the mistake of the rabbis was to sound the *shofar* after each benediction rather than after the recitation of all of them. (Cf. Maimonides, n. 241). This would not, however, change the force of the argument presented here.

[266] The Tosefta begins its discussion of the Temple proceedings with the words, "What did they say at the Temple?" (במקדש מה הן או'.). The use of the word "say" would seem to substantiate the emphasis on the different responses and not any difference in soundings.

[267] The Mishnah explicitly states that "Amen" was said in the procedure instituted by Ḥalafta and Ḥaninah. See above, p. 103. Hoenig has contended that the mistake of the rabbis was the saying of "Blessed is the name of the glory of His Kingdom" instead of "Amen." According to Hoenig, Ḥalafta and Ḥananiah attempted "to carry over Temple ritual into the newer milieu." Hoenig evidently assumed that the printed editions of the Mishnah, which state "they did *not* respond Amen after him" were correct (Cf. n. 230). See S. B. Hoenig, "The Suppositious Temple Synagogue," *JQR* 54 (1963), 127ff. Büchler contends that the rabbis erred "in more than one detail." He too has the reading, "they did not ..." See A. Büchler, *Types of Jewish-Palestinian Piety from 70 B.C.E. to 70 C.E.* (1922), pp. 222ff.

[268] According to Epstein, the words "Sound" (the plain note) priests (*kohanim*) sound!" and "Sound (the tremolo) sons of Aaron (*benei ʾaharon*) sound!" which also appear in the mishnaic version, belong to the First Mishnah (*mishnah riʾshonah*). Accordingly, a later *tanna* added these words from the older *mishnah* to the *maʿaseh* and closed the passage with the ruling of the *ḥakhamim*. See J. N. Epstein, *Mevoʾot Le-Sifrut Ha-Tannaʾim* (1957), pp. 45f.

[269] Epstein, in his analysis of the Mishnah (*ibid.*), concludes that "simple Israelites," not priests, sounded the *shofar* in the countryside. The reference to priests belonged to the earliest recension of the Mishnah, which described a Temple ceremony. Cf. J. Heineman, *Ha-Tefillah Bi-Tequfat Ha-Tannaʾim Ve-Ha-ʾAmoraʾim* (1966), p. 70f., who contends that the invocation formula was also recited by the priests at the Temple. If so, the entire fast day description would have been borrowed from the Temple proceedings. Green has recently suggested that before the Destruction the priests retained the right or "power" to bring rain. After 70, however, this power was transferred to the rabbis who taught that study of Torah could relieve a drought. See Green, "Palestinian Holy Men: Charismatic Leadership and Rabbinic Tradition," *Aufstieg und Niedergang der römischen Welt*, pt. 2, vol. 19.2 (1979), 640f.

Tosefta merely states: They respond, "Amen" after each blessing (and) they (?) sound the plain note, the tremolo and (again) the plain note. It is unclear who was responsible for the sounding of the *shofar* in the *gevulin.*[270] In all probability anybody could have sounded the instrument.[271] If in fact the rabbis only erred with respect to the repetition of the invocation, then it can be assumed that they followed the Tosefta's outline of the *gevulin* ritual in all other respects. Thus there is no way of determining who sounded the *shofarot* in Sepphoris and Sikhnin. Of course, there could have been priests living in these cities who took part in the ceremony.[272] However, the Tosefta and, for that matter, the Mishnah, cannot be considered conclusive evidence for the settlement of priests in Sepphoris and Sikhnin shortly after the destruction of the Temple.

The amoraic traditions must now be considered. B. *Taʿanit* 16b contains two *baraitot* each ending with the notice, "Such was the procedure introduced by Rabbi Ḥalafta in Sepphoris and Rabbi Ḥananiah in Sikhnin. And when the matter came before the sages, they said, 'Such was the practice only at the Eastern Gates and the Temple Mount.' " Unfortunately, both the printed editions and the manuscripts contain several different versions of the *baraitot*, none of which can be considered definitive.[273] It is apparent, though, that each *baraita*

---

[270] The omission of "they sound the plain note, the tremolo and the plain note" in some of the Mss. (above n. 246) only detracts slightly from the argument presented here. The description of the Temple procedure would still give a prominent role to the priests. In fact, the description brings to mind the water libation ceremony which was another Temple procedure in which the priests had a prominent role. See below, p. 114.

[271] According to Finesinger ("The Shofar," *passim*) the *ḥaẓoẓrah* (trumpet) and not the *shofar* was the preferred instrument of the priests during Temple times. After the Destruction, the popular will asserted itself, and the *shofar* became the exclusive instrument of worship. Finesinger traces the tension between the priestly use of the *ḥaẓoẓrot* and the preference of the people for the *shofar* back to biblical times. His theory would further support the view presented here that the *shofar* could have been sounded by anybody in the worship of the *gevulin*. For a different view, cf. below, nn. 272 and 297. Curiously, non-priests sound the *shofar* in the *War Scroll* (8:9,15). See Yadin, *Scroll of the War,* pp. 107ff.

[272] It should not be automatically assumed, however, that local priests would have been given priority when it came to the sounding of the *shofar*. In B. *Gittin* 59b a *tanna* of the school of R. Ishmael (early second century) reports that in sacred matters a *kohen* speaks first, recites the first blessing and receives first choice. (Cf. M. *Horayot* 3:8) Whether this applied to the sounding of the *shofar* is difficult to say. Furthermore, it is not known whether this view was prevalent in Ḥalafta's time. Still it is curious that the Babylonian *geonim* made a point of having the priests sound the *shofar* in fast day rituals. See B. M. Lewin, *ʾOẓar Ha-Geonim* (1928-62), *Taʿanit,* pp. 23ff. The *geonim* of the ninth-eleventh centuries (Sar Shalom, Sherira, Hai) may not have been familiar with the procedure of the Palestinian *gevulin* of earlier centuries. In any case, their testimony concerning their own practices has little bearing upon the procedure followed by Ḥalafta and Ḥaninah in the first century. Cf. n. 297. On the fast day liturgy outside Palestine during geonic times, see A. Marmorstein, "The Amidah of the Public Fast Days," reprinted in Petuchowski, *Contributions*, pp. 449-458.

[273] All of the printed editions and Mss. are seriously corrupt as shown in Malter's work, *Taʿanit,* pp. 61f. The printed editions actually have three *baraitot,* two of which seem to disagree over whether the *shofar* should be sounded after each benediction in the *gevulin* service. Mss. Oxford and London, however, have two *baraitot* which do not disagree in this regard. Because of the confusing versions available it has been decided not to present a text here but rather to draw some tentative conclusions based on Malter's assessment of the manuscript evidence.

contains a different tradition of the Temple proceedings. The mistake of Ḥalafta and Ḥananiah is dependent upon the perspective of the particular *baraita* to which its notice ("Such was the procedure...") is appended. According to the more consistent manuscripts,[274] the *baraitot* disagree as to whether the invocation was repeated or merely recited for the first time after the blessing. In either case, the mistake of the rabbis would have concerned the invocation. In the *gevulin*, the latter was said once, preceding the blessing. The rabbis either repeated the invocation or uttered it for the first time after the blessing, depending upon the *baraita* accepted.

At least one amoraic tradition indicates that the error of Ḥalafta and Ḥananiah had to do with the sounding of the *shofar*. The Babylonian Talmud preserves the following tradition in the tractate *Rosh Ha-Shanah*:[275]

> רב פפא בר שמואל סבר למיעבד עובדא כמתניתין אמר ליה רבא[276] לא אמרו אלא במקדש תניא נמי הכי במה דברים אמורים במקדש אבל בגבולין מקום שיש חצוצרות אין שופר מקום שיש שופר אין חצוצרות[277] וכן הנהיג רבי חלפתא בציפורי ורבי חנניא[278] בן תרדיון בסיכני וכשבא דבר אצל[279] חכמים אמרו לא היו נוהגין[280] כן אלא בשערי מזרח ובהר הבית בלבד אמר רבא ואיתימא רבי יהושע בן לוי מאי קראה דכתיב בחצוצרות וקול שופר הריעו לפני המלך ה׳ לפני המלך ה׳ הוא דבעינן חצוצרות וקול שופר אבל בעלמא לא

> Rav Papa bar Samuel sought to practice in accordance with our Mishnah. Rava said to him, "They (the *tannaim* of the Mishnah) only spoke in reference to the Temple." It has also been taught thus (*tanya᾽ nammi hakhi*):[281] When is this applicable? In the Temple (*ba-miqdash*), but outside of the Temple (*bi-gevulin*), wherever there are *ḥazoẓrot* there is no *shofar*; wherever there is a *shofar* there are no *ḥazoẓrot*. (And) such was the procedure introduced by Rabbi Ḥalafta in Sepphoris and Rabbi Ḥananiah ben Teradion in Sikhnin. And when the matter came before the sages[282] They said, "Such was the practice only at the Eastern Gates and the Temple Mount." Rava said, or, according to others, Rabbi Joshua ben Levi, "Which biblical verse (teaches this)? It is written (Ps. 98:6): 'With trumpets and the blast of a horn raise a shout before the Lord, the King.' We require *ḥazoẓrot* and the sound of a *shofar* 'before the Lord, the King' but in general not."

---

274 Mss. Oxford, London and the Margin of Munich 140, 141. See Malter, *ibid.*

275 B. *Rosh Ha-Shanah* 27a, ed. Vilna.

276 Ms. Munich has רבה but Rabbinovicz, *Diqduqei Soferim* (*Rosh Ha-Shanah* 27a) says that רבא is probably correct.

277 Ms. Munich has the opposite order: מקום שיש שופר אין חצוצרות מקום שיש חצוצרות אין שופר.

278 Ms. Munich reads חנינא.

279 Ms. Munich has וכשבאו לפני.

280 Mss. Munich, Oxford and London have עושין.

281 It is unlikely that Rava also reported the *baraita* which begins with the words *tanya᾽ nammi hakhi*. *Baraitot* beginning with these words are not usually part of the statement of the *amora* who has just spoken. See, however, Halivni, *Nashim*, p. 249 and *idem, Moᶜed*, p. 132, n. 3 for some exceptions to this rule.

282 Or according to Ms. Munich (n. 279): When they (the two rabbis) came before ...

This passage forms part of a discussion of the Mishnah describing the procedure for sounding the *shofar* and *ḥazoẓrot* on both, *Rosh Ha-Shanah* and fast days.[283] Since the *shofar* was to be emphasized on *Rosh Ha-Shanah*, those who sounded it stood in the middle, between the sounders of the *ḥazoẓrot*. On fast days both instruments were also used, but the *ḥazoẓrot* were given the central position. The Mishnah also describes the *shofar* itself. The *shofar* of *Rosh Ha-Shanah* was made from the horn of a wild goat and had a mouthpiece covered with gold. The *shofar* used on fast days was a ram's horn whose mouthpiece had been covered with silver. The ornate *shofarot* suggest that the Mishnah has in mind practices and procedures of the Temple. A *shofar* overlayed with gold or silver was most probably an instrument adapted for Temple ceremonies rather than one commonly used among the people.[284]

Rav Papa, a fourth century *amora*, intended to follow the directions of the Mishnah. It is not apparent when or, for that matter, what Papa wished to do. The reply of Rava, a contemporary of Papa, indicates that the *mishnah* only applied to the Temple. The *baraita* introduced by *tanya*ʾ *nammi hakhi* reveals that the use of *both* the *shofar* and the *ḥazoẓrot* was exclusively a Temple practice. Presumably, Papa wanted to use both instruments in Babylonia on *Rosh Ha-Shanah* and/or fast days.[285] The incident involving Ḥalafta and Ḥananiah is produced as a precedent indicating that the *ḥakhamim* had ruled that the Temple procedure was not to be emulated. The assumption is that Ḥalafta and Ḥananiah introduced the sounding of both, the *shofar* and *ḥazoẓrot*, in their respective cities.[286] The statement "Such was the procedure introduced by ...," is identical with that used in the Tosefta and in the *baraitot* of the Babylonian Talmud. The statement was incorporated into the present context no earlier than the fourth century, at which time it was interpreted as a reference to the incorrect usage of both types of instruments in the ritual outside of the Temple. The passage concludes with a proof text (Ps. 98:6) supplied by either Rava or Joshua ben Levi.[287]

Interestingly, a parallel discussion in the Palestinian Talmud[288] also concerns the carrying out of the requirements of the Mishnah. Rabbi Yose[289] wanted both

---

[283] M. *Rosh Ha-Shanah* 3:3-4.

[284] See Finesinger, "The Shofar," pp. 211f.

[285] It is not explicitly stated whether Papa wanted to follow the Mishnah in reference to a fast day or *Rosh Ha-Shanah*. The material preceding the passage discusses the composition of the *shofar* used on fast days. Thus the context, at least, suggests that Papa meant a fast day.

[286] Cf. Büchler, *Piety*, pp. 235f. It is not clear here whether Ḥalafta and Ḥananiah made their mistake on a fast day or on *Rosh Ha-Shanah*. See preceding note.

[287] Joshua ben Levi, who lived in the first half of the third century, could not have commented on Papa's practice. If he did provide the verse, he could only have done so in reference to Ḥalafta and Ḥananiah or, more probably, with regard to that part of the *baraita* which precedes the report concerning the rabbis. Cf. Alfasi on B. *Rosh Ha-Shanah* 27a. Alfasi omits the reference to Ḥalafta and Ḥananiah and has Joshua ben Levi comment on the earlier part of the *baraita*.

[288] P. *Rosh Ha-Shanah* 3, 58d.

[289] It is unclear which Yose is intended, but he must have been a contemporary of Joshua ben Levi as indicated by the account related here. Perhaps Yose ben Nehoraʾy is meant. On this person, see Albeck, *Mavo*ʾ *Le-Talmudim*, p. 168.

the *ḥaẓoẓrot* as well as the *shofarot* to be sounded in the presence of Joshua ben Levi on a fast day, but the latter refused to permit this practice because *ḥaẓoẓrot* were only to be used in the Temple.[290] Once again an *amora* was prevented from following the directions of the Mishnah because they were said to apply only to the Temple. Here, however, Yose is given no choice between the *ḥaẓoẓrot* and *shofarot*. Only the latter could be used. In contrast, the *baraita* quoted in the Babylonian episode permits Papa to implement whichever instrument he chooses as long as he refrains from using both. If Ḥalafta and Ḥananiah had really introduced the sounding of both instruments in Sepphoris and Sikhnin as contended in the *baraita*, it is strange that no mention of it is made in the Palestinian discussion. Yose could have been expected to refer to the procedure instituted by the two rabbis as a precedent for the use of both the *shofarot* and *ḥaẓoẓrot*. Or else, Joshua ben Levi could have noted the negative response of the *ḥakhamim* to the practice followed by Ḥalafta and Ḥananiah to support his view that only one type of instrument, the *shofar*, was to be used. Evidently, the Palestinian *amoraim* did not know of any unusual practice introduced by Ḥalafta and Ḥananiah regarding the use of the *shofar* or *ḥaẓoẓrah* on a fast day. Only in the Babylonian *gemara* is the statement, "Such was the procedure introduced by ...," understood as a reference to the copying of the Temple's procedure for sounding the instruments.[291]

Summary and Conclusion

The accounts appearing in Mishnah and Tosefta *Taᶜanit* strongly suggest that Ḥalafta and Ḥananiah incorrectly pronounced or repeated the invocation after the conclusion of each benediction. The discussion in the Babylonian *gemara* to *Taᶜanit* is confused, but it too seems to indicate that the invocation was the problem.[292] The Babylonian *gemara* to *Rosh Ha-Shanah*, however, clearly regards the sounding of *both* the *shofarot* and *ḥaẓoẓrot* as the issue. It could, of course, be argued that Ḥalafta and Ḥananiah copied the Temple ceremony in every respect. The appearance, however, of the statement, "Such was the procedure introduced by Rabbi Ḥalafta ...," in several different contexts, suggests that later generations did not fully comprehend the tradition concerning the two rab-

[290] This may have been the reason the verse was attributed to Joshua ben Levi in the Babylonian discussion. See n. 287. Cf. *Qorban Ha-ᶜEdah* on P. *Rosh Ha-Shanah* 3, 58d. Finesinger ("The Shofar," pp. 212f.) uses this passage as proof that the *shofar* supplanted the *ḥaẓoẓrot* after the Destruction.

[291] This, admittedly, is an argument from silence. Yose and Joshua ben Levi may not have been familiar with the tannaitic tradition concerning Ḥalafta and Ḥananiah. Even more likely, the reaction of the Palestinian *amoraim* to the tradition may not have been preserved in the Palestinian Talmud which has come down to us. Still, the view presented here is supported by the fact that the Mishnah and Tosefta do not seem to regard the error of Ḥalafta and Ḥananiah as having anything to do with the soundings or type of instruments used. Only the *baraita* preserved in the Babylonian schools claims otherwise.

[292] At least according to the better Mss. tradition. See above, n. 273.

bis. The statement, therefore, became associated with various practices believed to have been part of the Temple ceremony. At the root of the tradition was a report that Ḥalafta and Ḥananiah had each introduced practices reserved for the Temple into the local fast day ritual. What these practices were was unclear, so much so, that when the report reached Babylonia it was associated with a practice apparently unknown in the Palestinian tradition.[293]

The relevance of the entire tradition to our discussion of the priests of Sepphoris depends on who was supposed to have sounded the *shofarot* on the fast days observed in that city. It has been noted that the references to *kohanim* and *benei ʾaharon* seem more fitting in a description of the Temple ceremony than in a portrayal of a local ceremony. Not only does the Tosefta drop the designations from its outline of the countryside procedure, it also gives no indication that priests were responsible for the soundings outside of the Temple.[294] Elaborate ceremonies were, of course, commonplace at the Temple, in particular at the Eastern Gates where the annual water libation celebration known as *Simḥat Bet Ha-Shoʾevah* was held on the festival of Sukkot.[295] In fact, the *Simḥat Bet Ha-Shoʾevah* ceremony contains several elements of the fast day ritual. The Mishnah (*Sukkah* 5:4) states that two priests bearing trumpets (*ḥaẓoẓrot*) would stand at the gate leading from the Court of the Israelites into the Court of the Women and would proceed to sound a plain note, a tremolo and a plain note (תקעו, והריעו, ותקעו) at daybreak. They continued sounding these notes until they reached "the gate which leads out to the east" (לשער היוצא מזרח). When it is remembered that the purpose of the water libation ceremony was to induce rain, the similarities with the fast day ritual under discussion are even more striking. After all, Ḥalafta and Ḥananiah introduced the fast day ritual as a result of a drought. It seems likely then that the prominence given to the priests in the rabbinic descriptions of the fast day ritual must have also referred to the proceedings of the Temple.

There is no reason to assume that Ḥalafta and Ḥananiah deliberately attempted to copy the Temple ceremony in its entirety. The rabbis would have naturally turned to the tradition associated with the Temple in order to get an idea of the correct procedure. The later *tannaim* could hardly have blamed Ḥalafta and Ḥananiah for this. The sources, however, give no indication that these rabbis introduced a ceremony identical to that of the Temple in Sepphoris and Sikhnin. On the contrary, the rabbis are faulted for emulating the Temple ceremony in one particular matter. The rabbinic tradition does not impart a

---

[293] The Babylonian *geonim* Sherira and Hai also assume that the mistake concerned the sounding of the *shofar*. Precisely what they believe to have been the mistake of Ḥalafta and Ḥananiah is not clear from their responsa. See Lewin, *ʾOẓar Ha-Geonim*, p. 24 and cf. Lieberman, *Toseftaʾ Ki-Feshutah* V, 1074.

[294] Above, pp. 109f. and nn. 268, 269.

[295] For a discussion of the significance of this ceremony see R. Patai, "Control of Rain in Ancient Palestine," *HUCA* 14 (1939), 259 and *idem, Man and Temple* (1947), chap. 2.

unitary view of the rabbis' mistake, but the Palestinian traditions at least give the impression that the error was the copying of the Temple procedure for reciting the invocations. That Ḥalafta and Ḥananiah would have also introduced the soundings of the *shofar* cannot be doubted,[296] but that the horns were blown by priests (as in the Temple) should not be automatically assumed.

To be sure, local priests would certainly have been called upon to participate in the countryside ceremony.[297] The sources, however, cannot be regarded as evidence that such was the case in Sepphoris or Sikhnin. Even if priests did participate in these cities, there is no way of knowing whether they represented a significant settlement of priests or a particular *mishmar*. However, the fact that Sikhnin is not known to have been the location of a *mishmar* in later centuries suggests that the Ḥalafta-Ḥananiah tradition is inconsequential in terms of the later history of priests in that city and Sepphoris. In sum, the account of the fast day ritual introduced by Ḥalafta and Ḥananiah cannot be considered as evidence for the presence of priests in Sepphoris (or Sikhnin) in the post-Destruction period.

---

[296] The blasts of the *shofar* would almost certainly have been an intrinsic part of any rain inducing ceremony. See Patai, "Control," p. 274 and *idem, Man and Temple*, p. 35.

[297] Sherira and Hai certainly indicate that in their day priests participated. The responsa attributed to them (above, n. 293) specifically states, however, that this was "our custom" (מנהגנא דילנא). Nevertheless, Allon uses this responsa as proof that the priests blew the *shofar* in fast day ceremonies following the Destruction. He also notes that the *Targum Sheni* to Esther indicates that the priests blew the *shofar* on the fast day instituted by Esther and Mordecai. The *Targum*, however, is a late (perhaps eighth century) source. See Allon, *Meḥqarim* I, 108f.

CHAPTER THREE

THE PRIESTS OF THE THIRD AND FOURTH CENTURIES

The remaining reports of priests at Sepphoris reflect conditions which prevailed long after the first century. The following passage appears in the Palestinian Talmud:[298]

> מהו שיטמא כהן לכבוד הנשיא כד דמך ר׳ יודן נשיאה אכריז ר׳ ינאי ומר אין כהונה
> היום כד דמך ר׳ יודה[299] נשיאה בר בריה דר׳ יודה נשיאה[300] דחף ר׳ חייא בר אבא
> לר׳ זעירא[301] בכנישתא דגופנה דציפורין וסאביה[302] כד דמכת נהוראי[303] אחתיה דר׳
> יהודה נשיאה שלח ר׳ חנינא[304] בתר ר׳ מנא ולא סליק אמ׳ ליה אם בחייהן אין[305]
> מטמאין להן כל שכן[306] במיתתן אמ׳ ר׳ נסא במיתתן עשו אותן כמת מצוה

> Is it permissible for a priest to defile himself out of respect for (*mahu she-yitame᾿ kohen li-khevod*) the *Nasi* (patriarch)? When Rabbi Judah Nesiah died, Rabbi Yannai declared, "There is no priesthood (*kehunah*) today." When Rabbi Judah Nesiah the grandson of (the aforementioned) Rabbi Judah Nesiah died, Rabbi Ḥiyya bar Abba pushed Rabbi Zeira into[307] the Gofnah synagogue of Sepphoris and (consequently) rendered him unclean. When Nehora᾿y the sister of Rabbi Judah Nesiah died, Rabbi Ḥanina informed Rabbi Mana, but he did not come (to the funeral). He (Ḥanina) replied to him "If we do not defile ourselves (out of respect) for them (the *nesi᾿im*) in their lifetime, we certainly would not do so when they die." (Since we do in fact defile ourselves when they die, we may certainly honor the Nasi during his lifetime by attending the funeral of his sister, Nehora᾿y.)[308] Rabbi Nasa said, "(The only

---

[298] P. *Berakhot* 3, 6a, Ms. Leiden. A parallel *sugya* which includes this passage appears in P. *Nazir* 7, 56a. The *Nazir* text contains more difficulties. Some of these will appear in the notes below.

[299] A Genizah fragment containing this passage and Ms. Leiden on the *Nazir* parallel have יודן instead of יודה or יהודה throughout the text. See Ginzberg, *Seridei Ha-Yerushalmi* (1909), p. 32.

[300] From דמך until נשיאה appears in the margin in Ms. Leiden of the *Nazir* parallel.

[301] Ms. Leiden on *Nazir* has דחף ר׳ חייה לר׳ זעירה בר בה but this is definitely a mistake.

[302] Ms. Leiden on *Nazir* has ומסאביה.

[303] Ms. Leiden on *Nazir* has the name יהודיניי instead. According to Ginzberg, this is the correct reading since Nehora᾿y is a man's name. See L. Ginzberg, *Perushim Ve-Ḥiddushim Ba-Yerushalmi* (1941-61) II, 98.

[304] Ms. Leiden on *Nazir* has חנינה.

[305] The word אין appears above the line in Ms. Leiden.

[306] Ms. Leiden on *Nazir* has לא כל שכן which if understood as an interrogative would not change the interpretation presented here.

[307] The phrase דחף ב has been taken here to mean that Zeira was "pushed into" the Gofnah synagogue. The only other possible rendering would have Zeira "pushed *in*" the synagogue. This does not seem to have been the intention as both Ḥiyya and Zeira would have been automatically defiled by being in the synagogue when the pushing occurred. (According to biblical law, anyone in a tent having a corpse in it is rendered unclean. See *Numbers* 19:14. Cf. *Sifre Num.* 126.) The point of the passage, however, is that Ḥiyya forced Zeira to become *tame᾿*.

[308] This parenthetical note has been introduced here to explain Ḥanina's difficult statement. The latter was understood by *Penei Moshe* on P. *Berakhot* 3, 6a to mean that since one is not permitted to

reason we defile ourselves for the *nesiʾim*) when they die is because they are considered as an abandoned corpse'' (*met mizvah*, the burial of which is the responsibility of everyone, including priests).

According to biblical law, a priest could only participate in the funeral rites of a close blood relative.[309] The *gemara* from which our passage is excerpted discusses exceptions to this rule. Other individuals and circumstances are presented for whom or which a priest may deliberately become *tameʾ*. Each case is introduced with the words, ''Is it permissible for a priest to defile himself for ...'' (*mahu she-yitameʾ kohen le-...*).[310] Thus the entire *sugya* is formulated as a list. In each case, the reaction of a leading sage (or sages) in a particular circumstance is noted to indicate the *halakhah*. Almost all of these sages lived during the latter part of the third or fourth centuries.[311] While it is difficult to determine the particulars concerning the purported incidents, it can be regarded as certain that the list was formulated shortly after their occurrence since the Palestinian Talmud was edited by the beginning of the fifth century.[312]

That part of the list which is of interest here is the discussion of whether a priest is permitted to defile himself by participating in the funeral rites for a member of the patriarchal house. Three incidents are reported in chronological order. The first is the declaration of Yannai upon learning of the death of Judah Nesiah. According to I. Halevy and L. Ginzberg, Judah Nesiah is the grandson of the famous Judah Ha-Nasi who is credited with the compilation of the Mishnah.[313] Judah II Nesiah flourished in the first half of the third century and died ca. 260.[314] Rabbi Yannai's suspension of the *kehunah* upon the demise of Judah enabled any priest who wished to participate in the funeral of the patriarch to do so. Although it is not explicitly stated, the purported declaration of Yannai probably occurred in Sepphoris where the patriarchal house was located during much of the third (and fourth) centuries.[315] Accordingly, Yannai

---

defile oneself for a woman during her period of menstruation, that is while she is alive, a priest could certainly not become impure for a woman who has died: אם אין מטמא להן בחייהן בנדותן במיתתן לא כל שכן

This explanation seems forced since the reference to menstrual impurity would have to be read into the passage. The statement of Ḥanina is better understood if the words חייהן and מיתתן are taken as referring to the *Nesiʾim*. For the interpretation presented here, see below, pp. 119f.

309 See *Lev*. 21:1-6.

310 See P. *Berakhot* 3, 6a and P. *Nazir* 7, 56a.

311 The appearance of Yannai in our text would be an exception as he lived in the first half of the third century. It is clear, however, that the present text was formed after the other cases involving the patriarchal descendants occurred.

312 See above, p. 4, n. 21.

313 See I. Halevy, *Dorot Ha-Riʾshonim* V (1901), 28f. and L. Ginzberg, *Perushim Ve-Ḥiddushim* II, 95. Halevy takes Frankel to task for contending that Judah Ha-Nasi is meant. See Z. Frankel, *Mevoʾ Ha-Yerushalmi* (1870), p. 93b. Ginzberg is less adamant and concedes that the chronology in the text is difficult.

314 On the chronology of the patriarchal house, see Levine, ''The Jewish Patriarch,'' pp. 685ff. In the present discussion, members of the patriarchal house will be enumerated from R. Judah (I) Ha-Nasi on.

would have been directing his remarks at his fellow priests of Sepphoris who were anxious to participate in the funeral of the patriarch.[316]

At least one priest who attended a funeral of a patriarch at Sepphoris had second thoughts about defiling himself. When Judah III Nesiah, the grandson of Judah II Nesiah, died ca. 305, Rabbi Zeira had to be forced into participating in the funeral. His priestly colleague, Rabbi Ḥiyya bar Abba, who elsewhere is reported to have defiled himself in order to get a view of the Emperor Diocletian,[317] shoved him into the Gofnah synagogue where the corpse of the patriarch had evidently been brought.

The reference to Gofnah, a city of northern Judea during the Second Temple period, is particularly interesting. That there should be a synagogue of "foreigners" at Sepphoris is not in itself unusual. The "Babylonians" were also reported to have established their own place of worship at Sepphoris.[318] As Büchler has noted, what is remarkable is the fact that the incident is supposed to have occurred at this particular synagogue.[319] According to Josephus, Vespasian had settled priests who deserted the rebels of Jerusalem in Gofnah.[320] Both the Palestinian and Babylonian Talmudim preserve traditions regarding the settlement of large numbers of priests at Gofnah.[321] Coffins from the first and second centuries which have been found at Gofnah contain the following Aramaic and Greek inscriptions:[322] (1) יהודה בר אלעזר /Judah bar Eleazar (2)

[315] According to Halevy (*Dorot* V, 74f.), the patriarchal house remained in Sepphoris even after Tiberias became the major academic center in the days of R. Yoḥanan (mid-third century). Cf. Hyman, *Toledot* II, 611 and 614f. If Judah Ha-Nasi was intended here (see n. 313), the incident would almost certainly have occurred in Sepphoris as that patriarch is reported to have lived the last years of his life in the city. See above, p. 4, n. 20.

[316] Priests from outside of Sepphoris would no doubt have also been included among those participating in the funeral of the *Nasi*. However, for the most part, Yannai's pronouncement would have been directed at those priests residing in Sepphoris itself. If the issue of becoming *tame'* for the sake of the *Nasi* was as controversial as the source under discussion suggests, priests were unlikely to have come from very far away to pay their respects.

It should be noted that Yannai was probably a priest himself. See P. *Taʿanit* 4, 68a. According to Halevy (*Dorot*, V, 275f.), Yannai may have been at Sepphoris at one time or another but was a resident of Acbara.

[317] That Zeira was a priest is obvious from the context. As for Ḥiyya, it is related in the *gemara* preceding the text under discussion that he became unclean by stepping over graves in order to see the Emperor Diocletian. The incident was produced to illustrate that a priest could become unclean for the sake of a king. Interestingly, Ḥiyya bar Abba is found in the company of two other priests of Galilee, Ammi (Immi) Ha-Kohen and Assi, who are referred to in the Babylonian Talmud (*Megillah* 22a) as "the well known priests of the land of Israel" (כהני חישבי דארעא ישראל.). These two priests were apparently members of the academy of Tiberias. See Albeck, *Mavo La-Talmudim*, pp. 227ff. Ammi, Assi and Ḥiyya were said to have been sent by Judah III Nesiah to the towns and villages to inspect their educational systems. See P. *Ḥagigah* 1, 76c.

[318] P. *Shabbat* 6, 8a; *Genesis Rab.* 33:3 *et al.* See Klein, "*Ẓippori*," p. 50.

[319] Büchler, *Kohanim*, pp. 36f.

[320] *War* VI, 114-115.

[321] P. *Taʿanit* 4, 69a and B. *Berakhot* 44a.

[322] See S. Klein, *Jüdisch-palästinische Corpus Inscriptionum* (1920), pp. 53f. Cf. B. Z. Lurie, "*ʿArei Ha-Kohanim*," p. 11.

Σαλωμη Ιαχειμου/Salome (daughter of) Yakeim. As B. Z. Lurie has noted, Eleazar and Salome are names commonly found in priestly families.[323] "Yakeim" or "Yakim" is a designation of one of the *mishmarot*. Finally, the name "Bilgah" (בלגה) is inscribed on the wall of one of the Gofnah burial caves.[324] Bilgah, like Yakim, is a designation of a *mishmar*. It has been suggested that the Gofnah synagogue at Sepphoris was established by emigrants from the Judean city.[325] That the synagogue was frequented exclusively by priests cannot be proven.[326] However, in view of the fact that Gofnah was a prominent priestly residence, it can be safely assumed that the group of emigrants which eventually settled at Sepphoris included a number of priests. That the incident concerning the two priests, Zeira and Ḥiyya, occurred at the Gofnah synagogue is, to say the least, curious. Was this assemblage perceived as a special priestly gathering in honor of the late patriarch? That priests of several different *mishmarot* appear to have settled at Gofnah is also of interest. The *mishmar* usually associated with Sepphoris is *Yedaʿyah*.[327] If indeed priests of Gofnah did settle at Sepphoris, they may have represented *mishmarot* other than *Yedaʿyah*. Although the evidence is by no means conclusive, it can be suggested that priestly families did not necessarily settle wherever the *mishmarot* to which they belonged decided as a whole to establish residence. Other factors, such as a particular family's lay associations may have been influential. Thus priestly families belonging to *mishmarot* other than *Yedaʿyah* may have also settled at Sepphoris.

One other incident concerning the patriarchal house is reported. When Nehoraʾy, the otherwise unknown sister of the patriarch Judah Nesiah, died, Rabbi Ḥanina informed Rabbi Mana. The latter's refusal to attend the funeral suggests that a priest (which Mana evidently was)[328] need not defile himself out of respect for the reigning *Nasi*. Ḥanina and Mana, both rabbis of the late fourth century, are frequently found to disagree in the Palestinian Talmud. Nehoraʾy must have been the sister of Judah IV Nesiah who seems to have been *Nasi* during the time of Ḥanina and Mana. Little is known concerning Judah IV Nesiah and it cannot be established with certainty that he (or his sister) lived in

---

323 Lurie, *ibid.* Cf. Klein (*Corpus*, p. 54), who equates Salome with שלמציון.

324 Lurie, "*ʿArei Ha-Kohanim*," p. 11.

325 Büchler, *Kohanim*, p. 36.

326 Cf. B. *Sotah* 38b which speaks of a synagogue attended only by priests. This could, however, have been a hypothetical situation.

327 See above, p. 62. The rabbinic reports concerning *Yedaʿyah* and Sepphoris are discussed below, pp. 120ff.

328 According to Frankel, this R. Mana was Mana II the son of R. Yonah. Hyman, however, contends that Yonah was not a priest so that Mana II cannot have been intended. See Frankel, *Mevoʾ Ha-Yerushalmi*, p. 115a and Hyman, *Toledot* II, 614. Perhaps the source Hyman uses to show that Yonah was not a priest (P. *Maʿaser Sheni* 5, 56b) refers to a different Yonah. Or else, another Mana may indeed have been intended. See Hyman, III, 885. Curiously, R. Mani (Mana) the son of R. Yonah is said to have once been annoyed by the patriarchal house. See B. *Taʿanit* 23b. It would be no surprise if this figure and the R. Mana who refused to come to Nehoraʾy's funeral were one and the same!

Sepphoris.[329] Ḥanina, however, was the head of the academy at Sepphoris until he abdicated in favor of his colleague, Mana.[330] In the present context Ḥanina insists that a priest should defile himself for Nehoraʾy because she is the sister of the *Nasi*. Since a priest could defile himself for a *Nasi* who has passed away, he certainly should do so out of respect for the patriarch while he lives.[331] Rabbi Nasa, a contemporary of Ḥanina and Mana, disagrees and explains that it is incumbent upon a priest to defile himself *only* for a patriarch who has died since he is considered a *met mizvah* for whom all had to show their respect. Apparently, the defilement of a priest for the sake of a *Nasi* was a real issue the details of which remained undecided at the end of the fourth century. The issue, however, seems to have been of more than passing academic interest. The involvement of rabbis from Sepphoris in the discussion could have been the result of the city's association with the patriarchal house. The presence of a considerable number of priests in Sepphoris during the third and fourth centuries must, however, have also contributed to the interest in the problem.[332]

Yedaʿyah and Sepphoris

Still another report concerning the patriarchal house mentions priests living in Sepphoris. These priests, however, are specifically referred to as members of the *mishmar* of *Yedaʿyah. Qohelet* (Ecclesiastes) *Rabbah* relates the following:[333]

---

[329] Although, it is at least possible despite the upheavals in Galilee which involved Sepphoris in 351 C.E. After all, the other likely home of the patriarchate, Tiberias, was also involved in the turmoil of the time. Not much is known about Judah IV perhaps because of the general decline in the importance of the patriarchate during his lifetime. On this decline, see Avi-Yonah, *The Jews of Palestine*, pp. 225ff. According to Hyman (*Toledot* II, 615), Judah IV (III) was a resident of Caesarea. Hyman, however, assumes that the incident involved Judah III (II), who he claims lived in Sepphoris.

[330] Hyman, *Toledot* III, 886.

[331] Following the interpretation of Ginzberg, *Perushim Ve-Ḥiddushim* II, 98f. and Rabinovitz, *Shaʿarei Torat ʾEreẓ Yisrael*, p. 9. Weiss assumes that the patriarch was no longer alive when Nehoraʾy died. See I. H. Weiss, *Dor, Dor Ve-Dorshav* (1904) III, 102.

[332] The priests who honored Nehoraʾy by participating in her funeral probably were local residents since it is unlikely that they would have come from all over to pay respect to the Nasi's sister. Cf., however, Weiss (*ibid.*) who claims that Mana was in Tiberias when Ḥanina contacted him.

Another passage which appears in the *sugya* under discussion may also be relevant. It is related that R. Ḥezekiah, R. Kohen and R. Jacob bar Aḥa were walking along a street in Sepphoris and came to a cemetery arch (*kippah*). At this point, R. Kohen (obviously a priest) separated himself from his fellow scholars in order to avoid becoming unclean. The parallel in P. *Nazir* 7, 56a, however, has the "street of Caesarea" (בפלטיא דקיסרין) instead of "street of Sepphoris" (פלטיותא דצפורי.). Curiously in the Ms. Leiden text of *Nazir* the words בפלטיא דקיסרין appear almost directly under the words כיפתא דקיסרין which is part of a previous passage. This suggests the possibility of a scribal error. On the other hand, the fact that R. Ḥezekiah and R. Jacob bar Aḥa are mentioned would point to a Caesarean location for the episode. On the rabbis of Caesarea see S. Lieberman, "*Talmudah Shel-Kisrin*," Supplement to *Tarbiz* 2 (1931), p. 10 and cf. Levine, *Caesarea Under Roman Rule*, pp. 92 and 217, n. 361. Because the relevance of this passage for our discussion cannot be determined, it has not been discussed here. See, however, M. Hacohen, "*Ẓippori-Qeisaryah*," in *idem*, *ʾIshim U-Tequfot* (1977), p. 114.

[333] *Qohelet Rab.* to *Ecc.* 7:12, ed. Vilna. A parallel appears in 9:10 but it is obvious that the passage was reintroduced there because it mentions R. Judah Ha-Nasi.

ר׳ הוה דמיך בציפורין ואמרין ציפוראי כל דאתא ואמר דמך ר׳ אנן קטלין ליה אזל בר קפרא ועלל בכוותא ואדיק ליה ורישיה מיכרך ומניה בזיעין אמר אחינו בני ידעיה שמעוני שמעוני אראלים ומצוקים אחזו ידן בלוחות הברית גברה ידן של אראלים וחטפו את הלוחות אמרין ליה דמך רבי ואמר להו אתן אמריתון אנא לא אמינא ולמה לא אמר דכתיב ומוציא דבה הוא כסיל קרעון מניהון עד דאזל קליה דקריעה עד גופפתה מהלך שלשה מילין וקרא עליה ויתרון דעת החכמה תחיה בעליה

> "Rabbi" (Judah Ha-Nasi) was dying in Sepphoris and the Sepphoreans said, "We will kill whoever comes and says that Rabbi has died." Bar Kappara came and went to the window where he waited impatiently[334] with his head wrapped and his clothes rent.[335] (Unable to wait any longer) he said, "My brothers, sons of *Yedaʿyah*, Listen to me! Listen to me! The angels and the mortals seized the tablets of the covenant (i.e. Rabbi). The hands of the angels have prevailed and snatched the tablets." They said to him, "Rabbi has died." He replied, "You have said it, I have not said it." And why did he not say it? Because it is written (Pr. 10:18): "And he that uttereth a slander is a fool." They rent their clothes and their cry was heard all the way to Gof-fatah, three miles away. And this (Eccl. 7:12) applied to him (Bar Kappara): "And the excellence of knowledge is, that wisdom preserveth the life of him that hath it."

The Midrash is concerned with the meaning of Ecclesiastes 7:12 (end): "Wisdom preserveth the life of him that hath it." Examples of rabbis who used their wisdom to help themselves out of life threatening situations are provided. By alluding to the death of Judah instead of making an outright announcement, Bar Kappara avoided saying, "Rabbi has died," which would have evoked the extreme anger of the people of Sepphoris. Bar Kappara's metaphor is considered a shrewd form of wisdom which proves the point of the biblical verse.[336] The legend serves the *midrash* well.

The reference to the people of Sepphoris as the "sons of *Yedaʿyah*" is important to our discussion of the priests of Sepphoris. If an early third century *tanna* such as Bar Kappara could have actually addressed the residents of Sepphoris in such a manner, there would be reason to assume that the *mishmar* of *Yedaʿyah* had settled in Sepphoris by the end of the tannaitic period (ca. 200). Klein has even suggested that the mere fact that Bar Kappara could address the people as the "sons of *Yedaʿyah*" indicates that the community was largely composed of priests![337]

Several points have to be considered in assessing the historical value of Bar Kappara's words. First of all, the passage is clearly a legendary account utilized by the Midrash for its own purposes. True, the reference to the "sons of *Yedaʿyah*" is incidental to the actual story. Since, however, the account is found in *Qohelet Rabbah*, a work which in its present redaction stems from the eighth century at the earliest,[338] even incidental details must be considered suspect.

---

334 Cf. Jastrow, *Sefer Millim*, pp. 287f.

335 Signs of mourning.

336 On the metaphors of Bar Kappara, see Klein, "*Ẓippori*," pp. 72ff.

337 Klein, "*Baraitaʾ*," p. 9.

338 See M. D. Herr, "Ecclesiastes Rabbah," *Encyclopaedia Judaica* 6 (1972), col. 355.

Finally, the parallel version which appears in a work redacted earlier, omits the reference altogether. Thus the Palestinian Talmud has:[339]

> ציפריא אמרין מאן דאמ׳ לן ר׳ דמך אנן קטלינן ליה אדיק לון בר קפרא רישיה מכסי מאנוי מבזעין[340] אמר לון יצוקים ואראלים תפוסין[341] בלוחות הברית וגברה ידן של אראלים וחטפו את הלוחות אמרין ליה דמך ר׳ אמ׳ לון אתון אמריתון וקרעון ואזל קלא דקרעון לגו פפתה[342] מהלך תלתה מילין ר׳ נחמן בשם ר׳ מנא מעשה ניסין נעשו[343] באותו היום...

> The Sepphoreans said, "We will kill whoever tells us that Rabbi has died." Bar Kappara was impatient with them so he covered his head, rent his clothes and said to them: "Mortals and angels were grasping the tablets of the covenant, and the hands of the angels prevailed and snatched the tablets." They said to him, "Rabbi has died." He replied, "You have said it." And they rent their clothes, and their cry, which accompanied the rending, was heard as far away as Goffatah, a distance of three miles. Rabbi Naḥman in the name of Rabbi Mana said, "A miraculous event occurred on that day ..."

This rendering of the Bar Kappara story is briefer than the one found in *Qohelet Rabbah*. Here the story appears after a discussion of funeral arrangements, in particular, those pertaining to Judah. It is followed as Naḥman's remark indicates, by reports of miracles which occurred following the death of the *Nasi*. As we have already seen, many legends circulated concerning the deaths of members of the patriarchal house. That rabbinic tradition should pay special attention to the greatest of the patriarchs, Judah Ha-Nasi, is no surprise. The Midrash, however, has transformed this story into an account of the wisdom of Bar Kappara. By adding the biblical verses, the Midrash has effectively illustrated how wisdom preserved the life of Bar Kappara. It is curious that the Midrash follows up its account with the very material which appears after the talmudic version. The fact that this material, which serves no purpose in the discussion of wisdom, is reproduced by the Midrash, suggests that the latter drew upon the Talmud as its source.[344]

As for the reference to the "sons of *Yedaʿyah*," there can be no doubt that this was an editorial embellishment.[345] By the time *Qohelet Rabbah* was edited, the *mishmarot* and their places of residence had become a popular theme of *piyyut*

---

339 P. *Kilʾayim* 9, 32b, Ms. Leiden.

340 מבזעין is omitted in Ms. Vatican.

341 Ms. Vatican has תופסין.

342 Ms. Vatican has one word לגופפתה, which is probably correct. It appears to have been the name of a place. See Ratner, *ʾAhavat Ẓiyyon Vi-Yerushalayim, ad loc.*

343 Ms. Vatican has נעשה.

344 Or perhaps the Talmud and Midrash drew from a third source. On the parallels found in the Midrashim and the Palestinian Talmud, see Bokser, "Bibliographical Guide," pp. 182f.

345 It should be noted that the story of Bar Kappara's announcement of the death of Judah Ha-Nasi also appears in the Babylonian Talmud (*Ketubot* 104a) where again no reference is made to the "sons of *Yedaʿyah*."

literature.[346] Although the *mishmar* of *Yedaʿyah* could have taken up residence in Sepphoris before the end of the tannaitic period, the Bar Kappara legend cannot be regarded as evidence thereof.

The following excerpt from the Palestinian Talmud[347] refers to the settlement of the priestly division (*mishmar*) of *Yedaʿyah* at Sepphoris:

> אמ׳ ר׳ לוי יהויריב גברה מירון קרתה מסרביי מסר בייתא לשנאייא[348] אמ׳ ר׳ ברכיה[349] יה הריב עם בניו על שמרו וסרבו בו ידעיה עמוק ציפורים ידע יה עיצה עמוקה שבליבם והגלם לציפורין[350]

> Rabbi Levi said, "Yehoyariv is a (name of a) man. Meron is a city. Mesarebay means: He (God) delivered (*mesar*) His house (*baytaʾ*, i.e. Temple) to His enemies."[351] Rabbi Berakhiah said "(*Yehoyariv* means) God (*yah*) contended (*heriv*) with His children because they rebelled (*maru*) and defied (*seravu*) Him. *Yedaʿyah ʿAmoq Ẓipporim* (means) God (*yah*) knew (*yadaʿ*) the profound (*ʿamuqah*) design in their heart and exiled them to Sepphoris (*Ẓipporim*)."

Earlier in the *gemara*, a *baraita* in the name of Rabbi Yose (mid-second century) states that the destruction of both the First and Second Temples occurred while the *mishmar* of *Yehoyariv* was officiating on the Ninth of Av.[352] The comments of Levi (third quarter of the third century) and Berakhiah (late fourth century) seem to have been introduced because of their relevance to the designation "*Yehoyariv*." The rabbis, however, do not refer to the preceding *baraita*. Indeed, it has long been accepted that Levi and Berakhiah were interpreting the first two entries in the "*Baraita* of the Twenty-Four *Mishmarot*."[353] This *baraita* is actually a list of the priestly courses.[354] Each entry consisted of the number of the *mishmar* in the Temple rotation, its name and the town (or city) with which it was associated. In several cases, a secondary priestly title appeared alongside of the main designation by which the *mishmar* was known. The first two entries evidently read: First Division: *Yehoyariv Mesarebay Meron*; Second Division: *Yedaʿyah*

---

346 Discussed below, pp. 125ff.

347 P. *Taʿanit* 4, 68d, Ms. Leiden.

348 The Genizah version reads: מסרבייתיה לשנאיה. See L. Ginzberg, *Seridei Ha-Yerushalmi*, p. 184. (All references to the Genizah version in the following notes refer to the text in Ginzberg's work.)

349 Ed. Venice includes the word יהויריב at this point. Ms. Leiden has it in the margin. The Genizah version omits the word altogether.

350 The Genizah version has ואגלם כצפרין. The phrase might then be translated, "and exiled them like birds." Cf. the *piyyut* of Kallir (discussed below, p. 126) which reads: ונדדו כצפורים כהני ציפורים.

351 Following the reading of the Genizah version (n. 348).

352 P. *Taʿanit, ad loc.* Cf. *Seder ʿOlam Rabbah* 30. For an attempt to reconcile the difference between this tradition and others which claim that *Yehoyariv* served in the first weeks of *Tishrei* and *Nisan*, see L. Finkelstein, *New Light from the Prophets* (1969), pp. 106ff.

353 See Klein, "*Baraitaʾ*," pp. 16f. and J. A. Goldstein, "The Hasmoneans: The Dynasty of God's Resisters," *HTR* 68 (1975), 57 and more recently, *idem*, I *Maccabees* (*The Anchor Bible*), p. 20.

354 No complete version of the "*baraita*" exists. The assumption that the list represents a *baraita* was first proposed by S. Klein. See the discussion on p. 62 and the sources referred to in n. 1.

ʿAmoq Ẓipporim (Sepphoris). Levi and Berakhiah used the secondary designations in their interpretations. According to Levi, *Mesarebay* meant that God delivered (*mesar*) His house or Temple (*baytaʾ*) to the enemies. *Mesarebay* would then be a fitting epithet for the *mishmar* of *Yehoyariv* which was believed to have officiated during the last days of the Temple. Berakhiah's interpretation of *Yehoyariv-Mesarebay* may also allude to this tradition. It is his understanding of *Yedaʿyah ʿAmoq Ẓipporim*, however, which is of interest here. Berakhiah's pun yields the following: God (*yah*) knew (*yadaʾ*) the profound (*ʿamuqah*) design in their heart (that of the priests of the *mishmar*) and exiled them to Sepphoris. Berakhiah may have associated *Yedaʿyah* with the destruction of the Temple, but the details of the tradition he had in mind are unclear. Perhaps the "profound design" of the priests refers to their sympathy for the Roman cause. In any case, Berakhiah's pun seems to be no more than an attempt to connect the arrival of the *mishmar* at Sepphoris with some historical event of the past.[355] Berakhiah's comments reveal, however, that the priestly division of *Yedaʿyah* had not always been associated with Sepphoris and that the *mishmar* had certainly settled in that city by the time of the *amora*, in the late fourth century.

The terms *Mesarebay* and *ʿAmoq* may actually refer to individual *battei ʾavot* (families) which constituted sub-divisions of *Yehoyariv* and *Yedaʿyah*, respectively. The case of *ʿAmoq* is instructive. Klein has noted that the term appears among the names of the "chiefs of the priests and their brethren" (*raʾshei ha-kohanim va-ʾaḥeihem*) who returned with Zerubbavel (Nehemiah 12:7, 20).[356] Since *Yedaʿyah* (and, for that matter, *Yehoyariv*) also appears in this list,[357] it is unlikely that *ʿAmoq* was synonymous with that *mishmar*. J. Liver has called attention to the fact that other names in the priestly register of Nehemiah 12 appear as secondary designations in the *mishmarot* lists. These names could only have been assumed by some smaller subdivision, probably a *bet ʾav*, which had become incorporated into a larger *mishmar*.[358] Why particular *battei ʾavot* should have been singled out in the *mishmarot* lists is not known. Perhaps these *battei ʾavot* represented the largest or most important families of the *mishmarot*. It could also be maintained that certain *mishmarot* did not settle in their entirety in a given city but only became associated with that place once their predominant *bet ʾav* established residence there. Perhaps some of the *battei ʾavot* of a particular *mishmar* desired to settle elsewhere, for instance, in the adjoining countryside. The singling out of

---

355 Curiously, the medieval *paytan* Eleazar Kallir associated all twenty-four *mishmarot* with the Destruction in his elegy for the Ninth of Av. The part of this elegy dealing with Sepphoris is presented below, p. 126. Because of the involvement of the priests in Temple matters, it was only natural for the *mishmarot* to be associated with the Destruction.

356 See Klein, *Beiträge*, pp. 10f.

357 Verses 7, 8, 19 and 21.

358 Other examples provided by Liver are משמר אביה עדו כפר עוניאל and משמר דליה גנתון צלמין of which עדו (= עדוא, Neh. 12:4, 16) and גנתון (*Neh*. 10:7, 12:16 cf. 12:4) were *battei ʾavot*. See Liver, *Peraqim*, p. 47.

ʿAmoq could very well mean that the greatest proportion of priests of the *mishmar Yedaʿyah* who settled at Sepphoris belonged to that *bet ʾav.*[359]

References to the priests of Sepphoris and the *mishmar* to which they belonged also appear in the medieval liturgical poems known as *piyyutim*. Many of the *paytanim* (poets), especially those who were priests, composed *piyyutim* using a list of twenty-four *mishmarot* and their places of residence as their motif. Until the discovery of archeological fragments preserving similar lists, these *piyyutim* were the most important documentation of the *mishmarot* in existence.[360] The lists were apparently intended to preserve the order of the priestly rotation and the memory of the participation of the *mishmarot* in the Temple service. Presumably, the perpetuation of the tradition was necessary if the Temple was ever to be restored.[361] Indeed, at least until the eleventh century there was a custom in *Ereẓ Yisrael* to recall the priestly courses every Sabbath and to recite *piyyutim* concerning them.[362] The *mishmar* whose turn it would have been to serve that particular week at the Temple was especially noted.[363] The prayer would also include a petition: "May the merciful God restore the *mishmarot* to their place soon in our time, Amen."[364] As mentioned, several of the extant *piyyutim* mention the priests of Sepphoris (*Ẓipporim*). Thus the *paytan*, Eleazar Kallir,[365] wrote the following in the elegy over the Destruction of the Temple which he composed for the Ninth of *Av*.[366]

---

[359] In the case of *Yehoyariv*, however, the designation *Mesarebay* may be an actual nickname by which the *mishmar* was known. Goldstein has suggested that the term referred to the Hasmoneans who belonged to the *mishmar* of *Yehoyariv* and were dubbed "resisters" (*mesarebay*) of God" by their detractors. See Goldstein, "God's Resisters," pp. 56ff. and *idem*, I *Maccabees*, pp. 20f.

[360] See above, p. 62, n. 1. Fragments preserving parts of the list of *mishmarot* have been found at Caesarea, Ashkelon, Kissufim and Bet El-Ḥazar in Yemen. On the Caesarea inscription, see the already mentioned (n. 1) article of Avi-Yonah, "The Caesarea Inscription of Priestly Courses," or its Hebrew version in *ʾEreẓ Yisrael* 7 (1964), 24-28. The Ashkelon inscription is reported on by E. K. Sukenik in *Ẓion* 1 (1926-7), 16-17. For the fragment from Kissufim see Z. Ilan in *Tarbiz* 43 (1974), 225f. The inscription from Bet El-Ḥazar is reproduced and discussed in R. Degan, "*Ketovet Mi-Teman ʿal Mishmerot Ha-Kohanim*," *Tarbiz* 42 (1973), 302-307. Cf. H. Z. Hirschberg, "*ʿAl Ha-Ketovot Ha-Yehudiyot Ha-Ḥadashot She-Nitgalu Be-Teman*," *Tarbiz* 44 (1975), 151-158. It is presumed that these fragments once formed tablets which were affixed to the walls of synagogues in the places in which they were found. The tablets preserved the memory of the *mishmarot* and could very well have been the source used by the *paytanim*. See Avi-Yonah, "The Caesarea Inscription," p. 51.

[361] According to Baron, the priests who wrote these *piyyutim* were "reflecting their extraordinary readiness to spring into immediate action upon the advent of the Messiah and without delay to restore the ancient rituals into full operation." See S. Baron, *History* VII (1958), 90.

[362] See Klein, *ʾEreẓ Ha-Galil*, pp. 63f.

[363] Urbach has suggested that a chapter of Mishnah *Shabbat* (which is divided into twenty-four chapters) was read each Sabbath in honor of the *mishmar* whose turn it would have been. See E. E. Urbach, *Mishmarot U-Maʿamadot, Tarbiz* 42 (1973), 309ff.

[364] הרחמן ישיב את המשמרות למקומה (!) מהרה בימינו אמן See M. Zulay, "*Le-Toledot Ha-Piyyut Be-ʾEreẓ Yisrael,*" *Yediʿot Ha-Makhon Le-Ḥeqer Ha-Shirah Ha-ʿIvrit Bi-Yerushalayim* 5 (1939), 111.

[365] His dates are unknown but he is generally believed to have lived in the seventh century. See Baron, *History* VII, 264.

[366] The Ninth of *Av* commemorates the Destruction of both the First and Second Temples. See above, p. 123. For the complete text of the *piyyut* see Klein, *ʾEreẓ Ha-Galil*, pp. 181ff. and *idem,*

בכו תבכה מחמשת ספרים
כנהרג כהן ונביא ביום הכפורים
ועל דמו נשחטו פרחים כצפירים
ונדדו כצפורים כהני ציפורים

Bitterly wept[367] the five-fold books (of the Torah)
When the priest and prophet was killed on the Day of Atonement[368]
And over his[369] blood, the young priests[370] were slaughtered like goats
And the priests of Sepphoris migrated like birds.

Another *paytan*, Phineas ben Jacob Ha-Kohen ("the Priest") of Palestine (ca. eighth century) also composed *piyyutim* commemorating each *mishmar*. The stanza concerning the *mishmar* whose week it was to officiate at the Temple would be recited in conjunction with the *Birkat Kohanim* of the *Tefillah*. Sepphoris is mentioned thus:[371]

בשוֹבְבָך כהנים לידעיה עמוק צפורים
יַדַּע בגבורתך ותיודע ביופי הדרתך
יַקֵּר בביתך שלום רב לאוהבי תורתך

ידעיה עמׄ צפׄ
משמרת השניה

Yeda

Yedaʿyah ʿAmoq Ẓipporim
The Second *Mishmar*[372]

You have led away the priests of *Yedaʿyah ʿAmoq Ẓipporim* (Sepphoris)
Reveal Your (God's) might! And You will be known by the beauty of Your splendor
Honor Your house (Temple). A great peace to the lovers of Your Torah.

Beiträge, pp. 97ff. Also cf. G. Dalman, "*Die galiläischen heimatorte der 24 Priesterordnungen nach Kalir*," *PJB* (1922-3), pp. 80-89, which includes a German translation of the *piyyut*. For an English translation and annotation, see A. Rosenfeld, trans. and ed., *The Authorised Kinot for the Ninth of Av* (1965), pp. 99ff.

367 Cf. Lamentations 1:2. Each stanza of this *piyyut* borrows its introductory words from the beginning of verses in the first chapter of Lamentations.

368 The "priest and prophet" is a reference to Zechariah the son of Jehoiada who, according to II Chronicles 24:20-22, denounced the idolators in the courtyard of the Temple during the reign of Joash (835-798 B.C.E.). The latter had Zechariah stoned for his denunciation. Rabbinic sources relate how Nebuzaradan, the commander of Nebuchadnezzar's guard, attempted to appease the blood of Zechariah which he found seething in Jerusalem. Accordingly, Nebuzaradan slew some 94,000 people including the young priests. However, only after Nebuzaradan cried out to Zechariah, "Do you want me to kill them all?" did the seething stop. Some versions report that this experience prompted Nebuzaradan to convert to Judaism. The murder of Zechariah was supposed to have occurred on the Day of Atonement; hence the reference in the *piyyut* to that holiday. See *Lamentations Rab., Proem* 23; *Lamentations Rab.* 4:13; B. *Gittin* 57b; B. *Sanhedrin* 96b and P. *Taʿanit* 4, 69a-b. On Zechariah, see J. Heinemann and Y. M. Grintz, "Zechariah," *Encyclopaedia Judaica* 16 (1971), cols. 952-953.

369 Zechariah's, see previous note.

370 See n. 368.

371 The *piyyut* is presented in Zulay, "*Toledot Ha-Piyyut*," pp. 137ff. and Klein, *ʾEreẓ Ha-Galil*, pp. 188f. The text is alphabetical. Thus the stanza referring to Sepphoris starts with ב as the *mishmar* of *Yedaʿyah* was usually listed second after *Yehoyariv*.

372 The phrases "*Yedaʿyah ʿAmoq Ẓipporim*" and "The Second Mishmar" appear at the side of the stanza.

There are many other *piyyutim* concerning the *mishmarot.*[373] Those presented here, however, should serve to indicate how deeply entrenched was the association of Sepphoris with the *mishmar* of *Yedaʿyah* in the medieval period.

Summary

The issue of whether a priest could defile himself out of respect for the *Nasi* was of particular interest in Sepphoris during the third and fourth centuries. Evidently, a considerable number of priests were living in the city during that period. A number of them were likely to have been included among the worshippers at the Gofnah synagogue, which functioned during the early fourth century at Sepphoris. These priests may have belonged to a *mishmar* other than *Yedaʿyah.*

The reference to the "sons of *Yedaʿyah*," which appears in Bar Kappara's metaphor concerning the death of Judah Ha-Nasi, cannot be considered proof that priests of that *mishmar* had settled in Sepphoris by the end of the tannaitic period. The reference is only found in the metaphor produced in *Qohelet Rabbah.* This Midrash adapted material found in the Palestinian Talmud for its own purpose. Thus the earliest reference to the settlement of *Yedaʿyah* at Sepphoris appears in a statement attributed to the fourth century *amora*, Berakhiah. The latter's pun on the words *Yedaʿyah ʿAmoq Ẓipporim* indicates that the *mishmar* had not always been connected with Sepphoris. It is unclear whether Berakhiah actually believed that the "exile" of *Yedaʿyah* to Sepphoris had anything to do with the destruction of the Temple, although his pun may be so understood. In any case, the *mishmar* must have relocated at Sepphoris by the fourth century when Berakhiah took the group's relationship with the city for granted. The association of *ʿAmoq* with *Yedaʿyah* is of particular interest since it may indicate that the majority of priests who settled at Sepphoris belonged to that *bet ʾav*. The memory of the settlement of *Yedaʿyah-ʿAmoq* at Sepphoris is preserved in several medieval *piyyutim*.

---

373 See Zulay's article, "*Toledot Ha-Piyyut*," pp. 107-180 and the sources listed by E. Fleisher in "*Piyyut Le-Yannai Ḥazzan ʿAl Mishmerot Ha-Kohanim*," *Sinai* 64 (1969), 176, n. 1. *Yedaʿyah* also appears in a *piyyut* discussed by S. Abramson in "*Qerovot La-Ḥatan*," *Tarbiz* 15 (1943-4), 52. The residences of the *mishmarot* are not mentioned in this *piyyut*.

CHAPTER FOUR

CONCLUSION

While the sources may not permit the reconstruction of the history of the priests of Sepphoris in all its aspects, they do allow at least a glimpse of their relationship with the city. The earliest Sepphorean priest referred to by the sources is Joseph ben Elim, who may have been involved in some intrigue concerning the succession to the high priesthood in the time of Herod. It has been shown that ben Elim served temporarily as High Priest because, as a relative of the incumbent, he was the likely choice to substitute when the former was disqualified. Sepphorean priests should not be regarded as having attained any unique social status in Jerusalem during the Second Temple period.

The sources do not reveal whether ben Elim or, for that matter, the legendary ben Ḥamsan represented a large settlement of priests at Sepphoris during Temple times. Neither of these individuals is portrayed as having been a member of a particular *mishmar* whose residence was at Sepphoris. Indeed, no *mishmar* is known to have settled at Sepphoris or any other Galilean location during the Second Temple period.[374] Furthermore, it is not known whether the priests of the individual *mishmarot* chose to settle together even before 70. Interestingly, no locations are mentioned in the list of priestly courses found at Qumran.[375] Thus

---

[374] Klein has suggested that the Hasmoneans followed the Hellenistic practice of designating individual administrative units known as toparchies. In doing so, the Hasmonean kings merely utilized the areas designated by the *mishmarot* to divide the country into toparchies. Thus by the time of Alexander Yannai there were twenty-four toparchies corresponding to the number of *mishmarot*. Sepphoris, as the center of one of these toparchies, would have been the location of a *mishmar* as well. Klein goes to great lengths to identify the other *mishmarot*-toparchies and, in the end, claims that Galilee was divided into eight such divisions (including Sepphoris). There are several difficulties with this theory. First, it seems unlikely that eight of the twenty-four *mishmarot* would have been located in Galilee in the days of the Second Temple. Second, several of the locations in Galilee identified by Klein are not known to have been areas where priests resided either before or after 70. Cf. the article of Lurie cited earlier which finds little evidence for priests in Galilee before 70. Still, Klein's theory is suggestive and warrants reexamination. See his two studies, "*Ḥaluqat Yehudah Ve-Ha-Galil*," *Sefer Ha-Shanah Shel-ʾEreẓ Yisrael* 1 (1923), 24ff. and "*Ḥaluqat ʾEreẓ Yisrael Le-Maʿamadot*," *Sefer Ha-Shanah Shel-ʾEreẓ Yisrael* 2 (1924), 17ff. Cf. A. Schalit, "Domestic Politics and Political Institutions," *The World History of the Jewish People* VI, The Hellenistic Period (1972), 265 and *idem, Ha-Mishtar Ha-Romaʾi Be-ʾEreẓ Yisrael* (1937), pp. 23f. On the identification of the toparchies, see A. H. M. Jones, "The Urbanization of Palestine," *JRS* 21 (1931), 78f.

[375] See S. Talmon, "The Calendar Reckoning of the Sect from the Judaean Desert," *Scripta Hierosolymitana* 4 (1965) 170f. To be sure, it is apparent that the list was used by the sect in order to calculate their calendar. Accordingly, the priestly rotation was used to reckon the festivals. Thus it could be maintained that the sect had no interest in the locations. Nevertheless if the sect went so far as to adopt the priestly rotations of the Temple as their calendrical guide, there is no reason to assume that they would have balked at preserving the locations of the *mishmarot*, had there been any to preserve.

the *mishmar* to which ben Elim belonged may not have had a permanent residence.

Still, there is at least one source which may, if only indirectly, support the idea of a settlement of a substantial number of priests at Sepphoris during this period. In Part One[376] it has been contended that the "old archives of Sepphoris" were a repository for, among other things, marriage contracts which had been signed by notables of the community, in particular, priests and Levites or Israelites who gave their daughters in marriage into the priestly stock. It has been shown that the archives were in operation under Jewish auspices during the pre-70 period. The documents deposited in the archives could have contained signatures belonging to local priests. While this information is suggestive, it cannot be regarded as definitive since other notables, besides priests, could have served as witnesses to marriages.

It is more likely that the participation of ben Elim in the Temple worship was merely indicative of the interest and the involvement of Sepphoreans in general in religious matters. Other Sepphoreans are reported to have visited Jerusalem on occasion. Thus Yose (ben Ḥalafta, a Sepphorean) reports that an Israelite from Sepphoris named Arsela once led the scapegoat into the wilderness on the Day of Atonement.[377] This notice is of special interest since Yose's point in mentioning this tradition is to illustrate that Israelites as well as priests could be put in charge of the scapegoat. Here we have a lay Sepphorean serving in a role that his priestly neighbors would presumably have been entitled to.[378] Rabbinic sources also mention the "daughters of Sepphoris" (*benot Ẓippori*) who used to go to Jerusalem for the Sabbath.[379] While these traditions warrant a thorough elucidation, the preponderance of notices concerning priests or Israelites of Sepphoris worshipping in Jerusalem is significant in itself.[380]

The evidence for the era following the Destruction would seem to further support the contention that the reports concerning priests during the earlier period were the exception rather than the rule. The sources do not indicate that there

---

[376] pp. 47f.

[377] M. *Yoma*ʾ 6:3. Some editions do not indicate that Arsela was from Sepphoris, but the better Mss. do. See Rabbinovicz, *Diqduqei Soferim* on B. *Yoma*ʾ 66a.

[378] Nor should Arsela be considered a noble or influential Sepphorean because he was given such an honor. Participation in cultic affairs alone may not have been an indication of social status.

[379] P. *Maʿaser Sheni* 5, 56a and *Lamentations Rab*. 3:9.

[380] On the participation of Galileans in Temple worship, see S. Safrai, *Ha-ʿAliyah Le-Regel Bi-Yemei Ha-Bayit Ha-Sheni* (1965), pp. 42ff.

It should be noted that Klein assumes that priests also resided in the Galilean cities of Kabul, Shiḥin, Migdala and Kefar Nimrah before 70. This assumption is based on the fact that the people of these cities are reported to have provided for various needs of the priests of Jerusalem. This, however, cannot be considered conclusive evidence. See P. *Taʿanit* 4, 69a. The reference in the parallel (*Lamentations Rab*. 2:2) to *mishmarot* must certainly be a reading into the text of later circumstances. See Klein, *ʾEreẓ Ha-Galil*, pp. 51f., *idem*, "*Neue Beiträge zur Geschichte und Geographie Galiäas*," *Jeschurun* 10 (1923), 244. Cf. Safrai, *ʿAliyah Le-Regel*," pp. 51f. and Freyne, *Galilee*, p. 304, n. 81.

was a large scale settlement of priests at Sepphoris after the Destruction. The account concerning Ḥalafta and the fast day service at Sepphoris reveals nothing about the priests who might have been in Sepphoris at the end of the first-beginning of the second centuries. Ḥalafta incorrectly imitated a distinct part of the Temple's fast day ceremony. There is no reason to assume that he copied (or could have copied) the entire ceremony with its heavy dependence on the role of the priests. The fast day episode must, therefore, be rejected as evidence for an assemblage of priests at Sepphoris following the destruction of the Temple.

Given this fact, another question must be asked: Is there any evidence which would suggest the existence of other priestly communities in Galilee in the post-Destruction period? According to Klein, priests resided in the following Galilean locations between 70 and 135: (1) Tibᶜon (2) Guvta-ᵓAriaḥ (3) Kefar Menori (4) Kefar ᶜOtnay (5) Sikhnin (6) Kokhba and (7) Rom-Bet Anat.[381] There is no evidence, however, for large scale settlement of priests in any of these cities. Furthermore, the paucity of references only argues against the mass migration of priests to Galilee after the Destruction, a point Klein himself seems to agree with.[382] Thus external evidence provides no support for a priestly settlement at Sepphoris after the Destruction.

In the second century, however, we at least find an interest in the preservation of traditions concerning priests from Sepphoris who served at the Temple. Thus it is the second century Sepphorean *tanna*, Yose ben Ḥalafta, who reports the story of ben Elim. It was probably a second century *tanna* or circle of *tannaim* who originally associated the legend of ben Ḥamsan with the miracles pertaining to Simeon the Righteous.[383] Both of these traditions are negative in their attitude toward the priests concerned. Indeed, one wonders whether these stories represent a general bias against priests or perhaps a local prejudice against priests from Sepphoris. Unfortunately, the sources only permit speculation on this matter.[384]

---

[381] Most of Klein's proofs are merely suggestive and cannot be considered conclusive. See "*Neue Beiträge*," pp. 246ff. It should be noted that Kefar ᶜOtnay, while near the Galilee border, is not in Galilee proper.

[382] See Klein, "*Baraita*ᵓ," p. 8 and cf. *idem*, "*Neue Beitrage*," pp. 248f.

[383] The Tosefta has been shown to contain the earliest tradition concerning ben Ḥamsan. It has been argued that the *maᶜaseh* in which he appears was associated with a list of miracles concerning Simeon the Righteous which was composed in the second century. The *maᶜaseh*, therefore, is probably no later in origin than the end of the tannaitic period. See above, pp. 91 (esp. n. 157) and 100.

[384] Büchler has collected some evidence which suggests that the scholars of Galilee were antagonistic towards unlearned priests. Further study of this matter would certainly be worthwhile in view of the findings presented here. See A. Büchler, *Political and Social Leaders*, pp. 69f. In a different study, Büchler attempts to show that in the time of Yose ben Ḥalafta (mid-second century), Sepphorean slaves would often attempt to pass as priests in order to collect priestly dues. Büchler maintains that a frequent insult among the second century priests of Sepphoris was to call a priest a slave. Büchler's argument depends on some *baraitot* in B. *Ketubot* 28a-b which need further investigation. It should be noted, however, that no direct reference to Sepphoris is made (only "in the place" of Yose, see 28b), and at least some of the discussion may have been academic. See Büchler, "*Familienreinheit und Sittlichkeit in Sepphoris im zweiten Jahrhundert*," *MGWJ* 78 (1934), pp. 127f. In yet

It is not until the third and fourth centuries that we find a substantial number of references to priests living at Sepphoris. Thus the sources relate three stories pertaining to the behavior of priests at the death of a reigning *Nasi* or his sister. Two of these deal with incidents which occurred in Sepphoris. At the death of Judah II Nesiah (ca. 260), Yannai declared a temporary suspension of the priesthood so as to enable the local priests to participate in the funeral rights. Similarly, when Judah III Nesiah died (ca. 305) Ḥiyya bar Abba made sure that his priestly colleague, Zeira, paid his respects. The incident concerning Nehoraʾy should not be discounted as it provoked discussion among the scholars of Sepphoris concerning the participation of priests in the funerals of relatives of the *Nasi*.

Thus it is not surprising that we first hear of the *mishmar* of *Yedaʿyah* in relation to Sepphoris in the fourth century.[385] Bar Kappara's reference to *Yedaʿyah* in his announcement of the death of Judah (I) Ha-Nasi would have placed the *mishmar* in Sepphoris as early perhaps as 200 C.E. Unfortunately, the reference has been shown to be a later interpolation.[386] The list of twenty-four *mishmarot* and their Galilean locations has generally been presumed to represent the post-Bar Kokhba situation, when the priests were forced to leave Judea, giving up their immediate hopes for the rebuilding of the Temple.[387] While this is a persuasive hypothesis for the evolution of the priestly settlements of Galilee, the evidence, at least insofar as Sepphoris is concerned, points to a later date. The archeological data would seem to support this finding. Inscriptions containing parts of the list of the *mishmarot* and their locations have been found at Caesarea, Ashkelon, Kissufim and Bet al-Ḥaḍir (Yemen). Not one of these inscriptions has been dated earlier than the third century.[388] It is of course possible that these inscrip-

another work, Büchler has suggested that the term *ʿamei ha-ʾareẓ* was used after 135 C.E. especially to refer to priests who disregarded the laws pertaining to the priestly gifts. See Büchler, *ʿAm Ha-ʾAreẓ Ha-Galili* pp. 52-72. The evidence used in this study, however, has been called into question. See Freyne, *Galilee*, pp. 308 and 336, n. 12.

385 Berakhiah, it will be remembered, coined his pun in the late fourth century. See above, pp. 123f.

386 Nevertheless, the fact that the reference to *Yedaʿyah* was interpolated into the text testifies to the strength of the association of the *mishmar* with Sepphoris in later centuries.

387 Klein, "*Baraitaʾ*," pp. 8f. and 24ff. Cf. Kahana, "*Ha-Kohanim Le-Mishmeroteihem*," pp. 14f. Kahana suggests that the priests settled together in order to preserve the unity of the *mishmarot* in the event the Temple should someday be restored. On the depopulation of Judah and the emergence of Galilee as the prime area of Jewish settlement, see Baron, *History* II, 122f., Smallwood, *The Jews of Palestine*, pp. 473f. and E. E. Urbach, "*Mi-Yehudah Le-Galil*," *Sefer Zikaron Le-Yaʿaqov Fridman* (1974), pp. 59-75.

388 None of these inscriptions has preserved that part of the list containing *Yedaʿyah ʿAmoq Ẓipporim*. The fragment from Caesarea was found among Hellenistic debris in the area of the synagogue. It has been dated by N. Avigad to the third-fourth centuries. See Avi-Yonah, "The Caesarea Inscription," p. 51. On the dating of the Ashkelon inscription, see Sukenik in *Ẓion* 1 (1926-7), 16. For an assessment of the Kissufim fragment see Ilan in *Tarbiz* 43 (1974), 226. On the date of the inscription from Bet al-Ḥaḍir in Yemen see Hirschberg, "*Ha-Ketovot Ha-Yehudiyot*," p. 154.

tions are only indicative of the time when it became a practice to preserve the memory of the *mishmarot* in the synagogue. If so, they may not testify to the earliest appearance of the *mishmarot* in Galilee but rather to the origins of a liturgical custom. Perhaps further archeological discoveries will elucidate their value as historical witnesses. In the meantime, the evidence does not permit the dating of the arrival of *Yedaᶜyah-ᶜAmoq* at Sepphoris before the third century, at the earliest.[389]

To be sure, this conclusion is not incompatible with the accepted view of the origins of the "*Baraita* of Twenty-Four *Mishmarot*." As mentioned earlier, priests were not known to have settled in Galilee in great numbers before the Bar Kokhba period. In contrast, many priests are reported to have lived in Judea during the Yavnean era.[390] After the Bar Kokhba revolt many of the surviving priests undoubtedly left Judea and moved northward to Galilee, an area which had a long history of Jewish settlement but which certainly did not have as strong a connection with the Temple and its cult as its southern neighbor. That the priests consolidated their families and preserved the memory of their Temple rotation is not surprising. The question, however, is *when* did they first begin to consolidate? That is, at what point did the families of individual *mishmarot* unite and become associated with specific cities? This process may have been a gradual one especially in view of the fact that the families may not have settled together according to *mishmarot* when they dwelled in Judea.[391] The evidence pertaining to the priests of Sepphoris suggests that the priestly population of Galilee increased sometime after the Bar Kokhba revolt, but consolidation and relocation as *mishmarot* may have been a somewhat later development. It is also conceivable that the entire process of consolidation and centralization occurred at different times for each *mishmar.*[392] Perhaps an investigation of the priestly traditions pertaining to the other cities mentioned in the "*Baraita*" will help to elucidate this important aspect of Galilean history.

---

[389] The fact that the late-third century *amora* R. Levi associated the *mishmar* of *Yehoyariv* with the city of Meron (above, p. 123) suggests that the *mishmarot* were resettled in Galilee already before the time of Berakhiah (late fourth century). It is possible, however, that the individual *mishmarot* relocated at different times. See the ensuing discussion.

[390] These reports are collected by Büchler in "The Economic Condition of Judea After the Destruction of the Second Temple," reprinted in A. Corre, *Understanding the Talmud* (1975), pp. 76ff. For a discussion of the priests during the Yavnean period, see G. Allon, "*Nesiᵓuto Shel-Rabban Yoḥanan ben Zakkaᵓi*," *Meḥqarim* I, 255ff.

[391] Cf. above, p. 128. According to Allon (*ibid.*, p. 259) it cannot be determined where the priests concentrated after the Destruction.

[392] See n. 389.

EPILOGUE

The studies presented above utilized a critical approach to the rabbinic traditions pertaining to the *castra* and the priests of Sepphoris. The main purpose in elucidating these traditions was to ascertain what it was (if anything) they had to say about the *castra* and the priests. It had been contended earlier that the only way to accomplish this, given the difficult nature of the rabbinic sources, was to analyze each tradition separately, taking into consideration philological, literary, textual, and, finally, historical concerns. Some examples of how these concerns helped to elucidate the subject matter will now be reviewed.

Foremost in importance for the understanding of a text is a proper rendering and consideration of the words of which it is composed. Philology is an important aid for the comprehension of the meaning of a text. This was most apparent in the discussion of the *castra*. A study of the way in which the term *castra* is used in rabbinic literature revealed that a gentile institution was usually intended. Similarly, the term *ʿarchei* is used in reference to a non-Jewish archive. Only when these words appeared with the designation "*yeshanah*" (old) was it apparent that Jewish institutions were meant.

In the study of the priests, two important examples come to mind. It had been suggested that Joseph ben Elim substituted for the High Priest in the capacity of a *segan*. While ben Elim's participation in the Temple service is important in itself, the fact that he might have held an official position would have meant that a Sepphorean had achieved significant rank among the Jerusalem priesthood. Unfortunately, an investigation of the way in which the word "*segan*" is used in rabbinic sources suggests that the responsibilities of this office did not include that of substitute High Priest. Only one authority, Ḥananiah, maintained that the *segan*'s duties included this role, and he appears to have been expressing a minority opinion.[1]

The second example is the appellation "ben Ḥamsan" which had been applied to a priest from Sepphoris who attempted to obtain more than his fair share of the Shewbread and the Two Loaves. The word "*ḥamsan*" was shown to be a reference to this priest's greedy and unlawful behavior. Later traditions confused the word with various terms meaning "chick pea" or "bean," but the plain meaning was probably the original intention. It had been hypothesized that ben Ḥamsan was a member of the high priestly family known as Phiabi.[2] Accordingly, the name Phiabi was derived from the Latin word for bean (*faba*), and "ben Ḥamsan," with its chick pea/bean overtones, was an allusion to the high priestly

[1] Above, pp. 83ff.

[2] Above, pp. 100ff.

family. Once it was shown that the original sense of the appellation did not necessarily include the connotation of "chick-pea" or "bean," this theory had to be ruled out.[3]

The literary analysis of each tradition was extended to its context as well. Of course, it had to be shown that the passage and its context formed a unit. Redactors are often responsible for imposing the context upon a passage. However, when it can be shown that a passage belongs to a particular context, a better understanding of its contents is often made possible. For instance, the contexts in which both the *castra ha-yeshanah* and the *ʿarchei ha-yeshanah* appeared indicated that Jewish institutions which had been in existence prior to 70 C.E. were intended. The *castra ha-yeshanah* was included in a list of cities to which the laws pertaining to the redemption of houses in walled cities were applicable. An understanding of the biblical premise for these laws helped to clarify the assertion of the Mishnah that the *castra ha-yeshanah* had been walled "since the days of Joshua bin Nun."[4] In contrast, the *castra* of Sepphoris in both the Palestinian and Babylonian Talmudim is a gentile institution. The "men of the *castra*" who came to extinguish the fire which broke out on the premises of Joseph ben Simai on the Sabbath could only have been gentiles. Indeed, the question discussed in the *gemara* is whether a gentile may extinguish a fire for a Jew on the Sabbath.

Similarly, the *ʿarchei ha-yeshanah* was mentioned in the context of those institutions "beyond which" a man need not examine the descent of the woman he intends to marry. Once it was determined that a woman's paternal line included someone who was *ḥatum ʿed* (signed as a witness) in the *ʿarchei ha-yeshanah* of Sepphoris, this examination could be dispensed with. The most likely explanation of the phrase *ḥatum ʿed* is that it referred to someone who had signed a *ketubah* as a witness to a marriage. This person had to have been a priest or a Levite, or an Israelite who was permitted to marry his daughter into the priestly stock. *Ketubot* containing the signatures of these worthies were kept in an archive (*ʿarchei*). In view of the fact that the other institutions mentioned in the Mishnah were Jewish and belonged to the pre-70 era, it seems probable that the same was true of the *ʿarchei ha-yeshanah* of Sepphoris.

The most frequent textual difficulty encountered in the studies was that of parallel versions. The origins of the variants which appear in these versions had to be discerned in order to evaluate their reliability and relevance to the discussion. Had all rabbinic texts been edited by the same hands in the same time and place, perhaps the harmonization of these versions would be justified. Even then, serious questions would have to be asked about the manuscript tradition. After all, glosses could have been introduced in the process of transmission. In any event, rabbinic texts did not develop in a vacuum but instead include

---

[3] It was also suggested that the name Phiabi may not have been derived from *faba*. See p. 102.
[4] Above, pp. 16ff.

material spanning several centuries. The editors were Jews from diverse regions and academies of Palestine and Babylonia. For these reasons, each parallel was examined carefully before the reliability of any of its variants was discussed. Care was taken not to confuse verisimilitude with historicity and reliability. If it could not be shown that a variant was germane to a passage, it was considered an interpolation. Variants which proved to be interpolations were not always lacking in historical value, however; they often revealed something about the people responsible for them.

Two examples of these phenomena should suffice. The "men of the *castra*" of Sepphoris were said to have come to extinguish the fire on the premises of Joseph ben Simai in Shiḥin. The Palestinian traditions do not tell us who ben Simai was. They merely report on his pious behaviour. The tradition found in the Babylonian Talmud, however, explains that the men came to ben Simai's aid because he was the "*ʾepitropos* of the king." Several scholars identified this *ʾepitropos* with the "*ʾepitropos* of Agrippa the king" who appears in an entirely different context. They then concluded that ben Simai was the *ʾepitropos* of Agrippa II and that the *castra* of Sepphoris was under the jurisdiction of the Jewish king. However, the phrase "*ʾepitropos* of the king" was probably interpolated into the text of the Babylonian parallel to explain why the men of the *castra* came to ben Simai's aid. Furthermore, there is no evidence that the domains of Agrippa II were ever expanded to include Sepphoris.[5] The identification of Joseph ben Simai with the *ʾepitropos* of Agrippa II would have helped to date the non-Jewish *castra*. Unfortunately, the identification was unfounded.

In Part Two, the relationship of the *mishmar* of *Yedaʿyah* to Sepphoris was discussed. According to a late midrashic work (*Qohelet Rabbah*), Bar Kappara addressed the people of Sepphoris as "sons of *Yedaʿyah*" when he announced the death of Judah Ha-Nasi. Had Bar Kappara really addressed the Sepphoreans in this manner, we would have reason to believe that the *mishmar* had already established itself in Sepphoris before Judah Ha-Nasi's death at the beginning of the third century. Unfortunately, the version found in the Palestinian Talmud does not contain the reference to the "sons of *Yedaʿyah*." Furthermore, the Midrash shows signs of having used the talmudic version for its own purposes.[6] Moreover, it is not surprising that the reference to *Yedaʿyah* found its way into the medieval Midrash. By the time *Qohelet Rabbah* received its final form (ca. eighth century) the tradition connecting *Yedaʿyah* with Sepphoris had become a popular theme in *piyyut* literature. The reference to "sons of *Yedaʿyah*" found in the *Qohelet Rabbah* version may reflect the popularization of this theme.

The most prevalent literary form to appear among the traditions studied was the *maʿaseh*. An examination of how each tradition introduced with the word

---

[5] Above, pp. 39f.
[6] Above, p. 122.

maʿaseh (or *maʿaseh be*) was incorporated into a discussion often helped to elucidate the tradition. For instance, the fact that the ben Simai incident was introduced as a *maʿaseh* suggested that it was the premise for the mid-second century ruling that a gentile who comes to extinguish a fire on the Sabbath is not to be prevented from doing so. Joseph ben Simai was said to have prevented the "men of the *castra*" from extinguishing a fire on his premises. The *halakhah* seems to have been predicated upon the reaction of the *ḥakhamim* to Joseph's behavior. Regardless of whether this assessment is correct, it is evident that the *halakhah* had not yet been decided during the time of Joseph ben Simai. Thus the *maʿaseh* had to represent circumstances which preceded the mid-second century, when the *halakhah* appears to have been decided. This fact helped to establish the likelihood of a late first-early second century date for the *castra* intended in the incident.

The fast day ceremony in which Rabbi Ḥalafta of Sepphoris introduced a practice reserved for the Temple was also introduced as a *maʿaseh* in the Mishnah. In this case the *maʿaseh* form was used to contrast the procedure followed in the Temple with that of the *gevulin*. From the *maʿaseh* itself it was impossible to discern what it was that Ḥalafta incorrectly introduced into the ceremony at Sepphoris. However, once it was realized that the *maʿaseh* differed with the Mishnah with respect to the recital of the invocations, it became apparent that the mistake of Ḥalafta (and Ḥananiah) had to do with this aspect of the ceremony. In describing Ḥalafta's mistake, the *maʿaseh* depicted the entire Temple ceremony, which included the participation of the priests. The manner in which the *maʿaseh* was used in the Mishnah, however, indicated that Ḥalafta only copied this ceremony with respect to the invocations. This conclusion was corroborated after an examination of the parallel traditions.[7] Thus a source which had been used to indicate that priests settled in Sepphoris following the Destruction was shown to lack this information altogether.

The benefits of critically examined texts for the types of inquiries attempted here should be apparent. Only after the best text has been recovered can the historicity of the events it describes be considered. More often than not, however, external evidence (historical writings, archeology, etc.) may not be available as witnesses to a given tradition. In such cases critical studies are still worthwhile since only properly understood traditions can be used for historical reconstruction. The inquiries presented here attempted to illustrate how useful information can be derived from carefully studied rabbinic traditions. To be sure, the conclusions which resulted from these inquiries are not incontrovertible. All historical writing is in the final analysis dependent upon a certain degree of interpretation. It is important, however, that this interpretation be based upon as reliable an understanding of the source materials as possible. What matters is that the sources themselves permit the interpretation suggested.

[7] Above, pp. 106ff.

With regard to Sepphoris, these inquiries have further implications. It should be apparent that a thorough evaluation of all the relevant rabbinic traditions is warranted before a comprehensive account of the city's history can be undertaken. This conclusion, however, is not limited to the history of Sepphoris. The traditions pertaining to other cities mentioned in rabbinic literature would also benefit from this type of study. This, of course, is particularly true of cities, like Sepphoris, for which rabbinic literature is the primary source of information. But it is equally true of those cities for which an abundance of external evidence is available.

As a final note, the history of the cities of Ancient Israel have benefited greatly from the accomplishments of twentieth-century archeology. It stands to reason that the interpretation of archeological materials can only be enhanced by the availability of critically analyzed literary sources. This fact has long been recognized in the field of biblical studies but only recently has found expression among scholars whose field of interest is the talmudic period.[8]

---

[8] See E. M. Meyers, "The Use of Archeology in Understanding Rabbinic Materials," *Texts and Responses: Studies Presented to Nahum N. Glatzer*, ed. M. A. Fishbane and P. R. Flohr (1975), pp. 30ff. Cf. R. de Vaux, "On Right and Wrong Uses of Archeology," *Near Eastern Archaeology in the Twentieth Century*, ed. J. A. Sanders (1970), p. 78 and in the same volume, J. Neusner, "Archaeology and Babylonian Jewry," pp. 331f.

BIBLIOGRAPHY

Abel, F. M. *Géographie de la Palestine*. 2 vols. Paris, 1933.

Aboth de Rabbi Nathan. Edited by S. Schechter. Reprint ed., Hildesheim, 1979.

Abramson, S. "*Qerovot La-Ḥatan.*" *Tarbiz* 15 (1943-4), 50-62.

Albeck, H. *Mavoʾ La-Mishnah*. Reprint ed., Jerusalem and Tel Aviv, 1967.

——. *Mavoʾ La-Talmudim*. Tel Aviv, 1969.

——, ed. *Shishah Sidrei Mishnah*. Jerusalem and Tel Aviv, 1957-9.

Allon, G. *Meḥqarim Be-Toledot Yisrael*. 2 vols. Tel Aviv, 1967 and 1970.

——. *Toledot Ha-Yehudim Be-ʾEreẓ Yisrael Bi-Tequfat Ha-Mishnah Ve-Ha-Talmud*. 2 vols. Tel Aviv, 1952.

Alt, A. *Kleine Schriften zur Geschichte des Volkes Israel*. 3 vols. Munich, 1953-64.

Applebaum, S. "*ʿAl Burgi Ve-Burgarii Be-ʾEreẓ Yisrael.*" *Yediʿot Ha-Ḥevrah Ha-ʿIvrit La-Ḥaqirat ʾEreẓ Yisrael Va-ʿAtiqoteha* 18 (1954), 202-208.

——. "Judaea as a Roman Province; the Countryside as a Political and Economic Factor." *Aufstieg und Niedergang der römischen Welt*. Edited by H. Temporini and W. Haase. Pt. 2, vol. 8 (1977), 355-396.

Applebaum, S., and Gihon, M. *Israel and Her Vicinity in the Roman and Byzantine Periods*. Tel Aviv, 1967.

Aptowitzer, A. *Parteipolitik der Hasmonäerzeit in rabbinischem und pseudepigraphischem Schrifttum*. Vienna, 1927.

Arndt, W. F., and Gingrich, F. W. *A Greek-English Lexicon of the New Testament*. Chicago, 1979.

Avigad, N. "*Qever Benot Yaʿaqov She-Le-Yad Ẓippori.*" *ʾEreẓ Yisrael* II (1973), 41-44.

Avi-Yonah, M. "The Caesarea Inscription of the Twenty-four Priestly Courses." In *The Teacher's Yoke: Studies in Memory of Henry Trantham*, pp. 46-57. Edited by E. J. Vardaman, J. L. Garret, and J. B. Adair. Waco, Texas, 1964.

——. *The Holy Land, From the Persian to the Arab Conquest* (536 B.C.-A.D. 640), *A Historical Geography*. Reprint ed., Grand Rapids, 1977.

——. "*Ketovet Mi-Qeisaryah ʿAl ʿEsrim Ve-ʾArbaʿah Mishmerot Ha-Kohanim.*" *ʾEreẓ Yisrael* 7 (1964), 24-28.

——. *The Jews of Palestine*. New York, 1976.

——. *Map of Roman Palestine*. Jerusalem, 1939.

——. "Sepphoris." *Encyclopedia of Archaeological Excavations in the Holy Land* 4 (1978), 1051-1055.

——. "Sepphoris." *Encyclopaedia Judaica* 14 (1971), 1177-1178.

——. "A Sixth Century Inscription from Sepphoris." *IEJ* 11 (1961), 184-187.

Babylonian Talmud. Ed. Vilna. Reprint ed., New York, 1973.

Babylonian Talmud. Codex Munich 95. Reprint ed., Jerusalem, 1971.

Bacher, W. *ʾAggadot Ha-Tannaʾim*. Translated by A. Z. Rabbinowitz. Jerusalem, 1922.

——. *Die ʾAgada der Tannaiten*. 2 vols. Strassburg, 1884-90.

Bar Daroma, H., trans. *Gevulot Ha-ʾAreẓ*. Jerusalem, 1965.

Bar-Kochva, B. "Notes on the Fortresses of Josephus in Galilee." *IEJ* 24 (1974), 108-116.

Barnes, T. D. "The Date of Herod's Death." *JTS*, n.s. 19 (1968), 204-209.

Baron, S. *The Jewish Community*. 3 vols. Philadelphia, 1942.

Baron, S. *A Social and Religious History of the Jews*. 17 vols. New York, Philadelphia, 1937-1980.

Beer, M. "*ʿAl Manhigim shel-Yehudei Ẓippori Be-Meʾah Ha-Shelishit.*" *Sinai* 74 (1974), 133-138.

Ben Yehuda, E. *Millon Ha-Lashon Ha-ʿIvrit Ha-Yeshanah Ve-Ha-Ḥadashah*. 8 vols. New York, 1960.

Bickerman, E. *From Ezra to the Last of the Maccabees*. New York, 1962.

Blau, L. *Die jüdische Ehescheidung und der jüdische Scheidebrief*. 2 vols. Strassburg, 1911-12.

Bloch, H. *Die Quellen des Flavius Josephus in seiner Archäologie*. Leipzig, 1879.

Bloch, R. "Methodological Note for the Study of Rabbinic Literature." Translated by W. S. Green and W. J. Sullivan. In *Approaches to Ancient Judaism: Theory and Practice*, pp. 51-75. Edited by W. S. Green. Missoula, 1978.

Boelter, F. W. "Sepphoris-Seat of the Galilean Sanhedrin." *Explor* (Published by Garret Evangelical Theological Seminary) 3 (Winter, 1977), 36-43.
Bokser, B. M. "An Annotated Bibliographical Guide to the Study of the Palestinian Talmud." *Aufstieg und Niedergang der römischen Welt*. Edited by H. Temporini and W. Haase. Pt. 2, vol. 19.2 (1974), 139-256.
The Book of Isaiah. New *JPS* trans. Philadelphia, 1973.
The Book of Psalms. New *JPS* trans. Philadelphia, 1972.
Brandt, W. *Mandäische Schriften*. Göttingen, 1893.
Bright, J. *A History of Israel*. Reprint ed., Philadelphia, 1974.
Brown, F.; Driver, S.; and Briggs, C. *A Hebrew and English Lexicon of the Old Testament*. Reprint ed., Oxford, 1975.
Büchler, A. *ʿAm Ha-ʾAreẓ Ha-Galili*. Translated by I. Eldad. Jerusalem, 1964.
——. "*Die Schauplätze des Bar-Kochbakrieges und die auf diesen bezogenen jüdischen Nachrichten*." *JQR* 16 (1904), 143-205.
——. "The Economic Condition of Judea After the Destruction of the Second Temple." Reprinted in *Understanding the Talmud*, pp. 73-106. Edited by A. Corre. New York, 1975.
——. "*Familienreinheit und Sittlichkeit in Sepphoris im zweiten Jahrhundert*." *MGWJ* 78 (1934), 126-164.
——. "*Ha-Kohanim Va-ʿAvodatam*. Translated by N. Ginton. Jerusalem, 1966.
——. *Meḥqarim Bi-Tequfat Ha-Mishnah Ve-Ha-Talmud*. Translated by B. Z. Segal. Jerusalem, 1967.
——. *The Political and the Social Leaders of the Jewish Community of Sepphoris in the Second and Third Centuries*. Oxford, 1909.
——. *Studies in Jewish History*. London, 1956.
——. *Types of Jewish-Palestinian Piety from 70 B.C.E. to 70 C.E.* Reprint ed., New York, 1968.
——. "*Über die Minim von Sepphoris und Tiberias im zweiten und dritten Jahrhundert*." In *Festschrift zu Hermann Cohens Siebzigstem Geburtstage*, pp. 271ff. Berlin, 1912.
Buttenwieser, M. "Priest." *The Jewish Encyclopedia* 10 (1905), 192-197.
Case, S. J. "Jesus and Sepphoris." *JBL* 45 (1925), 14-22.
Cheesman, L. *The Auxilia of the Roman Army*. Oxford, 1914.
Clermont-Ganneau, C. "*Mosaïque juive à inscription de Sepphoris*." *CRAIBL* (1909), 677-683.
Cohen, B. *Law and Tradition in Judaism*. New York, 1959.
——. *Mishnah and Tosefta: A Comparative Study, Part I—Shabbat*. New York, 1935.
Cohen, S. J. D. *Josephus in Galilee and Rome: His Vita and Development As a Historian*. Leiden, 1979.
Corpus Inscriptionum Judaicarum. 2 vols. Edited by J. B. Frey. Rome, 1936-52.
Corpus Inscriptionum Semiticarum. 7 vols. Paris, 1881-1962.
Corpus Papyrorum Judaicarum. 3 vols. Edited by V. Tcherikover, A. Fuks, and M. Stern. Cambridge, 1957-64.
Dalman, G. "*Die galiläischen Heimatorte der 24 Priesterordnungen nach Kalir*." *PJB* (1922-3), 80-89.
——. *Grammatik des jüdisch-palästinischen Aramäisch und aramäische Dialektproben*. Darmstadt, 1960.
Danby, H., trans. *The Mishnah*. Reprint ed., Oxford, 1974.
Degan, R. "*Ketovot Mi-Teiman ʿAl Mishmerot Ha-Kohanim*," *Tarbiz* 42 (1973), 301-307.
Derenbourg, J. *Essai sur l'histoire et la géographie de la Palestine* I. Paris, 1867.
De Vaux, R. *Ancient Israel*. 2 vols. New York, 1965.
De Vries, B. "*Beʿayat Ha-Yaḥas bein Ha-Toseftaʾ U-Vein Ha-Talmudim*." *Tarbiz* 27 (1958), 148-170.
Elon, M. *Ha-Mishpat Ha-ʿIvri: Toledotav, Meqorotav, ʿEqronotav*. 2 vols. Jerusalem, 1978.
——. "*Maʿaseh*." *Encyclopaedia Judaica* 11 (1971), 641-649.
Encyclopaedia Judaica (German). Berlin, 1928-34.
Encyclopaedia Judaica. 16 vols. Jerusalem, 1971-72.
Encyclopedia of Archaeological Excavations in the Holy Land. 4 vols. Edited by M. Avi-Yonah and E. Stern. Englewood Cliffs, N.J., 1975-8.
Encyclopedia Talmudit. 14 vols. Jerusalem, 1951-73.
Epstein, A. *Review of Die Priester und der Cultus im letzen Jahrzent des Jerusalemischen Tempels*, by A. Büchler. *MGWJ* 40 (1896), 138-144.
Epstein, J. N. *Diqduq ʾAramit Bavlit*. Jerusalem, 1960.
——. *Mavoʾ Le-Nusaḥ Ha-Mishnah*. 2 vols. Jerusalem and Tel Aviv, 1964.
——. *Mevoʾot Le-Sifrut Ha-Tannaʾim*. Jerusalem and Tel Aviv, 1957.
Feldblum, M. *Perushim U-Meḥqarim Ba-Talmud*. New York, 1969.

Feliks, J. "Beans." *Encyclopaedia Judaica* 4 (1972), 355.

——. "Legumes." *Encyclopaedia Judaica* 19 (1971), 1575-1576.

Finesinger, S. B. "The Shofar." *HUCA* 8-9 (1931-2), 193-228.

The Five Megilloth and Jonah: A New Translation (JPS). Edited by H. L. Ginsberg. Philadelphia, 1969.

Filmer, W. E. "The Chronology of the Reign of Herod the Great." *JTS*, n.s. 17 (1966), 283-298.

Finkelstein, L. *New Light from the Prophets*. New York, 1969.

Fleisher, E. "*Piyyut Le-Yannai Ḥazzan ʿAl Mishmerot Ha-Kohanim.*" *Sinai* 64 (1969), 176-184.

Foerster, G. "*Ha-Galil ʿErev Mered Bar Kokhba: Ha-ʿEdut Ha-'Arki'ologit.*" *Cathedra* 4 (1977), 77-80.

Fohrer, E. *Die Provinzeinteilung des assyrischen Reiches*. Leipzig, 1920.

Frankel, Z. *Mevoʾ Ha-Yerushalmi*. Breslau, 1870.

Freyne, S. *Galilee from Alexander the Great to Hadrian* 323 B.C.E. to 135 C.E.: *A Study of Second Temple Judaism*. Notre Dame, 1980.

Frick, F. S. *The City in Ancient Israel*. Missoula, 1977.

Fuchs, L. *Die Juden Aegyptens in ptolemäischer und römischer Zeit*. Vienna, 1924.

Fuerst, J. *Glossarium Graeco-Hebraeum*. Strassburg, 1890.

Ginsberg, H. L., ed. *The Five Megilloth and Jonah*. Philadelphia, 1969.

Ginzberg, L. *The Legends of the Jews*. 7 vols. Reprint ed., Philadelphia, 1968.

——. *Ginzei Schechter*. 3 vols. New York, 1928-9.

——. *Perushim Ve-Ḥiddushim Ba-Yerushalmi*. 4 vols. New York, 1941-61.

——. *Seridei Ha-Yerushalmi*. New York, 1909.

Glare, P. G. W., ed. *Oxford Latin Dictionary*. 5 vols. to date. Oxford, 1968-76.

Goldstein, J. A. "The Hasmoneans: The Dynasty of God's Resisters." *HTR* 68 (1975), 53-59.

——. *I Maccabees*. New York, 1976.

Goodblatt, D. "The Babylonian Talmud." *Aufstieg und Niedergang der römischen Welt*. Edited by H. Temporini and W. Haase. Pt. 2, vol. 19.2 (1974), 257-336.

Gorodazki, Z. "*ʿOreq Ha-Ḥayyim Shel-Ẓippori.*" *Ha-Tevaʿ Ve-Ha-ʾAreẓ* 19 (July-August, 1977), 226-229.

Graetz, H. "*Agrippa* II *und der Zustand Judäa's nach dem Untergang Jerusalems.*" *MGWJ* 30 (1881), 481-499.

——. *Geschichte der Juden*. 11 vols. Leipzig, 1897-1911.

——. "*Zur Geschichte der nachexilischen Hohenpriesten.*" *MGWJ* 30 (1881), 49-64; 97-112.

Green, W. S., ed. *Approaches to Ancient Judaism: Theory and Practice*. Missoula, 1978.

——. "Palestinian Holy Men and Rabbinic Tradition." *Aufstieg und Niedergang der römischen Welt*. Edited by H. Temporini and W. Haase. Pt. 2, vol. 19.2 (1979), 619-647.

Greenwald, L. *Toledot Ha-Kohanim Ha-Gedolim*. Columbus, 1932.

Gulak, A. *Le-Ḥeqer Toledot Ha-Mishpat Ha-ʿIvri Bi-Tequfat Ha-Talmud*. Jerusalem, 1929.

Guttman, S. *Gamala*. Tel Aviv, 1977.

Guttmann, A. "Jerusalem in Tannaitic Law." *HUCA* 40-41 (1969-70), 251-275.

——. "The Patriarch Judah I, His Birth and His Death. A Glimpse into the Chronology of the Talmudic Period." *HUCA* 25 (1954), 239-261.

——. *Studies in Rabbinic Judaism*. New York, 1976.

Guttmann, M. *ʾEreẓ Yisrael Be-Midrash Ve-Talmud*. Breslau, 1929.

Hacohen, M. "*Ẓippori-Qeisaryah.*" In *idem*, *ʾIshim U-Tequfot*. Jerusalem, 1977, pp. 113-122.

Haenchen, E. *The Acts of the Apostles: A Commentary*. Philadelphia, 1971.

Halevy, I. *Dorot Ha-Riʾshonim*. 5 vols. Frankfurt am Main, 1898-1937.

Halivni, D. *Meqorot U-Mesorot*. 2 vols. Tel Aviv, 1968-1975.

Har-El, M. "The Zealots' Fortresses in Galilee." *IEJ* 22 (1972), 123-130.

Harper Jr., G. M. "Village Administration in the Roman Province of Syria." *Yale Classical Studies* 1 (1928), 105-168.

Hecker, M. "*Kevish Romaʾi Legio-Ẓippori.*" *Yediʿot Ha-Ḥevrah La-Ḥaqirat ʾEreẓ Yisrael Va-ʿAtiqoteha* 25 (1961), 175-186.

Heinemann, J. *Ha-Tefillah Bi-Tequfat Ha-Tannaʾim Ve-Ha-ʾAmoraʾim*. Jerusalem, 1966.

Heinemann, J. and Grintz, Y. M. "Zechariah." *Encyclopaedia Judaica* 16 (1971), cols. 952-953.

Herr, M. D. "Ecclesiastes Rabbah." *Encyclopaedia Judaica* 6 (1972), 355.

Hildesheimer, H. "*Geografyah Shel-ʾEreẓ Yisrael.*" In *Gevulot Ha-ʾAreẓ*, pp. 1-115. Translated by H. Bar Daroma. Jerusalem, 1965.

Hirschberg, H. Z. "*ʿAl Ha-Ketovot Ha-Yehudiyot Ha-Ḥadashot She-Nitgalu Be-Teiman*," *Tarbiz* 44 (1975), 151-158.

——, ed. *Kol ʾEreẓ Naftali*. Jerusalem, 1968.

Hoehner, H. W. *Herod Antipas*. Cambridge, 1972.

Hoenig, S. "The Ancient City-Square: The Forerunner of the Synagogue." *Aufstieg und Niedergang der römischen Welt*. Edited by H. Temporini and W. Haase. Pt. 2, vol. 19.1 (1979), 448-476.

——. "Historical Inquiries: I. Ḥeber Ir II. City Squares." *JQR* 48 (1957), 123-139.

——. "The Suppositious Temple Synagogue." *JQR* 54 (1963), 115-131. Reprinted in *The Synagogue: Studies in Origins, Archeology and Architecture*. Edited by J. Gutmann. New York, 1975, pp. 55-71.

The Holy Scriptures. 1915 JPS trans. Reprint ed., Philadelphia, 1955.

Hölscher, G. "*Die Hohenpriesterliste bei Josephus und die evangelische Chronologie*." *Sitzungsberichte der Heidelberger Akademie der Wissenschaft*, 1940.

Horowitz, I. Z. "*Ẓippori*." *ʾOẓar Yisrael* 9 (1913), 51-54.

Hyman, A. *Toledot Tannaʾim Ve-ʾAmoraʾim*. 3 vols. Reprint ed., Jerusalem, 1964.

Jastrow, M. *Sefer Millim*. Reprint ed., New York, 1971.

Jeremias, J. *Jerusalem in the Time of Jesus*. Translated by F. H. Cave and C. H. Cave. Philadelphia, 1969.

Jones, A. H. M. *The Cities of the Eastern Roman Provinces*. Reprint ed., Oxford, 1971.

——. *The Greek City from Alexander to Justinian*. Oxford, 1940.

——. "The Urbanization of Palestine." *JRS* 21 (1931), 78-85.

Josephus. *Jewish Antiquities*. 6 vols. Translated by H. St. Thackeray, R. Marcus, A. Wikgren, and L. Feldman. Cambridge: Loeb Classical Library, 1930-65.

——. *The Jewish War*. 2 vols. Translated by H. St. J. Thackeray. Cambridge: Loeb Classical Library, 1927.

——. *The Life/Against Apion*. Translated by H. St. Thackeray. Cambridge: Loeb Classical Library, 1926.

Judeich, W. *et al. Altertümer von Hierapolis*. In *Jahrbuch des deutschen archäologischen Instituts*. Supplementary issue no. 4, Berlin, 1898.

Juster, J. *Les Juifs dans l'empire romain*. 2 vols. Paris, 1914.

Kahana, T. "*Ha-Kohanim Le-Mishmeroteihem U-Le-Meqomot Hityashvutam*." *HUCA* 48 (1978-9), 9-29.

Kaminka, A. *Meḥqarim Ba-Miqraʾ U-Va-Talmud U-Ve-Sifrut Ha-Rabanit*. 2 vols. Tel Aviv, 1938-51.

Kenyon, F. G. *Greek Papyri in the British Museum*. 1893-

Klausner, J. *Historiyah Shel-Ha-Bayit Ha-Sheni*. 5 vols. Reprint ed., Tel Aviv, 1976.

Klein, S. "Akra." *Encyclopaedia Judaica* I (Berlin, 1928-34), cols. 38-40.

——. "*ʿArei Ha-Kohanim Ve-Ha-Leviyim Ve-ʿArei Miqlat*.', *Koveẓ Ha-Ḥevrah Ha-ʿIvrit La-Ḥaqirat ʾEreẓ Yisrael Va-ʿAtiqoteha*, 1935, pp. 81-107.

——. "*ʿArim Muqafot Ḥomah Mi-Yemot Yehoshuʿa bin Nun*." *ʾAzkarah Li-Khevod Ha-Rav Kook*, 1937, pp. 67-77.

——. "*Baraitaʾ Shel-ʾArbaʿah Ve-ʿEsrim Mishmarot*." In *idem, Maʾamarim Shonim La-Ḥaqirat ʾEreẓ Yisrael, Meḥqarim ʾEreẓ-Yisreʾelim*, 1924, pp. 1-29.

——. *Beiträge zur Geographie und Geschichte Galiläas*. Leipzig, 1909.

——. *ʾEreẓ Ha-Galil*. Reprint ed., Jerusalem, 1967.

——. *ʾEreẓ Yehudah*. Tel Aviv, 1939.

——. "*Galiläa von der Makkabäerzeit bis 67*." *Jüdische Studien, Joseph Wohlgemuth*. Frankfurt am Main, 1928, pp. 47-102.

——. "*Ḥaluqat ʾEreẓ Yisrael Le-Maʿamadot*." *Sefer Ha-Shanah Shel-ʾEreẓ Yisrael* II (1924), 17-25.

——. "*Ḥaluqat Yehudah Ve-Ha-Galil*." *Sefer Ha-Shanah Shel-ʾEreẓ Yisrael* I (1923), 24-41.

——. *Jüdisch-palästinische Corpus Inscriptionum*. Vienna and Berlin, 1920.

——. "*Kastra*." *Encyclopaedia Judaica* IX (Berlin, 1928-34), cols. 1034-1036.

——. *Maʾamarim Shonim La-Ḥaqirat ʾEreẓ Yisrael, Meḥqarim ʾEreẓ-Yisreʾelim*. Vienna, 1924.

——. "*Neue Beiträge zur Geschichte und Geographie Galiläas*." *Jeschurun* 10 (1923), 129-146; 231-290.

——. *Sefer Ha-Yishuv* I. Jerusalem, 1939.

——. "*Teḥumei Ha-ʾAreẓ Be-Mishnat Ha-Tannaʾim*." In *Gevulot Ha-ʾAreẓ*, pp. 119-176. Translated by H. Bar Daroma. Jerusalem, 1965.

——. "*Ẓippori*." In *idem, Maʾamarim Shonim La-Ḥaqirat ʾEreẓ Yisrael, Meḥqarim ʾEreẓ-Yisreʾelim*, 1924, pp. 44-76.

——. "*Zum jüdischen Heerwesen in der mischnischen Zeit.*" *Jeschurun* 10 (1923), 88-90.
——. "*Zur Geographie Palastinas in der Zeit Mischna.*" *MGWJ* 61 (1917), 139ff.
Kohut, A. *ʿArukh Ha-Shalem.* 9 vols. Reprint ed., Israel, 1970.
Krauss, *Antoninus und Rabbi.* Frankfurt am Main, 1910.
Krauss, S. "*Die römischen Besatzungen in Palästina.*" *MWJ* 19-20 (1892-3), 227-244; 105-133.
——. *Griechische und lateinische Lehnwörter im Talmud, Midrasch, und Targum.* 2 vols. Berlin, 1898-9.
——. "*Ha-Kerakh Ha-ʿIr, Ve-Ha-Kefar Ba-Talmud.*" *He-ʿAtid* 3 (1922), 1-50.
——. *Paras Ve-Romi Ba-Talmud U-Va-Midrashim.* Jerusalem, 1948.
——. "Priests and Worship in the Last Decade of the Temple at Jerusalem." *JQR*, o.s. 8 (1896), 666-678.
——. *Talmudische Archäologie.* 3 vols. Leipzig, 1910-12.
——. "Sepphoris." *The Jewish Encyclopedia* 11 (1905), 198-200.
——. "*Über Siedlungstypen in Palästina in talmudischer Zeit.*" *MGWJ* 82 (1938), 173-190.
Kutcher, E. Y. *Studies in Galilean Aramaic.* Jerusalem, 1976.
Lampe, G. W. H., ed. *A Patristic Greek Lexicon.* 5 vols. Oxford, 1961-8.
Lebrecht, F. *Bether, die Fragliche Stadt im Hadrianisch-juedischen Kriege,* 1877.
Levine, L. I. *Caesarea Under Roman Rule.* Leiden, 1975.
——. "The Jewish Patriarch (Nasi) in Third Century Palestine." *Aufstieg und Niedergang der römischen Welt.* Edited by H. Temporini and W. Haase. Pt. 2, vol. 19.2 (1974), 649-688.
——. "R. Simeon b. Yoḥai and the Purification of Tiberias: History and Tradition." *HUCA* 49 (1978), 143-185.
Levy, J. *Wörterbuch über die Talmudim und Midraschim.* 4 vols. Leipzig, 1883.
Lewin, B. M. *ʾOẓar Ha-Geonim.* 13 vols. Haifa, 1928-62.
Lichtenstein, H. "*Die-Fastenrolle, eine Untersuchung zur jüdisch-hellenistischen Geschichte.*" *HUCA* 8-9 (1931-32), 257-351.
Liddel, H. G. and Scott, R. *A Greek-English Lexicon.* Reprint ed., Oxford, 1976.
Lieberman, S. *Greek in Jewish Palestine.* Reprint ed., New York, 1965.
——. *Ha-Yerushalmi Ki-Feshuto.* Jerusalem, 1934.
——. *Hellenism in Jewish Palestine.* New York, 1962.
——. "The Martyrs of Caesarea." *Annuaire de l'Institut de Philologie et d'Histoire Orientales et Slaves* 7 (1939-44), 395-445.
——. "Palestine in the Third and Fourth Centuries." *JQR* 36-37 (1946-47), 329-370; 31-54.
——. "*Redifat Dat Yisrael.*" *Salo Baron Jubilee Volumes* III (1975), 213-245.
——. "*Talmudah Shel-Kisrin.*" *Tarbiẓ* 2 (1931). Supplement.
——. *Text and Studies.* New York, 1974.
——. *Toseftaʾ Ki-Feshutah.* 8 vols. New York, 1955-73.
Lifschitz, B. "*Ligyonot Romiyim Be-ʾEreẓ Yisrael.*" *Yediʿot Ha-Ḥevrah La-Ḥaqirat ʾEreẓ Yisrael Va-ʾAtiqoteha* 23 (1959), 53-67.
——. "*Sur la date du transfert de la legio VI Ferrata en Palestine.*" *Latomus* 19 (1960), 109-111.
Liver, J. "The Israelite Tribes." In *The World History of the Jewish People* III, *Judges*, pp. 183-211. Edited by B. Mazar. New Brunswick, N.J., 1971.
——. *Peraqim Be-Toledot Ha-Kehunah Ve-Ha-Leviyyah,* Jerusalem, 1969.
Loew, E. *Die Flora der Juden.* 4 vols. Vienna and Leipzig, 1924-34.
Lurie, B. Z. "*ʿArei Ha-Kohanim Bi-Yemei Bayit Sheni.*" *HUCA* 44 (1973), Hebrew section, 1-19.
Luttwak, E. N. *The Grand Strategy of the Roman Empire.* Baltimore, 1976.
Maimonides, M. *Mishneh Torah.* Ed. Vilna. Reprint ed., Jerusalem, 1955.
Malter, H. *Massekhet Taʾanit min Talmud Bavli.* New York, 1930.
Mantel, H. "The High Priesthood and the Sanhedrin in the Time of the Second Temple." In *The World History of the Jewish People* VII, *The Herodian Period*, pp. 264-281. Edited by M. Avi-Yonah and Z. Baras. New Brunswick, N. J., 1975.
——. *Studies in the History of the Sanhedrin.* Cambridge, 1961.
Margaliot, R. *Le-Ḥeqer Shemot Ve-Kinnuyim Ba-Talmud.* Jerusalem, 1944.
Marmorstein, A. "The Amidah of the Public Fast Days." Reprinted in *Contributions to the Scientific Study of Jewish Liturgy*, pp. 449-458. Edited by J. J. Petuchowski. New York, 1970.
Mason, H. J. *Greek Terms for Roman Institutions: A Lexicon and Analysis.* Toronto, 1974.
Mazar, B. *ʿArim U-Gelilot Be-ʾEreẓ Yisrael.* Jerusalem, 1975.

——. "The Cities of the Priests and the Levites." *Vetus Testamentum*, Supplement 7 (1960), 193-205.

Mechilta D'Rabbi Ismael. Edited by H. S. Horovitz and I. A. Rabin. Jerusalem, 1960.

Meiseles, I. "Talmud, Recent Research." *Encyclopedia Judaica Yearbook*, 1974, pp. 266-270.

Melamed, E. Z. "*Ha-'Ma-ʿaseh' Ba-Mishnah Ke-Maqor La-Halakhah*." *Sinai* 46 (1959-60), 152-166.

Meshorer, Y. "*Matbeʿot Ẓippori Ke-Maqor Histori*." *Zion* 43 (1978), 185-200.

——. "Sepphoris and Rome." In *Greek Numismatics and Archaeology, Essays in Honor of Margaret Thompson*, pp. 159-171. Belgium, 1979.

Meyers, E. "Galilean Regionalism as a Factor in Historical Reconstruction." *BASOR* 221 (1976), 93-101.

——. "The Cultural Setting of Galilee: The Case of Regionalism and Early Christianity." *Aufstieg und Niedergang der römischen Welt*. Edited by H. Temporini and W. Haase. Pt. 2, vol. 19.1 (1979), 686-702.

——. "The Meiron Excavation Project: Archeological Survey in Galilee and Golan, 1976." *BASOR* 230 (1978), 1-24.

Meyers, E. *et al.* "Preliminary Report on the 1977 and 1978 Seasons at Gush Ḥalav (el-Jish)," *BASOR* 233 (1979), 33-58.

Meyers, E. and Strange, J. F. "Survey in Galilee, 1976." *Explor* (Published by Garret Evangelical Theological Seminary) 3 (Winter, 1977), 7-17.

Midrash Bereshit Rabbaʾ. Edited by J. Theodor and H. Albeck. Jerusalem, 1965.

Midrash Debarim Rabbah. Edited by S. Lieberman. Ms. Oxford, no. 147. Reprint ed., Jerusalem, 1974.

Midrash Echa Rabbati (*Lamentations Rabbah*). Edited by S. Buber. Reprint ed., Tel Aviv, 1963-4.

Midrash Rabbah. Ed. Vilna. 2 vols. Reprint ed., New York, 1952.

Midrash Tanḥumaʾ. Edited by S. Buber. Reprint ed., Jerusalem, 1963-4.

Midrash Va-Yiqraʾ Rabbah. 5 vols. (in 3). Edited by M. Margaliot. Jerusalem, 1971-2.

Mishnah, editio princeps. Napoli (Naples), 1492; reprint ed., Jerusalem, 1970.

Mishnah, Ms. Cambridge or *The Mishnah on Which the Palestinian Talmud Rests*. Edited by W. H. Lowe. Reprint ed., Cambridge, 1966.

Mishnah, Codex Jerusalem. A Ms. vocalized according to Yemenite tradition. Jerusalem, 1970.

Mishnah, Mishna Codex Kaufmann. 2 vols. Edited by G. Beer. Reprint ed., Jerusalem, 1969.

Mishnah, Ms. Parma (De Rossi 138). 2 vols. Jerusalem, 1970.

Mishnah. Ed. Vilna. 12 vols. Reprint ed., New York, 1952-3.

Momigliano, A. "Herod of Judaea." *The Cambridge Ancient History* 10 (1976), 316-339.

Moore, G. F. "Simeon the Righteous." In *Jewish Studies in Memory of Israel Abrahams*, pp. 348-364. 1927.

Morgenstern, J. "The Gates of Righteousness." *HUCA* 6 (1929), 1-37.

Mukhtar, K. "*Ẓippori Bi-Yemei Bayit Sheni, Ha-Mishnah Ve-Ha-Talmud*." M.A. thesis, Tel Aviv University, 1974.

Naḥmanides, M. *Ḥiddushei Ha-Ramban*. 2 vols. New York, 1966-7.

Narkis, M. "*ʾAnshei Ẓippori Ve-ʾEspasionos*." *Yediʿot Ha-Ḥevrah Ha-ʿIvrit La-Ḥaqirat ʾEreẓ Yisrael Va-ʿAtiqoteha* 17 (1953), 109-120.

Naveh, J. *ʿAl Peseifas Ve-ʾEven*. Tel Aviv, 1978.

Neusner, J. *Development of a Legend: Studies on the Traditions Concerning Yohanan ben Zakkai*. Leiden, 1970.

——. *Eliezer ben Hyrcanus*. 2 vols. Leiden, 1973.

——. *From Politics to Piety*. New York, 1978.

——. *A History of the Mishnaic Law of Holy Things*. 6 vols. Leiden, 1978-9.

——. *A History of the Mishnaic Law of Purities*. 22 vols. Leiden, 1974-7.

——. *A Life of Yohanan ben Zakkai*. Leiden, 1970.

——. *The Rabbinic Traditions about the Pharisees* before 70. 3 vols. Leiden, 1971.

——. *There We Sat Down*. Reprint ed., New York, 1978.

Oppenheimer, A. *The ʿAm Ha-Aretz: A Study in the Social History of the Jewish People in the Hellenistic-Roman Period*. Leiden, 1977.

——. "*Ha-Yishuv Ha-Yehudi Ba-Galil Bi-Tequfat Yavneh U-Mered Bar-Kokhba*." *Cathedra* 4 (1977), 53-83.

Otto, W. *Herodes: Beiträge zur Geschichte des letzten jüdischen Königshauses*. Stuttgart, 1913.

Palestinian Talmud. Ed. Krotoschin. Reprint ed., Jerusalem, 1960.
Palestinian Talmud. Ms. Leiden. Reprint ed., Jerusalem, 1971.
Palestinian Talmud. Ms. Vatican. Reprint ed., Jerusalem, 1970.
Palestinian Talmud. Ed. Venice. Reprint ed., Jerusalem, 1960.
Palestinian Talmud. With commentaries. See *Talmud Yerushalmi*.
Parker, H. M. D. *The Roman Legions*. Cambridge, 1928.
Patai, R. "Control of Rain in Ancient Palestine." *HUCA* 14 (1939), 251-286.
——. *Man and Temple*. Toronto and New York, 1947.
Perles, J. "*Baᶜal Ha-Pol-Amtsnamen*." *MGWJ* 21 (1872), 256-257.
Pesiqtaʾ (*De-Rab Kahana*). Edited by S. Buber. Reprint ed., New York, 1949.
Pesiqtaʾ De-Rab Kahanaʾ. 2 vols. Edited by B. Mandelbaum. New York, 1962.
Petuchowski, J. J., ed. *Contributions to the Scientific Study of Jewish Liturgy*. New York, 1970.
Photius. *Bibliotheca*. Edited by R. Henry. Paris, 1959.
Preisigke, G. *Wörterbuch der griechischen Papyrusurkunden usw. aus Ägypten*. 4 vols. Edited by E. Kiessling. Berlin, 1925-58.
Pritchard, J., ed. *Ancient Near Eastern Texts* (*ANET*). Princeton, 1969.
The Prophets: Neviʾim. New JPS translation, Philadelphia, 1978.
Rabbinovicz, R. N. *Sefer Diqduqei Soferim*. 2 vols. Reprint ed., New York, 1976.
Rabinowitz, Z. W. *Shaᶜarei Torat ʾEreẓ Yisrael*. Jerusalem, 1940.
Ratner, B. *ʾAhavat Ẓiyyon Vi-Yerushalayim*. 10 vols. Reprint ed., Jerusalem, 1967.
Reshumot Yalqut Ha-Pirsumim. Israel, 1964.
Rhoads, D. M. *Israel in Revolution* 6-74 *C.E.* Philadelphia, 1976.
Romanoff, P. "Onomasticon of Palestine." *PAAJR* 7 (1936), 147-227.
Rosenfeld, A., trans. and ed. *The Authorized Kinot for the Ninth of Av*. London, 1965.
Rostovtzeff, M. *The Social and Economic History of the Roman Empire*. 2nd ed. 2 vols. Oxford, 1957.
Saarisalo, A. "Topographical Researches in Galilee." *JPOS* 9-10 (1929-30), 27-40; 5-10.
Safrai, S. *Ha-ᶜAliyah Le-Regel Bi-Yemei Ha-Bayit Ha-Sheni*. Tel Aviv, 1965.
——. "*Ha-ᶜIr Ha-Yehudit Be-ʾEreẓ Yisrael Bi-Tequfat Ha-Mishnah Ve-Ha-Talmud.*" *In Milḥemet Qodesh U-Martirologyah Be-Toledot Yisrael U-Ve-Toledot Ha-ᶜAmim, Ha-ᶜIr Ve-Ha-Qehillah*, pp. 227-236. Jerusalem, 1967.
——. "The Relations Between the Roman Army and the Jews of ʾEreẓ Yisrael after the Destruction of the Second Temple." In *Roman Frontier Studies: The Proceedings of the Seventh International Congress held at Tel Aviv*, 1971, pp. 224-230.
——. "The Temple and the Divine Service." In *The World History of the Jewish People* VII, *The Herodian Period*, pp. 282-337. Edited by M. Avi-Yonah and Z. Baras. New Brunswick, N.J., 1976.
——. "The Temple." In *The Jewish People in the First Century* II, pp. 865-907. Edited by S. Safrai and M. Stern. Philadelphia, 1976.
Safrai, S., *et al. The Jewish People in the First Century*. 2 vols. Philadelphia, 1974, 1976.
Saldarini, A. J. " 'Form Criticism' of Rabbinic Literature." *JBL* 96 (1977), 257-274.
Sandberg, A. C., Jr. "Josephus' Galilee Revisited." *Explor* (Published by Garret Evangelical Theological Seminary) 3 (Winter, 1977), 44-55.
Sanders, E. P. *Paul and Palestinian Judaism*. Philadelphia, 1977.
Schachter, M. *Ha-Mishnah Ba-Bavli U-Va-Yerushalmi: Hashvaʾat Nusḥaoʾteha*. Jerusalem, 1959.
Schalit, A. "Domestic Politics and Political Institutions." In *The World History of the Jewish People* VI, *The Hellenistic Age*, pp. 255-297. Edited by A. Schalit. New Brunswick, N.J., 1972.
——. *Ha-Mishtar Ha-Romaʾi Be-ʾEreẓ Yisrael*. Jerusalem, 1937.
——. *Hordos Ha-Melekh: Ha-ʾIsh U-Poᶜolo*. Jerusalem, 1978.
Schechter, S. *Documents of Jewish Sectaries*. Reprint ed., New York, 1970.
Schiffman, L. H. *The Halakhah at Qumran*. Leiden, 1975.
Schultz, E. G. "*Mittheilungen über eine Reise durch Samarien und Galilaea*." *ZDMG* 3 (1848), 49ff.
Schürer, E. *Geschichte des jüdischen Volkes im Zeitalter Jesu Christi*. 3 vols. Leipzig, 1901-9.
——. *The History of the Jewish People in the Age of Jesus Christ* (175 B.C.-A.D. 135). Vol. I. Edited by G. Vermes and F. Millar. Edinburgh, 1973.
Schwabe, M. "*Eine griechische Inschrift aus Sepphoris*." *JPOS* 15 (1935), 88-97.
Schwarz, A. "*Der Segan*." *MGWJ* 64 (1920), 30-55.

Seder ʿOlam Rabbah. Edited by B. Ratner. Reprint ed., New York, 1966.

Seeck, O., ed. *Notitia Dignitatum*, Berlin, 1876.

Seyrig, H. "Irenopolis-Neronias-Sepphoris." *Numismatic Chronicle* 10 (1950), 284-289.

——. "Irenopolis-Neronias-Sepphoris, An Additional Note." *Numismatic Chronicle* 15 (1955), 157-159.

Sifraʾ De-Be Rab. Edited by I. H. Weiss. Vienna, 1862.

Sifraʾ De-Be Rab. Ed. Venice, 1545; reprint ed., Jerusalem, 1971.

Sifraʾ De-Be Rab (*Torat Kohanim*). With commentaries. Jerusalem, 1958-9.

Sifraʾ De-Be Rab. Codex Assemani 31 of the Vatican Library. Reprint ed., Jerusalem, 1932.

Sifraʾ De-Be Rab. Codex Assemani 46 of the Vatican Library. Edited by L. Finkelstein. New York, 1956.

Sifre De-Be Rab (Numbers). Edited by H. S. Horovitz. Jerusalem, 1966.

Sifre on Deuteronomy. Edited by L. Finkelstein. Reprint ed., New York, 1969.

Smallwood, E. M. "High Priests and Politics in Roman Palestine." *JTS* n.s. 13 (1962), 14-34.

——. *The Jews Under Roman Rule*. Leiden, 1976.

Sophocles, E. A. *Greek Lexicon of the Roman and Byzantine Periods*. 1914.

Speidel, M. P. "The Rise of Ethnic Units in the Roman Imperial Army." *Aufstieg und Niedergang der römischen Welt*. Edited by H. Temporini and W. Haase. Pt. 2, vol. 3 (1974), 202-231.

Sperber, D. "*Mishmarot* and *Maʿamadot*." *Encyclopaedia Judaica* 12 (1971), 89-93.

——. "On the πύργος as a Farm Building." *AJSr* 1 (1976), 359-361.

——. *Roman Palestine* 200-400: *The Land*. Ramat Gan, 1978.

——. *Roman Palestine* 200-400: *Money and Prices*. Ramat Gan, 1974.

——. "Social Legislation in Jerusalem during the Latter Part of the Second Temple Period." *Journal for the Study of Judaism in the Persian, Hellenistic and Roman Periods* 6 (1975), 86-95.

Stemberger, G. "Galilee—Land of Salvation." In *The Gospel and the Land: Early Christianity and Jewish Territorial Doctrine*, pp. 409-438. Edited by W. D. Davies. 1974.

Stern, M. "Aspects of Jewish Society: The Priesthood and Other Classes." In *The Jewish People in the First Century* II, pp. 561-630. Edited by S. Safrai and M. Stern. Philadelphia, 1976.

——. *Greek and Latin Authors on Jews and Judaism*. Jerusalem, 1974.

——. "*Mediniyuto Shel-Hordos Ve-Ha-Ḥevrah Ha-Yehudit Be-Sof Yemei Bayit Sheni*." *Tarbiz* 35 (1966), 235-253.

——. "The Reign of Herod and the Herodian Dynasty." In *The Jewish People in the First Century* I, pp. 216-307. Edited by S. Safrai and M. Stern. Philadelphia, 1974.

Strack, H. L. *Introduction to the Talmud and Midrash*. Philadelphia, 1931.

Strack, H. L. and Billerbeck, P. *Kommentar zum neuen Testament aus Talmud und Midrash*. 5 vols. Munich, 1922-56.

Sukenik, E. L. "*Mi-Seridei Ẓippori*." *Tarbiz* 3 (1931), 107-109.

——. "*Shetei Maẓevot Yehudiyot Mi-Ẓippori*." *Yediʿot Ha-Ḥevrah Ha-ʿIvrit La-Ḥaqirat ʾEreẓ Yisrael Va-ʿAtiqoteha* 12 (1945-6), 62-64.

Sussman, Y. "*Ketovet Halakhatit Me-ʾEmeq Bet Sheʾan*." *Tarbiz* 43 (1973-4), 88-158.

Tadmor, H. "*Kibbush Ha-Galil Bi-Yedei Tiglat Pileser Ha-Shelishi Melekh ʾAsshur*." In *Kol ʾEreẓ Naftali*, pp. 62-67. Edited by H. Z. Hirschberg. Jerusalem, 1968.

Talmon, S. "The Calendar Reckoning of the Sect from the Judean Desert." *Scripta Hierosolymitana* 4 (1965), 162-199.

Talmud Yerushalmi ʾO Talmud Ha-Maʿariv Ve-Yesh Qorin lo Talmud ʾEreẓ Yisrael. With commentaries. Ed. Vilna Romm. Reprint ed., New York, 1958-60.

Tanhumaʾ. Edited by S. Buber. 2 vols. Reprint ed., Jerusalem, 1964.

Targum Yerushalmi. Edited by M. Ginsburger (*Targum Pseudo-Jonathan ben Usiël zum Pentateuch*. Reprint ed., Jerusalem, 1968-9).

Ta-Shma, I. M. "*Rishonim*." *Encyclopaedia Judaica* 14 (1971), 192-193.

Tcherikover, V. *Ha-Yehudim Be-Miẓrayim Bi-Tequfat Ha-Helenistit Ha-Romit Le-ʾOr Ha-Papyrologyah*. Jerusalem, 1963.

The Torah. New *JPS* trans. Philadelphia, 1962.

Toseftaʾ. 4 vols. Edited by S. Lieberman. New York, 1955-73.

Toseftaʾ. Edited by M. Zuckermandel. Reprint ed., Jerusalem, 1962-63.

Urbach. "*Mishmarot U-Maʿamadot*." *Tarbiz* 42 (1973), 302-327.

——. "*Mi-Yehudah Le-Galil.*" In *Sefer Zikaron Le-Yaʿaqov Fridman*, pp. 59-75. Jerusalem, 1974.

Urman, D. "The Golan during the Roman and Byzantine Periods: Topography, Settlements, Economy." Ph.D. dissertation, New York University, 1979.

Vardaman, E. J., *et al. The Teacher's Yoke: Studies in Memory of Henry Trantham.* Waco, Texas, 1964.

Waterman, L., *et al. Preliminary Report of the University of Michigan Excavation at Sepphoris, Palestine, in 1931.* Ann Arbor, 1937.

Webster, B. *The Roman Imperial Army of the First and Second Centuries A.D.* London, 1969.

Weiss, I. H. *Dor, Dor, Ve-Dorshav.* Vilna, 1904.

Williamson, H. G. M. "The Historical Value of Josephus' Jewish Antiquities XI 297-301." *JTS* 28 n.s. (1977), 49-66.

Wycherley, R. E. *How the Greeks Built Cities.* Reprint ed., New York, 1962.

Yadin, Y. *The Scroll of the War of the Sons of Light Against the Sons of Darkness.* Translated by B. Rabin and C. Rabin. Oxford, 1962.

Yalqut Shimʿoni. 2 vols. Reprint ed., Jerusalem, 1960.

Yom Tob ben Abraham. *Ḥiddushei Ha-Ritbaʾ ʿAl Ha-Shas.* 3 vols. Edited by E. Lichtenstein. Jerusalem, 1974-6.

Ziegler, I. *Die Königsgleichnisse der Midrasch beleuchtet durch die römische Kaiserzeit.* Breslau, 1903.

Zulay, M. "*Le-Toledot Ha-Piyyut Be-ʾEreẓ Yisrael.*" *Yediʿot Ha-Makhon Le-Ḥeqer Ha-Shirah Ha-ʿIvrit Bi-Yerushalayim* 5 (1939), 107-180.

INDEX OF CITATIONS*

I. HEBREW SCRIPTURES

* The author expresses his appreciation to the Research Foundation of the University of Connecticut for providing funds towards the preparation of the indices.

II. QUMRAN LITERATURE

III. APOCRYPHA

IV. JOSEPHUS

V. NEW TESTAMENT

VI. OTHER CHRISTIAN SOURCES

VII. RABBINIC LITERATURE

A. Mishnah

B. Tosefta

C. Palestinian Talmud

D. Babylonian Talmud

E. Targumim

F. Midrashim

G. Other Rabbinic Sources

VIII. OTHER ANCIENT SOURCES

GENERAL INDEX